CANADA'S NATIONAL SECURITY IN THE POST-9/11 WORLD

STRATEGY, INTERESTS, AND THREATS

After the terrorist attacks of 9/11, which targeted the heart of financial and military power in the United States, Canada once again proved its credentials as a key American ally. With the imminent end of its combat role in Afghanistan, however, it is time to take stock of how Canada has adapted to the exigencies of the post-9/11 world and to consider the future directions for its foreign, defence, and security policies.

This timely exploration and reassessment of Canada's approach to strategic affairs offers a diverse set of nuanced, sometimes controversial, and always insightful perspectives on the most pressing security challenges that Canada currently faces. Bringing together noted experts on these issues – including a Canadian senator, a past minister of national defence, former high-level military officers, and top scholars – this collection provides powerful ideas and guidance for the difficult task of formulating an overarching national security strategy.

DAVID S. MCDONOUGH is a SSHRC post-doctoral fellow in the Department of Political Science (Balsillie School of International Affairs) at the University of Waterloo.

EDITED BY DAVID S. MCDONOUGH

Canada's National Security in the Post-9/11 World

Strategy, Interests, and Threats

UNIVERSITY OF TORONTO PRESS
Toronto Buffalo London

ISBN 978-1-4426-4135-8 (cloth)
ISBN 978-1-4426-1063-7 (paper)

Printed on acid-free, 100% post-consumer recycled paper
with vegetable-based inks.

Library and Archives Canada Cataloguing in Publication

Canada's national security in the post-9/11 world : strategy, interests,
and threats / edited by David S. McDonough.

Includes bibliographical references and index.
ISBN 978-1-4426-4135-8 (bound). – ISBN 978-1-4426-1063-7(pbk.)

1. National security – Canada – History – 21st century.   I. McDonough,
David S., 1978–

UA600.C3455 2012   355'.0330710905   C2011-907910-0

This book has been supported by a subsidy in aid of publication from the
Canadian International Council and Canadian Defence and Foreign Affairs
Institute through the Strategic Studies Working Group.

University of Toronto Press acknowledges the financial assistance to its
publishing program of the Canada Council for the Arts and the Ontario
Arts Council.

   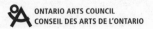

University of Toronto Press acknowledges the financial support of the
Government of Canada through the Canada Book Fund for its publishing
activities.

Contents

Foreword

It was in the aftermath of the 9/11 attacks that Canada first found itself fighting alongside its key allies, most notably the United States, against a difficult and deadly opponent in the arid plains of Afghanistan. Nearly a decade later, the U.S.-led 'war on terror' continues to pose significant foreign and defence policy challenges at home and abroad, sparking debate about our future role.

For better or worse, Canada's military contribution to the Afghan combat campaign has finally come to an end. We have already withdrawn much our armed forces in 2011, though a smaller training mission is expected to continue until 2014.

Our involvement in Afghanistan has, without doubt, required a 'whole of government' approach to policymaking, which must remain intact and perhaps even be augmented in the years to come. Regardless, it is clear that the Canadian role in Afghanistan will be irrevocably changed. With the end of our combat role, Afghanistan has already been the major preoccupation for Canadian diplomats and military planners alike for nearly ten years. The Canadian armed forces, which have performed so marvellously in this difficult stabilization and counter-insurgency campaign, will surely benefit from some much needed rest and recapitalization. Having said that, it is with great sorrow that Canada, like other countries, has suffered a number of casualties in this mission.

Upon our withdrawal, the Afghan mission will no longer be the centrepiece for Canada's foreign and defence policy in the post-9/11 world, irrespective of whether non-military resources are increased to that country. Clearly, Canada's global role must be reassessed in the context of this new environment.

Surprisingly, there is very little substantive debate, let alone consensus, on the future directions of our foreign and defence policies. Of urgency is the need to formulate a new post-Afghan role for the Canadian Forces returning from their combat mission in Kandahar. There is a significant opportunity to situate such a military policy within a broader national security strategy – something we hope officials and policymakers in Ottawa will recognize and act upon.

Unfortunately, few non-governmental organizations in Canada are now capable of the sort of coherent strategic analysis needed at this important juncture. And government departments, despite significant resources, face other internal challenges, which do not enable them to undertake this sort of sweeping strategic analysis and planning necessary for a truly 'whole of government' approach to national and international security matters.

The Strategic Studies Working Group, a joint partnership between the Canadian International Council and the Canadian Defence and Foreign Affairs Institute, therefore took it upon itself to initiate the Canadian National Security Strategy Project to take leadership and advance the discussion over Canada's global role in the twenty-first century. This edited volume, the final product of a multi-year endeavour, represents an insightful and timely contribution to this preliminary debate. The fourteen chapters of this book cover a range of salient issues, and each has done so in a thoughtful and original manner. The book brings together a diverse grouping of experts from Canada's defence and security studies community to stimulate dialogue. They are united, if not necessarily in their respective conclusions and prescriptions, in their common concern for Canadian national interests and the need to instil a greater degree of strategic thinking to Canadian policymaking.

I applaud them for their participation in this important project and believe that they bring a perspective that will be invaluable to the continuing national debate of the future of our foreign and defence policies.

Blake C. Goldring, MSM, is chairman & CEO, AGF Management Ltd, an honorary colonel of the Royal Regiment of Canada, and a member of the CIC Senate.

Acknowledgments

This book is the culmination of the Canadian National Security Strategy Project, a multi-year Strategic Studies Working Group (SSWG) initiative launched by the Canadian International Council (CIC) and the Canadian Defence and Foreign Affairs Institute. The project was meant to go beyond simply environmental analysis, to which many non-government organizations and government departments confine themselves, and instead focus on the strategic analysis of Canada's national security concerns. This involved the identification of national values and security interests and an analysis of interests, values, and the environment from which policy implications are derived.

The results of the project, consisting of the fourteen chapters of this volume, bring together a broad range of approaches to how Canada could adopt strategic planning and analysis to better approach major national and international security challenges of the post-9/11 world. The chapters and policy recommendations are certainly diverse, reflecting the eclectic topics and the different perspectives of the authors. But all the chapters are clearly united in their concern – as reflected in the book's title – that Canada should develop a coherent security *strategy* (or strategies) capable of identifying national *interests* and actual or potential *threats* to those interests. The chapters in this volume, I believe, are an important step in that direction.

This volume could not have been compiled without the hard and diligent work of numerous individuals. In particular, I would like to offer my most sincere thanks to my friend and colleague Thomas Adams, who was instrumental in gathering and editing the contributions of the authors featured here, and bringing to ultimate completion this volume and thereby the project itself. Tom's other duties at the

CIC's Research Program forced him to gradually reduce and eventually disengage from his role in this volume, and it was only as a result of his own gracious modesty – given the quantity and quality of his editorial contributions – that his name does not appear on its cover.

I would like to give special thanks to Brigadier-General (Ret'd) Don Macnamara, former SSWG chairman; Professor David Bercuson, current SSWG chairman and director of programs at the Canadian Defence and Foreign Affairs Institute; and CIC President Jennifer Jeffs, all of whom were unwavering in their support for this project and instrumental in the successful completion of this volume. The foreword to this book was graciously provided by Blake Goldring, chairman and CEO of AGF Management and member of the CIC Senate, and to him I offer my sincerest gratitude.

I would also like to thank each of the authors for their fine contributions: Thomas Adams, David Bercuson, Douglas Bland, Charles Doran, Jim Fergusson, Ann Fitz-Gerald, Douglas Goold, J.L. Granatstein, Joseph Jockel, Brian MacDonald, Don Macnamara, Alexander Moens, David Pratt, Hugh Segal, Elinor Sloan, Joel Sokolsky, Craig Stone, and Alex Wilner. It was certainly a delight to be able to collaborate with some of the most notable voices within Canada's security and defence community; and from the perspective of an editor, I am doubly thankful that their fine contributions required so little in the way of editing!

I would like to offer my thanks for the institutional and financial support for the project and this volume by the CIC and its Senate, the Canadian Defence and Foreign Affairs Institute, and the Strategic Studies Working Group. Thanks also to to Daniel Quinlan and the staff at the University of Toronto Press for their help in guiding this manuscript through the publication process, Sean Clark for his work on the index, and two anonymous reviewers for their many helpful suggestions.

David S. McDonough
Waterloo, ON

Abbreviations

3-D	defence, diplomacy, and development
AOR	auxiliary oiler replenishers
AWACS	Airborne Warning and Control System
BMD	ballistic missile defence
BPG	Binational Planning Group
BRIC	Brazil, Russia, India, and China
Canada COM	Canada Command
CBSA	Canada Border Services Agency
CIC	Canadian International Council
CIDA	Canadian International Development Agency
CF	Canadian Forces
CFDS	*Canada First Defence Strategy*
CFEF	Canada First Expeditionary Force
CSIS	Canadian Security Intelligence Service
DFAIT	Department of Foreign Affairs and International Trade
EEC	European Economic Community
ESDP	European Security and Defence Policy
EU	European Union
FLQ	Front de libération du Québec
G8	Group of Eight
G20	Group of Twenty
IRB	industrial regional benefit
ISAF	International Security Assistance Force
JSTAR	Joint Surveillance and Target Attack Radar System
LIFG	Libyan Islamic Fighting Group
LPH	Landing Platform Helicopter
LSD(A)	Landing Ship Docks (Auxiliary)

NACD	non-proliferation, arms control and disarmament
NATO	North Atlantic Treaty Organization
NORAD	North American Aerospace Defence Command
OAS	Organization of American States
OECD	Organisation for Economic Co-operation and Development
PSC	Public Safety Canada
PWGSC	Public Works and Government Services Canada
R2P	Responsibility to Protect
RCMP	Royal Canadian Mounted Police
SSWG	Strategic Studies Working Group
START	Stabilization and Reconstruction Task Force
USN	U.S. Navy
USNORTHCOM	U.S. Northern Command
WMD	weapons of mass destruction

CANADA'S NATIONAL SECURITY
IN THE POST-9/11 WORLD

STRATEGY, INTERESTS, AND THREATS

Introduction

DAVID S. MCDONOUGH

Canada was forced to deal with a succession of difficult strategic decisions after the terrorist attacks of 11 September 2001. There was the
abrupt tightening of the Canada-U.S. border in the immediate aftermath of the 9/11 attacks, which forced Canada to adopt 'smart border'
measures to maintain the high cross-border traffic so critical to its economy. There was the Canadian decision to avoid direct participation in
or endorsement of American missile defence plans, though this refusal
was certainly softened by the agreement for North American Aerospace
Defence Command's (NORAD) early warning and assessment functions
to be used for any interception. Most prominently, Canada confronted
the prospect of an expeditionary military role within the U.S.-led 'war
on terror.' While careful to avoid publicly supporting or deploying
troops to the regime-change campaign in Iraq, Canada would find itself
with a lengthy and increasingly dangerous military deployment to
Afghanistan.[1]

Canada is clearly not unaware of possible threats to its national security in the post-9/11 world, whether conceived as endangering its economic security (given the possibility of Canada-U.S. border closures)
or sovereign independence (in the face of U.S. plans for continental
missile defence), or even further broadened to include its preference
for 'forward defence' operations – whether this is the counterterrorism
and stabilization mission in Afghanistan or the recent humanitarian
effort to enforce a UN-authorized no-fly zone in Libya. Participation in
such expeditionary missions, with their sometimes questionable association to the national interest, has certainly contributed to the curious
Canadian tendency to view national and international security as being
one and the same. As members of a Canadian parliamentary committee

once said, there is 'practically no point in thinking of national security as distinct from international security.'[2] But it remains to be seen whether such conflation will continue at a time when Canadian homeland security – in terms of territory and populace – is itself under threat; especially as it pertains to catastrophic terrorism, though one should not underestimate the potential challenge posed by an American ally grown increasingly fixated on national security.

It is difficult to deny that national security has proven to be a persistent, albeit intermittent, driver of Canada's foreign and defence policy. It was present at the creation of the de facto Canada-U.S. security alliance, where the spectre of British defeat at the hands of fascist powers in the Second World War led to renewed interest in continental defence initiatives, most notably through the Ogdensburg Agreement and Hyde Park Declaration.[3] It certainly guided Canadian efforts at the United Nations, particularly as a means to uphold an institutional world order that could satisfy the wishes of the great powers and thereby minimize the possibility of another global military conflagration. And when that hope seemed to prove illusory, given the evidence of Soviet belligerence, Canada would find itself a founding member of a multilateral military alliance, the North Atlantic Treaty Organization (NATO), and more closely entwined in defence arrangements with the United States under NORAD.

National security is therefore not as foreign a concept to the Canadian historic experience as one might expect. That being said, it is also rarely the most salient issue to preoccupy policymakers, who are often overly eager to tighten the purse strings of the foreign affairs and defence portfolios at the first opportunity, whether this was at the first glimmer of détente in the bipolar U.S.-Soviet confrontation in the 1960s and 1970s or the more substantial peace dividend – now known as the 'decade of darkness' – brought about by the end of the Cold War and the Soviet Union's eventual collapse. Indeed, Canada's recent interest in security matters arose only in response to the immediate exigencies of the post-9/11 strategic environment, particularly the threat posed by terrorism, the proliferation of weapons of mass destruction (WMD), and the challenge of Canada's admittedly vulnerable geostrategic position next to a global superpower. Otherwise, one can certainly surmise that Canadian policymakers would continue to drift towards rhetorical platitudes about human security, a 'pinchpenny' approach to international commitments, and continued retrenchment of the Foreign Service, military, and other security-relevant federal agencies.[4]

It was only a few short decades ago that notable commentators bemoaned the lack of a Canadian strategic tradition, with Colin Gray even coining the memorable term *strategic theoretical parasitism* to describe Canada's penchant for relying on the strategic thinking of its erstwhile great power patrons.[5] Comments of this sort have not gone unchallenged. Andrew Richter, for one, has ably demonstrated Canadian contributions to strategic thought, particularly from its most notable of defence scientists R.J. Sutherland, and provided a strong defence Canada's political-military strategy during the early years of the Cold War.[6]

Yet there is certainly more than a grain of truth in such admittedly exaggerated criticism. True, Canada has shown itself surprisingly willing to assess its national security requirements and adjust its policies accordingly. But such strategic acumen has, for the most part, arisen only when the threats to its security – as in the Second World War, early Cold War period, and perhaps more debatably, in the post-9/11 period – are unambiguous and the direct costs of inaction high. In less extreme situations, Canada has shown a strong inclination to forgo the strategic planning altogether, preferring instead to place emphasis on Canadian 'values' rather than to admit that this country could have something as 'grubby' as 'self-interested aims in foreign policy.'[7]

Such strategic inattention may be an understandable response to Canada's otherwise fortuitous geostrategic position, with what amounts to an almost involuntary security guarantee from its superpower ally. But it would still be imprudent to prematurely discard the utility of strategy or strategic planning, which could help policymakers to identify and prioritize security interests – the necessary means to achieve security-enhancing political goals – and the threats that could endanger Canadian national security. As Douglas and Christopher Ross usefully remind us, 'There is nothing in the definition of grand strategy which specifies the type of state able to engage in such planning . . . State actors of any size should be able, in theory, to engage in such planning: even middlepowers.'[8]

The need for a more refined Canadian approach to strategic matters was forcefully argued by R.B. Byers, who used the memorable term *capability-commitment gap* in reference to Canada's frequent failure to connect the necessary capability with its commitments, and went on to advocate the development of a 'security policy' as a possible means to rectify this strategic deficit. As Byers describes it, security policy is meant to serve as a 'bridge' between defence policy and foreign policy, and therefore encompasses 'those political-strategic objectives and instruments which have been identified and established by the government as central to national security interests.'[9] With its emphasis on a means-ends chain directed at achieving political-strategic objectives, there can be little doubt that Byers was essentially making reference to strategy – and grand strategy at that.

The security policy concept was meant to provide a strategic means-ends framework to bridge Canada's foreign and defence policies. A definitive account would sadly not be completed by Byers himself. But the concept, refashioned as 'international security policy,' would later become the subject of a seminal 1995 collection, edited by David Dewitt and David Leyton-Brown and dedicated to Rod Byers's memory, titled *Canada's International Security Policy*.[10] That collection brought together some of the most prominent Canadian scholars of military and strategic affairs to discuss different facets of Canada's international security policy, though the diversity of the contributors and broad content of the subject matter did prevent the prescription of an overarching international security policy or strategic framework to guide policymakers on these pertinent questions.

Since the publication of the Dewitt and Leyton-Brown collection, scholars have found themselves adopting the term *international security policy*, though more often as a description for – as opposed to a prescriptive framework or heuristic device that guides – Canada's collection of foreign, defence, and security policies. Yet consensus remained elusive on the strategic content or planning underlying Canadian initiatives on these matters. Some have noted the continuity that underlies Canada's approach to international security, as evident in the 'internationalist' behaviour pursued by successive Canadian governments since the end of the Second World War, as well as the various policy-planning documents (both white and green papers) that have been periodically released during this period.[11] Others detect a notable shift towards a more 'sanctimonious' or 'narcissistic' approach to international security affairs.[12]

In any event, few would attribute anything approaching strategically sound policy-planning to Ottawa. Canada's national style, to borrow a term used by British strategist Colin Gray, has generally been considered ad hoc, 'situational,' and ultimately 'reactive' to world events. In the words of Daniel Madar and Denis Stairs, this makes 'the recourse to grand strategies ... the prerogatives of the greater states.'[13] Of course, successive governments, beginning under Pierre Trudeau's leadership, have sought to improve this process through bureaucratic reforms aimed at achieving greater efficiency and tighter coordination. Yet the results of these measures, ranging from introducing a policy-planning element within External Affairs to an effort by that department to be a central agency, have often proven less than satisfactory.[14] True, there has been a definite increase in the role of certain central agencies, such as the Privy Council Office and Prime Minister's Office, in the country's foreign and defence policymaking – though whether this fact actually results in any greater strategic direction, as opposed to the continued disaggregation of policymaking, remains to be seen.[15]

There are those scholars, however, who are much more open to the idea of a Canadian grand strategy that could provide a uniting theme to the country's foreign, defence, and security policies. David Haglund has been perhaps the most prominent proponent of a uniquely Canadian approach to grand strategy, embodied in the concept of a 'North Atlantic Triangle' and actualized in key historical and symbolic metaphors, such as the counterweight and the linchpin, that have helped guide policymakers on these important questions.[16] Others may avoid the terminology of grand strategy, but in a complementary fashion still posit the existence of a uniquely Canadian strategic culture that informs and guides policymakers on crucial matters of national security.[17] Most recently, former Defence Minister David Pratt has brought renewed attention on the benefits of a grand strategy for policymakers navigating today's uncertain security environment.[18] Some analysts with more limited ambitions have instead turned to the notion of niche diplomacy; this entails a reprioritization of and greater selectivity in choosing among Canadian foreign policy goals, which at times of fiscal austerity would better accord with Canada's more modest foreign and defence capabilities.[19] There might be little that is grand with niche diplomacy, but it still remains strategic in its prescription – at least, if its attention to carefully match means and ends is any indication. Indeed, even among scholars more critical of current government policies, there has been a visible effort to follow Byers's footsteps in the worthwhile endeavour to inculcate a greater degree of strategy and strategic acumen to Canadian policymaking – Don Macnamara and Ann Fitz-Gerald, who have kindly provided chapters for this volume, being perhaps foremost among them.

This volume represents an important addition to this long-standing effort to advance Canadian strategic thought on security matters. It brings together a diverse group of experts to discuss and provide an array of perspectives on Canada's particular place in the global system, its interests and the threats and potential threats to them, and ways for Canada to counter those threats and maintain and advance its national interests. Though many books discuss the topics of the individual chapters of this volume, not since the publication of Dewitt and Leyton-Brown's book has someone brought these topics together under a guiding framework that offers the beginnings of a more coherent strategic approach to Canadian national and international security affairs.

At this point, however, it seems prudent to provide greater historical context and clarity to the term that thematically unites this volume – the concept of strategy itself.

Strategy and Grand Strategy

'Strategy,' according to Prussian strategist Carl von Clausewitz, is 'the use of engagements for the object of the war.'[20] This definition nicely encapsulates the core of what is traditionally meant by strategy, and has survived remarkably well since it first appeared in 1832. Other authors may prefer slightly different wordings – Colin Gray makes reference to 'the use that is made of force and the threat of force for the ends of policy,' while John Lewis Gaddis terms it 'the process by which ends are related to means, intensions to capabilities, objectives to resources.'[21] That being said, the Clausewitzian distinction between tactical means and strategic ends remains at its core. This definition may contain a certain 'battlefield' flavour, but the concern with bridging tactical and/ or operational means to political ends precludes the notion that the Prussian officer was wedded to operational or even tactical thinking.[22]

Signs of a 'higher level' of strategy would be more fully spelled out by British military theorist Sir Basil Liddell Hart, who added to Clausewitz's definition by emphasizing the need 'to co-ordinate and direct all the resources of a nation, or band of nations, towards the attainment of the political object of the war.'[23] By expanding the notion of means to include military *and* non-military instruments of power, Liddell Hart did an admirable job in advancing a 'grand' perspective of strategy. As he notes, 'Fighting power is one of the instruments of grand strategy – which should take into account of and apply the power of financial pressure, of diplomatic pressure, of commercial pressure, and, not least of ethical pressure, to weaken the opponent's will.'[24]

The idea of grand strategy has since grown to incorporate a more holistic view of both tactical means *and* political ends. No longer is it limited to achieving political ends only within immediate wartime circumstances, but can include a much broader set of political goals during times of war and peace. As Paul Kennedy observed, 'The crux of grand strategy lies in *policy*, that is, in the capacity of the nation's leaders to bring together all the elements, both military and non-military, for the preservation and enhancement of the nation's long-term (that is, in wartime *and* peacetime) best interests.'[25] Whether one conceives of the relationship between military and non-military means and political policy ends as a 'bridge,' 'dialogue,' or a 'means-ends chain,' questions of grand strategy should neither be mistaken for strictly military matters nor be limited to what Clausewitz calls the 'grammar of war.'[26]

Yet there is a danger that the definitional broadening of grand strategy could be taken too far. For instance, if the definition of grand strategy was broadened to include all available resources and instruments in pursuit of all available international goals, there would be little to differentiate it from the concept of foreign policy – especially if one includes such 'low politics' issues as environmental protection or foreign aid to poor and strategically inconsequential regions under this rubric.[27] One solution is to narrow what one includes in the 'means' of grand strategy. While concerned with a plethora of different foreign policy goals, grand strategy in this formulation, as propagated by scholars such as John Mearsheimer and Robert Art, would be focused solely on the role of military instruments in achieving these goals.[28] Yet an undue emphasis on military means does seem to be an overly restrictive way to look at grand strategy, insofar as it would begin to resemble nothing so much as military policy. Indeed, by culling non-military instruments from the equation, this conception also loses a critical core of what made grand strategy unique: different instruments of national power can be synergistically directed towards certain political ends.

A potentially more useful approach is to maintain a broad perspective on the 'means' of grand strategy, and to balance this equation with more restricted political ends. Colin Dueck, for instance, defines grand strategy as a 'calculated relationship of ends and means' applied against potential opponents in narrow circumstances in which force might potentially be used. He is also careful to not precipitately discard non-military instruments from his definition, but 'only insofar as they are meant to serve the overall pursuit of national goals in the face of potential armed conflict with potential opponents.'[29] Clearly, this would make it very difficult to mistake grand strategy for foreign policy.

This definition also nicely emphasizes the need to reconcile political ends with *limited* means. Countries do not possess unlimited resources that can be placed at the disposal of policymakers; such individuals must instead set goals and priorities in a domestic environment characterized by resource scarcity and political constraints. If such a claim applies in the American case, it would be an even more apt description for middle powers like Canada that are sorely lacking in both strategic reach and resources. The clear emphasis on an opponent also serves as a reminder that strategy is played against another player who has the ability to react, respond, and potentially undo one's best-laid plans, thereby giving reason for the notion that strategy possesses a 'paradoxical logic.'[30]

Yet it would be an overstatement to assume that only those foreign policy concerns that involve conflict and the possible use of force can be considered 'in the realm of strategic interaction.'[31] For instance, Canadian security may no longer be threatened directly by American military aggrandizement, but there is little doubt that policymakers in Ottawa are clearly aware that 'unwanted' help from a larger ally like the United States could endanger its sovereign independence.[32] A broader view of security – which can encompass direct military threats, unwanted military assistance, and even the infringement of sovereignty – might prove analytically more useful in understanding questions of grand strategy. Barry Posen, for example, makes reference to the need for grand strategy to be centrally concerned with state security, but is also careful not to make explicit what actually constitutes a security threat.[33] As Don Macnamara makes clear in this volume, Canadian interests involve a broad set of different priorities, not all of which are necessarily threatened by military force.

Ultimately, grand strategy can perhaps best be conceptualized as a means-ends chain that helps policymakers identify the long-term, security-enhancing foreign policy goals and interests; the threats or challenges to those goals from adversaries and allies alike; and the relevant resources, capabilities, and instruments of statecraft (military and non-military, national and allied)[34] to achieve these goals. It nicely complements Byers's conception of a security policy and, for this author, can be used synonymously with *national security strategy*, the latter term occasionally used by contributors in this volume.[35]

Grand strategy can be seen as a *framework for action* that embodies a particular way of rational thinking, in which means and ends, and the linkage between the two, are identified. But it can equally be seen as a particular *type of behaviour*, which a state exhibits or, in a more prescriptive capacity, should pursue in its foreign, defence, and security policies. This volume is largely agnostic on this methodological and definitional issue. It is concerned instead with applying strategy (grand or otherwise) prescriptively (as a framework for or type of behaviour) on a range of national and international security issues. In so doing, we hope to demonstrate how strategic principles may help safeguard Canadian national security and advance the country's security interests, and thereby provide a guide on how to better inculcate strategy and national security concerns into Canada's foreign and defence policies.

Canada's National Security at Home and Abroad

This volume is divided into five parts, each of which consists of up to three chapters that address different facets of the section theme. Part One is concerned with providing 'A Framework for National Security' to guide Canadian policymakers on the crucial strategic issues of the day. As its title suggests, the uniting theme of this section is the need for academic scholars and policymakers to better conceptualize how strategic thinking and planning may be usefully applied in the formulation and implementation of Canada's foreign and defence policies. In particular, this involves the development of a means-ends framework that induces policymakers to identify and prioritize diverse national interests, recognize threats and potential threats to such interests, and identify those instruments of statecraft or 'means' to counter security threats and safeguard and advance security-enhancing political goals.

The notion that a middle power like Canada has the wherewithal let alone the pressing need to formulate a grand strategy may indeed seem presumptuous, especially to readers familiar with the arcane and often futile debates over U.S. grand strategy that take place in Washington.[36] But as Charles Doran and David Pratt argue in chapter 1, the need for Canadian policymakers to formulate a grand strategy and to do so in concert with its key allies, most notably the United States, has never been more vital – especially given the shifting and potentially unstable international structure that emerged at the end of the Cold War. To aid in this worthwhile endeavour, the authors provide some useful guidelines for the formulation of grand strategy in the Canadian context, as well as offering their thoughts on those powers that might pose the greatest challenge (as well as potential opportunity) in the future, most especially Germany, Japan, and China.

Both authors make clear that Canadian policymakers formulating the country's grand strategy should be strongly cognizant of its national interests, and possible threats and risks to such interests. This theme is taken up in further detail in chapter 2. As Don Macnamara argues, the Canadian government should recall that its primary obligation remains the security of its citizens and territory; this remains the sine qua non for any other goal that policymakers in the polity may seek to pursue. As he goes on to argue, a national security strategy would be the most important step in fulfilling that most crucial of obligations. Such a strategy should in turn be concerned with identifying and prioritizing different national interests,[37] and being situated with those behavioural inclinations – in the case of Canada, a notable proclivity to pursue 'forward defence' in order to counter threats abroad rather than at home – embedded in the country's strategic culture.

In pursuit of a grand or national security strategy, policymakers would do well to develop a strategic framework that recognizes what Hugh Segal has termed the 'balance of freedoms': to ensure that individuals at home and abroad are able to live with freedom from fear (e.g., violence) and the freedom from want (e.g., poverty or hunger). The balance of freedoms requires a deployable military and security capacity for operations abroad, because upholding freedom from fear may require the use of legitimate force by the international community; but since violence is often closely associated with poverty, Canada should also pay equal attention to reducing global poverty. As Segal makes clear, however, there remains an urgent need for reinvestment in Canadian international security capabilities and development of a strategic planning structure that can manage risk amidst such global uncertainty.

Part Two of this volume, by providing an overview of Canadian defence and security policy from a domestic and continental perspective, turns readers' attention to 'The Home Front.' In that regard, it is closely associated with what numerous Canadian policy-planning documents have frequently termed the first two priorities of the Canadian Forces (CF) – the defence of Canada and the defence of North America – with the third priority, contribution to international peace and security, being the subject of subsequent sections of this book. But the defence of Canada, while normally referring to protecting the country from external threats, can also refer to the important domestic role played by the Canadian military, and not simply in an 'aid of the civil powers' capacity.

This last point, that the Canadian military can have an important and indirect role in securing other important political goals aside from straightforward territorial security, is made clear by Craig Stone in chapter 4. The *Canada First Defence Strategy* offers a long-term funding framework that promises the planned spending of $490 billion over nearly the next twenty years; it is therefore clear that there will need to be accelerated military procurements to replace existing capabilities, in the years ahead. As this recapitalization slowly unfolds, Stone argues, a more robust linkage between military procurement and domestic industry could strengthen the Canadian economy and make it more competitive internationally, thereby enhancing Canada's national interests.

While policymakers should remain cognizant on the relationship between defence procurement and economic security, they should be equally aware of the increasingly important homeland security and defence role played by the CF and other departments and agencies, most notably the Canadian Coast Guard and the Royal Canadian Mounted Police. This is the subject of chapter 5, by Elinor Sloan, who argues that the terrorist attacks of 11 September 2001 and the melting of the polar ice cap have driven policymakers to focus more steadily on ensuring the security of the home front. She goes on to demonstrate that homeland security and homeland defence remain distinctive if still related concepts, and subsequently outlines ways in which policy has evolved and initiatives have been formulated to deal with threats to the homeland.

That being said, Canada is not alone, by dint of its uniquely fortuitous geostrategic location in North America, in confronting these security threats. In chapter 6, Joseph Jockel and Joel Sokolsky provide an overview of Canadian involvement in joint defence initiatives with the United States. As they note, Canada-U.S. arrangements have historically been looser and less integrative, often reflecting Louis St Laurent's memorable phrase, from his famous Gray Lecture, 'like farmers whose lines have a common concession line.'[38] Indeed, the only exception to this trend has been the *binational* 'NORAD anomaly,' to use James Fergusson's words.[39] And despite some preliminary discussions in the Binational Planning Group on expanding the responsibilities of this venerable command, both authors detect a clear trend towards looser bilateral defence cooperation for the foreseeable future.

Part Three, 'Regions and Players of Interest,' focuses on those key geostrategic regions of the world – the Euro-Atlantic, the Asia-Pacific, and South Asia – where Canada has important security interests and confronts threats and potential threats to those interests. Canada has traditionally been heavily involved in Euro-Atlantic affairs, initially as a result of its imperial linkages with the United Kingdom and later through its close partnership with the United States, as clearly demonstrated with its sizable military expeditions to Europe during two world wars, its sizable peacetime military deployment in Western Europe during the Cold War, and its duties – first with the UN and later with NATO – in the violent break-up of Yugoslavia in the 1990s. But at the cusp of the second decade of the twenty-first century, other regions of the world are competing for Canadian attention. One needs only to look at the nearly decade-long deployment of the Canadian Forces, along with its NATO partners, far from the frontlines of Europe in Afghanistan. With the simultaneous rise of China and India, it is clear that Canadian policymakers, especially the more strategically astute among them, will be even more focused on the geostrategic shifts in the Pacific, most notably in East Asia and South Asia respectively.

Alexander Moens in chapter 7 begins the section with an overview of Canada's traditional Euro-Atlantic region of concern. Canada may be no longer centrally concerned with strategic threats emanating from Europe, but should still recognize that its role in NATO remains of vital interest for an effective Canadian contribution to international security. This is especially true as a result of the gradual post–Cold War transformation of the Atlantic alliance, which has shifted from static collective defence directed at the Soviet Union to a cooperative security arrangement across the entire breadth of the European continent, in addition to being a global expeditionary-oriented coalition arrangement for 'out-of-area' operations. Partnership with the European Union is still of major concern for Canadian policymakers, but primarily as a means to address non-military (and especially economic) interests.

But, according to both Thomas Adams in chapter 8 and Douglas Goold in chapter 9, Canada should also recognize that economic trade, commerce, and indeed core international security dynamics have decisively shifted to the Asia-Pacific. China is at the heart of this geostrategic transformation, as Thomas Adams argues. But it is unfortunate that Canada's leaders have failed to grasp the complexities of the Asia-Pacific security environment and the ways in which Canadian interests have the potential to be harmed there. Douglas Goold, who keenly shows South Asia's growing importance and risk to Canadian interests, reiterates these concerns. It would be unfortunate indeed, he concludes, if Canadian policymakers failed to understand how globalization has only reinforced South Asia's growing strategic importance on economic and security spheres.

As examined in Part Four of this volume, 'Expeditionary Missions and the Future of the CF,' Canada's commitment to international security and stability – while often based on economic and institutional involvement – has periodically included a notable willingness to send military forces abroad. Indeed, scholars like Sean Maloney have coined the term *forward security*[40] in reference to Canada's evident inclination for the deployment of expeditionary forces to a range of international locales; since the end of the Cold War, these missions have increasingly focused on the need for the robust stabilization of failing or failed states, of which the Afghan mission remains only the latest and perhaps among the most ambitious. Military planners need to ensure that, as core capabilities are rebuilt in the decades ahead, the CF maintains a balanced force structure capable of fulfilling this important expeditionary role, while not overlooking its domestic and continental responsibilities.

Canada maintains a distinguished history of deploying its armed forces in global expeditionary coalitions. As illustrated by David Bercuson and J.L. Granatstein in chapter 10, Canada has often undertaken such missions – sometimes under the UN, though increasingly with its NATO allies – in pursuit of its national interest. Not only does confronting national security threats abroad help ensure that these threats do not materialize at home, but deploying as part of a coalition confers diplomatic and political benefits as well as influence and prestige. As the authors conclude, it is critical for Canadian officials to avoid the mistake of retrenching Canadian expeditionary capabilities as a result of some misconceived 'peace dividend.' Previous governments, both Liberal and Conservative, have often failed to resist such a temptation; and with the end of Canada's military deployment to Afghanistan in 2011, this warning is especially poignant.

Military expeditions over the last few decades have often taken the form of stabilization operations within states that, if not necessarily having totally failed, are often on the cusp of such failure. The mission in Afghanistan, after decades of having been ravaged by war, is a case in point. But as Ann Fitz-Gerald notes in chapter 11, while policymakers have been able to make the link between conducting stabilization operations abroad and serving Canadian national interests, the absence of several key elements of a clear strategic policy prevents Canada – and indeed other countries – from fully achieving key stabilization objectives. As she concludes, strategic planning and indeed policy needs to be coordinated across government departments and agencies involved in Canada's 'whole-of-government' approach to such missions.

Part Five looks further afield at those diverse and increasingly salient 'Issues, Risks, and Threats' that may pose increasingly serious implications for Canadian national security, and the security of our major allies and partners, as the post-9/11 era enters its second decade. Canadian policymakers must first be ever vigilant against threats that might emerge from within its borders and in its immediate region, whether defined in its traditional sense as North America or even broader to encompass the Americas itself. Yet it is equally important to look further afield – to the threat posed by catastrophic terrorism, so vividly demonstrated during 9/11, and the challenge of WMD proliferation that has haunted policymakers since the beginning of the nuclear age. WMD proliferation and global terrorism remain the twin scourges of the post-9/11 world and will continue to be so for the foreseeable future.

Policymakers were rightly preoccupied with planning the end of the CF combat role, even as a smaller contingent of Canadian Forces continues to be deployed in a training capacity. The Conservative government's *Canada First Defence Strategy* emphasizes the long-term recapitalization of a number of the CF's major platforms, notwithstanding certain doubts on the availability of continued government funding that was hinted in the 2010 Budget.[41] As Douglas Bland and Brian MacDonald remind us in chapter 12, it is important for policymakers to begin addressing what parameters should guide the future direction of the CF. There is certainly an urgent need to develop a military force structure, they conclude, that is geared towards expeditions abroad and would be equally flexible for potential challenges at home.

In chapter 13, James Fergusson and David McDonough undertake a strategic assessment of the ways in which WMD proliferation – particularly horizontal proliferation to rogue states and terrorists, as opposed to vertical proliferation among the established nuclear powers – might endanger Canadian national security. While Canada has a historic tradition of supporting the global non-proliferation regime to curb and control the spread of WMD, Fergusson and McDonough examine additional ways in which Canada can ensure its security interests and reinforce its vital partnership with its superpower ally. Most controversially, they assess the benefits that could be accrued from an independent Canadian military contribution to a continent-wide ballistic missile defence system, and offer their thoughts on the role that the Canadian military may play as geostrategic competition moves into outer space.

Since the 9/11 terrorist attacks, the international community (and especially the United States and its allies) has been fixated on the threat of transnational Islamist groups undertaking catastrophic terrorist attacks – most likely conventional, but potentially involving rudimentary but still deadly WMD or radioactive dispersal devices – against soft Western targets. In chapter 14, Alex Wilner undertakes a detailed examination of how the terrorist security threat has evolved during this period and how each of its three dimensions (international, regional, and home-grown) threatens Canadian interests. There is an urgent need for Canada, in close cooperation with other countries, to counter this threat, and he usefully provides the outline of a Canadian counterterrorism strategy.

In the post-9/11 world, the international environment and its security dimensions have taken on a broad and increasingly complex character – one needs only to witness the convulsions gripping the Middle East and North Africa to understand the fluid and often unexpected geostrategic dynamics that Canadian policymakers must now navigate. The development of appropriate security policies that address the protection of Canada's national interests, as well as the strategic analysis that underpins and unites such policies, are therefore equally complex and demanding. Indeed, they will have to go well beyond a military-only dimension to involve what has been termed the 'whole-of-government approach,' and will need to deal with both domestic and international security. In today's strategic environment, the 'home' and 'away' games are equally necessary and so is the formulation of a more coherent and strategic approach to national security in Canada. It is to this important task that the chapters of this volume will now turn.

NOTES

1 That being said, Canada did command the multinational naval Task Force 151, which was charged to support both Operation Enduring Freedom *and* Operation Iraqi Freedom in the Persian Gulf. In addition, there were 30 Canadian military personnel at U.S. Central Command in Qatar, as well as up to 150 military exchange personnel with the United States, the United Kingdom, and Australia, with some involved directly in Iraq (most notably then Major-General Walter J. Natynczyk, who commanded 30,000 troops in Iraq). See Janice Gross Stein and Eugene Lang, *The Unexpected War: Canada in Kandahar* (Toronto: Viking Canada, 2007), chap. 5; and Julian Beltrame, 'Canada to Stay Out of Iraq War,' *MacLean's*, 31 Mar. 2003.

2 This refers to the 1986 report of the Special Joint Committee of the
   Senate and the House of Commons on Canada's international relations,
   titled *Independence and Internationalism*. Cited in Joseph Jockel and Joel
   Sokolsky, 'Dandurand Revisited: Rethinking Canada's Defence Policy in
   an Unstable World,' *International Journal* 48, no. 2 (1993): 383. For more on
   the Canadian tendency to have an expansive definition of what constitutes national security, see Kim Richard Nossal, 'Defending the "Realm":
   Canadian Strategic Culture Revisited,' *International Journal* 59, no. 3
   (Summer 2004): 503–20.

3 See Galen Roger Perras, *Franklin Roosevelt and the Origins of the Canadian-
   American Security Alliance, 1933–1945: Necessary, But Not Necessary Enough*
   (Westport, CT: Praeger, 1998).

4 The term *pinchpenny diplomacy* was coined in Kim Richard Nossal,
   'Pinchpenny Diplomacy: The Decline of "Good International Citizenship"
   in Canadian Foreign Policy,' *International Journal* 54, no. 1 (Winter 1998–9):
   88–105.

5 Colin Gray, 'The Need for Independent Canadian Strategic Thought,'
   Canadian Defence Quarterly 1 (Summer 1971): 6. Also see John Gellner,
   'Strategic Analysis in Canada,' *International Journal* 33, no. 3 (1978):
   493–505.

6 Andrew Richter, *Avoiding Armageddon: Canadian Military Strategy and
   Nuclear Weapons, 1950–63* (Vancouver: UBC Press, 2002). For a good exam-
   ple of R.J. Sutherland's geo-strategic insight, see his 'Canada's Long-Term
   Strategic Situation,' *International Journal* 18, no. 3 (Summer 1962): 199–223.

7 David Haglund, *The North Atlantic Triangle Revisited: Canadian Grand
   Strategy at Century's End*, Contemporary Affairs no. 4 (Toronto: Irwin
   Publishing / Canadian Institute of International Affairs, 2000), 10.

8 Douglas Ross and Christopher Ross, 'From "Neo-Isolationism" to
   "Imperial Liberalism": "Grand Strategy Options" in the American
   International Security Debate and the Implications for Canada,' in
   *The Dilemmas of American Strategic Primacy: Implications for the Future
   of Canadian–American Cooperation*, ed. Douglas A. Ross and David S.
   McDonough (Toronto: Royal Canadian Military Institute, 2005), 165.

9 R.B. Byers, *Canadian Security and Defence: The Legacy and the Challenges*,
   Adelphi Paper 214 (London: International Institute for Strategic Studies,
   1986), 5. For his earlier thoughts on the foreign and defence policy bridge,
   see Byers, 'Defence and Foreign Policy in the 1970s: The Demise of the
   Trudeau Doctrine,' *International Journal* 33 (1977–8): 312–38.

10 See David Dewitt and David Leyton-Brown, eds., *Canada's International
   Security Policy* (Scarborough, ON: Prentice Hall, 1995).

11 See William Hogg, 'Plus ça change: Continuity, Change and Culture in Canadian Foreign Policy White Papers,' *International Journal* 59, no. 3 (Summer 2004): 521–36. For a good overview on the continuity of Canada's strategic behaviour, see Nossal, 'Defending the "Realm,"' 503–20.

12 See Kim Richard Nossal, 'Right and Wrong in Foreign Policy 40 Years On: Realism and Idealism in Canadian Foreign Policy,' *International Journal*, 62, no. 2 (Spring 2007): 263–77; and Douglas Ross, 'Foreign Policy Challenges for Paul Martin: Canada's International Security Policy in an Era of American Hyperpower and Continental Vulnerability,' *International Journal* 58, no. 4 (Autumn 2003): 550.

13 Daniel Madar and Denis Stairs, 'Alone on Killers' Role: The Policy Analysis Group and the Department of External Affairs,' *International Journal* 32 (1976–7): 730. For more on 'national style,' see Colin Gray, *Nuclear Strategy and National Style* (Lanham, MD: University Press of America, 1986).

14 For a good overview on the Trudeau government's emphasis on developing more rational policy planning, see David Dewitt and John Kirton, *Canada as a Principal Power: A Study in Foreign Policy and International Relations* (Toronto: Wiley, 1983).

15 For a good overview on the role of these two agencies, see Nelson Michaud, 'The Prime Minister, PMO, and PCO: Makers of Canadian Foreign Policy?' in *Handbook of Canadian: Foreign Policy*, ed. Patrick James, Nelson Michaud, and Marc O'Reilly, 21–48 (Toronto: Lexington Books, 2006).

16 For example, see Haglund, *North Atlantic Triangle Revisited*, and David Haglund, 'The North Atlantic Triangle Revisited: (Geo)Political Metaphor and the Logic of Canadian Foreign Policy,' *American Review of Canadian Studies* 29, no. 2 (Summer 1999): 211–35.

17 Justin Massie, 'Making Sense of Canada's "Irrational" International Security Policy: A Tale of Three Strategic Cultures,' *International Journal* 64, no. 3 (Summer 2009): 625–45; and Nossal, 'Defending the "Realm."'

18 See David Pratt, 'Canadian Grand Strategy and Lessons Learned,' *Journal of Transatlantic Studies* 6, no. 1 (Apr. 2008): 61–78; and David Pratt, 'Is There Grand Strategy in Canadian Foreign Policy?' *Journal of Military and Strategic Studies* 10, no. 2 (Winter 2008): 1–24. Also see his co-authored chapter (with Charles Doran) in this volume.

19 See Evan Potter, 'Niche Diplomacy as Canadian Foreign Policy,' *International Journal* 52, 1 (Winter 1996–7): 25–38.

20 Carl von Clausewitz, *On War*, trans. Michael Howard and Peter Paret (Princeton, NJ: Princeton University Press, 1976), 178, as cited in Colin Gray, *Modern Strategy* (Oxford: Oxford University Press, 1999), 17.

21 Gray, *Modern Strategy*, 17; and John Lewis Gaddis, *Strategies of Containment: A Critical Appraisal of Postwar American National Security Policy* (New York: Oxford University Press, 1982), viii.

22 Gray, *Modern Strategy*, 17 and 104.

23 Basil Liddell Hart, *Strategy*, 2nd ed. (New York: Signet/New American Library, 1974), 335–6.

24 Ibid., 336.

25 Paul Kennedy, 'Grand Strategies in War and Peace: Towards a Broader Definition,' in *Grand Strategies in War and Peace*, ed. Paul Kennedy (New Haven, CT: Yale University Press, 1992), 5 (emphasis in original).

26 Colin Gray concludes, 'Strategy is the *bridge* that relates military power to political purpose,' as well as the 'product of *dialogue* between policy and military power.' Gray, *Modern Strategy*, 17, and 'Inescapable Geography,' in Colin Gray and Geoffrey Sloan, eds., *Geopolitics, Geography and Strategy* (London: Frank Cass, 1999), 169 (emphasis added). Meanwhile, Barry Posen has termed grand strategy a 'political-military, *means-ends chain.'* Posen, *The Sources of Military Doctrine: France, Britain, and Germany Between the World Wars* (Ithaca: Cornell University Press, 1986), 13 (emphasis added).

27 Robert Art, 'A Defensible Defense: America's Grand Strategy after the Cold War,' *International Security* 15, no. 4 (Spring 1991): 7.

28 See Robert Art, *A Grand Strategy for America* (Ithaca: Cornell University Press, 2003); and John Mearsheimer, *Liddell Hart and the Weight of History* (Ithaca: Cornell University Press, 1988).

29 Colin Dueck, *Reluctant Crusader: Power, Culture, and Change in American Grand Strategy* (Princeton: Princeton University Press, 2006), 10.

30 See Edward Luttwak, *Strategy: The Logic of War and Peace* (Cambridge, MA: Harvard University Press, 1987).

31 Dueck, *Reluctant Crusaders*, 10.

32 This concern is at the core of what Nils Ørvik has termed the 'defence against help' strategy. See Nils Ørvik, 'Defence against Help: A Strategy for Small States?' *Survival* 15, no. 5 (Sept.–Oct. 1973): 228–31, and Nils Ørvik 'The Basic Issue in Canadian National Security: Defence against Help, Defence to Help Others,' *Canadian Defence Quarterly* 11, no. 1 (Summer 1981): 8–15. For a good analysis of this concept, see Donald Barry and Duane Bratt, 'Defence against Help: Explaining Canada–US Security Relations,' *American Review of Canadian Studies* 38, no. 1 (Mar. 2008): 63–89.

33 Posen, *Sources of Military Doctrine*, 13, 220.

34 The notion of including national and allied resources as part of a state's grand strategy is noted in Ross and Ross, 'From "Neo-Isolationism" to

"Imperial Liberalism,"' 165. This point is also hinted at by Liddell Hart, who notes the need to take into account the coordination and direction of 'all the resources of a nation, *or band of nations.*' Hart, *Strategy,* 336 (emphasis added).

35 Indeed, in a previous paper, both Don Macnamara and Ann Fitz-Gerald make clear that their use of the term *national security strategy* is synonymous with *grand strategy.* See their 'A National Security Framework for Canada,' *IRPP Policy Matters* 3, no. 10 (October 2002): 1–40.

36 For an overview of the U.S. grand strategy debate, see David S. McDonough, 'Beyond Primacy? Hegemony and "Security Addiction" in US Grand Strategy,' *Orbis* 52, no. 3 (Winter 2009): 6–22.

37 For a complementary classification of American national interests, see Robert Art, *A Grand Strategy for America* (Ithaca: Cornell University Press, 2003), chap. 2.

38 For good analyses of St Laurent's Gray Lecture, see Adam Chapnick, 'The Gray Lecture and Canadian Citizenship in History,' *American Review of Canadian Studies* 37, 4 (Winter 2007): 443–57; and Hector Mackenzie, 'Shades of Gray? "The Foundations of Canadian Policy in World Affairs" in Context,' *American Review of Canadian Studies* 37, no. 4 (Winter 2007): 459–74.

39 James Fergusson, *Beneath the Radar: Change and Transformation in the Canada–US North American Defence Relationship* (Calgary: Canadian Defence and Foreign Affairs Institute, Dec. 2009), 5.

40 See Sean Maloney, 'In the Service of Forward Security: Peacekeeping, Stabilization and the Canadian Way of War,' in *Canadian Way of War: Serving the National Interest,* ed. Bernd Horn (Toronto: Dundurn, 2006), 297–323.

41 Canada, Department of National Defence, *Canada First Defence Strategy* (Ottawa: 2008).

PART ONE

A Framework for National Security

1 The Need for a Canadian Grand Strategy

CHARLES F. DORAN AND DAVID PRATT

What do we mean by *grand strategy*?[1] Coming out of a period of bipolarity, members of the international system are still trying to comprehend where they stand in structural terms. If unipolarity is a reality, what does it entail? To the extent that it is an acknowledgment of the U.S. willingness and capacity to lead in world affairs, that observation is a useful premise to start the discussion. Vast inequalities of power do exist. But how are Canada and the other prominent democracies to respond to change on their own power cycles and to those of the new rising states in the twenty-first century?

Grand strategy manifests the values, interests, and aspirations of a country and its citizens. It encompasses the foreign policy role that the country would like to play and an assessment of its capability to play that role, which is grounded in structural reality – a reality that itself is ever evolving.[2] It incorporates a notion of the threats that a country faced historically and the risks it is likely to confront in the future. Grand strategy also transmits a country's sense of purpose and the place it holds both morally and politically in the international system. As Paul Kennedy has summarized, 'The crux of grand strategy lies therefore in *policy*, that is, in the capacity of the nation's leaders to bring together all of the elements, both military and nonmilitary, for the preservation and enhancement of the nation's long-term (that is in wartime *and* peacetime) best interests. ... it operates at various levels, political, strategic, operational, tactical, all interacting with each other to advance (or retard) the primary aim.'[3] Grand strategy requires prescient understanding and use of that combination of hard- and soft-power tools that Joseph Nye recommends under the label 'smart power.'[4] The very long view of grand strategy can become a reality only through policies envisioned and implemented in the near term.

The reader may object: surely grand strategy is for the United States, or the European Union, or China, but not for Canada. According to that view, grand strategy is only for the largest states in the system, the 'great powers.' But international relations theory has long challenged the exclusivity of these ideas about grand strategy, for 'whether a state has yet to develop economically or is already developed, whether a state is an importer of security or a great power, whether a state primarily views the system through a regional or a global lens, whether a state is a new entry into the global trading system or an experienced participant in globalization – it is traversing a "cycle of relative power and role" vis-à-vis a system of states, both regionally and globally.'[5] Middle powers too have interests. They must act even more circumspectly than the great power. They must husband their resources and marshal them to best effect. They too have roles to play and miles to go before each generation tallies its challenges and its accomplishments.

Properly conceived, grand strategy provides a government with an understanding of structural change within the international system. It generates an estimate of how this change is likely to unfold in the near term and with what impact on the country and its interests. Following the Napoleonic wars, the British foreign secretary, Lord Castlereagh, sought at the Congress of Vienna (1815) to pursue a grand strategy of concert among the former belligerents, leading to annual meetings – much like those of the Group of Eight (G8) today and perhaps the Group of Twenty (G20) in the future – to try to resolve problems of world order without plunging Europe once again into war.

U.S. President George Washington in his Farewell Address attempted to promote a grand strategy for the fledgling American polity that simultaneously identified the principal problems the young country would face and provided a possible solution. That grand strategy involved the principle of avoiding 'permanent alliances' and reflected a clear vision of the near-term structural changes impinging on the nation's foreign and domestic policies at a time when it was weak and preoccupied with economic matters. Washington's meaning was that the United States ought not to get involved in the war between France and Britain, but for reasons of diplomatic delicacy, the individual countries were not mentioned. Each country put pressure to bear on the United States, with France wanting the Americans to honour their alliance commitments under the 1778 Treaty of Alliance, and Great Britain wanting – if not quite an alliance – then at least for Washington to continue its otherwise non-committal position towards France. Washington's grand strategy was to avoid any substantive alliance commitments, or as Thomas Jefferson would later term 'entangling alliances,' and therefore war with either European power. This perspective contained all the elements of grand strategy – affecting not only European relations but North American relations, not only military considerations but economic ones, not only tactical issues but strategic ones at the highest level.

Sir John A. Macdonald is not known as a grand strategist, but he probably deserves such a title. Like George Washington, he was pre-occupied with economic growth and avoiding conflict. Macdonald's National Policy of high tariffs and a transcontinental railway was intended to knit the country together from east to west and lay the foundations for growth and prosperity. Unlike Washington, however, Macdonald could not politically or strategically disavow the imperial connection with Britain and declare neutrality. The earliest signs of Canadian grand strategy began to emerge after the Treaty of Washington in 1871. Negotiated by American and British diplomats, it has been characterized by American jurist John Bassett Moore as 'the greatest treaty of actual and immediate arbitration the world has ever seen.'[6] It brought an end to what historian Frank Underhill described as the Anglo-American 'Hundred Years War'[7] and importantly demilitarized the Canada-U.S. border. Since the Americans agreed to both Sir John A's participation within the British delegation and to his title 'Prime Minister of the Dominion of Canada,' the treaty also amounted to de facto recognition by the United States of Canadian sovereignty.

The Treaty of Washington was the first step toward British–American détente and the creation of a 'zone of peace' (perhaps the world's first), where Canada, the United States, and Britain had reasonable expectations that disputes would be settled peacefully.[8] Building on American historian John Bartlet Brebner's concept of the 'North Atlantic Triangle,' David Haglund's 'bookkeeper's puzzle' summarized the challenges that faced Canadian grand strategy in the decades after Confederation: 'This puzzle consisted in how best to manage relations with both Britain and the United States so as to be able to invoke the assistance of the former against the latter's political (and perhaps military) pressure while at the same time ensuring that British desire for Anglo American rapprochement would not result in a "sacrifice" of Canadian interests.'[9]

Although not always successful (the Alaska Boundary Dispute being a case in point), successive Canadian governments were generally able to protect the country's vital interests as power shifted from Imperial Britain to Pax Americana. U.S. dominance after the Second World War created new challenges for Canadian grand strategy, which were deftly managed by Prime Minister Louis St Laurent and his secretary of state for external affairs, Lester Pearson. From Confederation to the present day, felicitous Canada–U.S. relations – from the North American Aerospace Defence Command (NORAD) to the North American Free Trade Agreement – have been at the core of Canadian grand strategy.[10] But Canada's commitment to multilateralism and security cooperation, through the United Nations and the North Atlantic Treaty Organization (NATO), respectively, has also been critical as a means of moderating or tempering the U.S. inclination toward unilateralism and as an instrument for expressing Canadian values, interests, and aspirations.

Grounding Grand Strategy in Structural Reality

One frequently hears about 'power shifts' in the international affairs literature. But what is meant by *power shift*? Is power really shifting from North America and Europe to Asia? Or is power merely shifting from one state to another, if at all, and if so, to what extent and toward which states? Do shifts necessarily imply disorder and increased probability of war? Where would Canada find itself in such a loosely configured reordering of power?

Analysts also speak of 'hegemony' and often attribute hegemony to the United States, especially following the collapse of the Soviet Union and the end of bipolarity. But what purportedly does such hegemony entail? If it implies a disproportionate capacity for initiative and leadership, then it makes sense. If it is to mean here political domination and control, then it is not tenable. Equally problematic, the proponents of the hegemonic interpretation usually think in terms of a pair of states – a declining hegemon and a rising challenger – and argue that major war is highly likely if not inevitable when a 'power transition' occurs, replacing one hegemon with a new hegemon.[11] According to that structural understanding, the United States is a declining hegemon and China the rising challenger, with Canada and other countries caught between these larger structural forces. The 'hegemonic-transition' characterization of structure and structural change has many advocates, probably both in China and the United States, because it appears intuitive. But its hegemonic perspective is incorrect and misleads.

Certainly a better way of capturing the dynamic of structural change is needed than is offered by notions of either 'power shift' or 'hegemonic transition.' Another way of capturing this dynamic, and what it means for Canada, is in terms of the 'cycle of relative [state] power and role' introduced earlier in the chapter. In this understanding, each state is located on a cycle of power relative to other states, which, over long periods, traces the state's evolution as a major power. According to this dynamic view of structural change, the state power cycles evolve as part of a 'single dynamic' that maps the structural trends of history. Two 'principles of the power cycle' explain how differential absolute growth sets the cycles in motion, creating a particular non-linear pattern of rise and decline for the component state cycles. In brief, a single state growing faster than the systemic norm initiates change in the power cycles throughout the system, altering the systemic norm and the competitive relationships reflected on each relative power cycle trajectory. Moreover, the trends on the state cycles encode the perspective of statecraft. When decision-makers contemplate future change on a state power cycle, they form expectations regarding its future security and foreign policy role outlook.[12]

Structural change takes place over long periods of history. Since the middle of the eighteenth century, France has been in relative decline. Britain peaked in its relative power somewhere in the middle of the nineteenth century. Although it remains an economic powerhouse, as a pre-eminent imperial power, Germany passed through its entire cycle from rise, to peak, to relative decline in less than a century. It took some 175 years for the United States to reach the upper turning point in its relative power around 1970. However, since it is by far the most powerful state in the system, its nascent relative decline has not altered its position of predominance very much. It remains the most powerful state in the system by a wide margin both in economic and (especially) military terms.

To the great surprise of many analysts who were predicting in the 1980s that Japan would become number one, replacing the United States in that position, Japan for a variety of internal and external reasons peaked in the 1990s. What happened? Because of its very high absolute growth rate, China, at the bottom of the central system of major powers, was taking power share away from Japan, as always happens in such cases, causing Japan's relative rise to flatten; Japan's internal growth challenges foreshortened the interval of its rise even more. China is located somewhere in the rapidly rising section of its own relative power cycle curve. But other countries in Asia are rising rapidly as well. South Korea has had meteoric growth. India, from a massive population base like China, is growing at a remarkable rate economically.

Normally, given a certain lag for adjustment to take place, a nation's foreign policy role follows the pattern of change on its cycle of relative power. China, for example, enjoyed a gradual, steady increase in its foreign policy role since its 'opening up' under Deng Xiaoping, starting in the late 1970s. In part to offset the decline in its foreign policy role in the early Cold War years, Europe formed the European Economic Community in 1958. To the extent that they are able to negotiate together, member states thus tried to aggregate their power on matters such as setting the rules of international economic regulation. The abrupt decline in power of Russia in 1989 led to a corresponding abrupt decline in its foreign policy role, a reality that the Putin/Medvedev government through its oil politics has assertively been attempting to reverse.

Where is Canada located on its own cycle of relative power? Although one-tenth the size of the United States in overall economic and population terms, Canada is following a pattern of change on its power cycle that is probably quite congruent with that of the United States. But because of its smaller size, Canada has felt the pressure of the rising states in the developing world even more directly than that of the United States and the European countries. That is why Canada (along with the United States) was gratified when French President Sarkozy offered support for upgrading the status of the G20, an organization that had been in existence for a decade.[13] Canada, at the bottom of the G8, was rapidly feeling the pressure from India, Brazil, and South Korea for admission.

Supported by careful data collection and analysis, power cycle theory holds a number of important theoretically justified and empirically tested conclusions regarding the relationship between movement on the state power cycle and the likelihood of involvement in war.[14] A principal conclusion is that when the relative power of a state abruptly shifts from accelerating rise (or decline) to decelerating rise (or decline), or when it abruptly shifts from rise to decline, the likelihood of war sharply increases. It is at such 'critical points' on a state power cycle that structural change is most wrenching and the probability of war is greatest. Each critical point corresponds in the state's experience to the time when the tides of history have shifted in the international system. Everything changes for state and system when expectations regarding future security and role are shattered. A confluence of such critical change in a short time creates monumental structural change known as systems transformation – periods that historically have been associated with wars of the greatest magnitude, intensity, and duration. For example, the amount of structural change in the two decades prior to the First World War, and likewise during the interwar period before the outbreak of the Second World War, was extraordinary, yielding a systems transformation in each case that undermined the equilibrium of each international system. Since the origin of the modern state system in the sixteenth century, six systems transformations have occurred: the Thirty Years War (1618–48), Louis XIV's wars (1670–1713), the Napoleonic Wars (1795–1815), the First World War (1914–19), the Second World War (1939–45), and the events at the end of the Cold War (1989–91). Only the latest systems transformation ended in a peaceful outcome.

Regarding the policy conclusions to be drawn from present and future structural change for Canadian grand strategy, several are paramount:

- Structural change on a massive scale cannot be prevented. Canada can prepare for such change, make intelligent strategic choices, and provide for its security, but no country can halt ongoing structural change. To believe otherwise is to indulge in fantasy or wishful thinking.
- Canada must adopt a grand strategy that will protect its interests. While no country can provide an exact prediction regarding structural change or future events, it is possible to assess trends and prepare for contingencies. A grand strategy allows one to place these trends and contingencies into a coherent framework for policy initiative.
- Canada possesses assets that will help to promote its interests. Canada contains a single population composed of two primary cultural-linguistic groupings – francophones and anglophones – each of which is highly literate, productive, and wealthy by global standards. Canada is an attractive place to live, both for its natural environment and reasons associated with its quality of life. From an economic point of view, Canada's proximity to the richest markets in the world provides it with leverage and stature. Canada also has seemingly unbounded natural resources such as iron, nickel, phosphate, natural gas, hydropower, and uranium. Its output of oil from the oil sands will in the next decades prove hugely valuable, provided that it does not mishandle either the politics or the environmental aspects of these extraordinary endowments.
- Canada must not isolate itself in international politics. Instead, in the midst of global structural change – especially in the context of such change – it must work with other governments possessing

roughly similar interests and the capability to promote a shared (common) world view that supports democracy, human rights, the rule of law, and pluralism.

Guidelines for Canadian Grand Strategy

At least five guidelines for formulating Canadian grand strategy ought to be kept in mind.

*Need for Flexibility and Awareness of Changing
Circumstances Abroad*

Since 1945, one cataclysmic change has altered the entire structure of the international system: the collapse of the Soviet Union and the end of the Cold War. Other equally momentous structural changes may confront the international system in the twenty-first century. Canadian grand strategy must be flexible enough to cope with such events, safeguarding the Canadian foreign policy interest in adapting to new systemic circumstances.

Need for High Level of Acceptance within the Country

Formulation of grand strategy is important only to the extent that the citizens of a country accept the general terms of that strategy. Citizens from Quebec and Alberta must accept the arguments of grand strategy as much as those from Ontario or Nova Scotia. Francophone and anglophone must equally share confidence in the notion of grand strategy. New Canadians, as much as those whose roots in Canada pre-date Confederation, must be comfortable with the principles that underlie the grand strategy. If foreign policy 'stops at the water's edge,' as U.S. Senator Arthur Vandenberg once said, then some degree of consensus across political parties is necessary for grand strategy to succeed.

*Need for Grand Strategy to Contain a Clear Conception
of Threats, Interests, and Values*

Like other liberal democracies, Canada shares a strong commitment to human rights, representative government, and a market economy. Canada does not flinch in its defence and promotion of these values. It implicitly acknowledges the lessons of democratic peace theory that mature, liberal democracies do not use force against each other. In its relationship to the United States and other democracies, Canada has always stressed the value of interdependence. But Canada has gone further and emphasized the need to interact peacefully and productively with non-democracies such as China, for example, on trade and commerce, even though these governments may not fully meet the high standards Canada sets for the treatment of its own citizens. Canada joins other governments in condemning nuclear proliferation, the sale of nuclear materials for hostile purpose, acts of environmental degradation, terrorism, piracy, the trafficking in drugs and persons, and aggression in all its forms. For these reasons, relations with North Korea, Iran, Myanmar, and Somalia, among other countries, are strained and often subject to actions short of force to try to obtain redress. Moreover, as its record in two world wars, Korea, and more recently in Afghanistan shows, Canada is willing to oppose aggression and employ force to defend its territory, its citizens, and its values when the threat is genuine and dire.

In world affairs, the Canadian interest is not hard to define. Canada is willing to join its allies and partners to preserve the kind of international order that has prevailed since 1945. Just as in international trade where, through specialization and exchange, the smallest trading partners benefit disproportionately by being able to fulfil their objectives in production consumption, so in matters of world order, it is the smallest members who benefit most because they need the kind of world order Canada cherishes to preserve their independence, territorial sovereignty, and well-being. Since the mid-twentieth century, Canada has flourished. Certainly its interest is to see that type and quality of world order preserved.

For Canada, threats can arise from a number of quarters. If a government similar to Nazi Germany or Imperial Japan were to attempt to mount a military campaign of aggression against neighbours, that would be the equivalent of aggression against Canada. Such effort to obtain global military domination would be intolerable. If a totalitarian ideology such as fascism or communism were to threaten neighbours and partners, that would jeopardize the Canadian capacity to interact and to prosper. If flagrant acts of terrorism against friends and allies, such as occurred in 9/11 against the United States, were once again to occur, that would undermine the interests and values that Canada has long sought to preserve and promote. If damage to the physical environment such as continued global warming or to the health of its population through a pandemic were to occur, that would threaten Canada and cause it to take immediate action with friends and global partners to employ the best of modern technology to eliminate the threats. In none of these cases could Canada stop these depredations alone. A cornerstone of Canadian security is that it must be achieved in combination with other like-minded neighbours and friends.

Need for Grand Strategy to Possess Unity of Purpose and Provide Predictability

Properly articulated, grand strategy informs and prepares. Yet for Canada, since its security is to be obtained by cooperation with others, the formulation of grand strategy is complicated in particular by the ambiguity of the American strategic vision, which fails to specify clearly whether the new administration, for instance, is altering the core of Bush administration policies and strategy in relation to the 'war on terror.' While President Obama's officials are now characterizing American military engagement as 'overseas contingency operations,' there continues to be no defining central feature to U.S. grand strategy. While each new U.S. administration adds novelty to foreign policy conduct (as President Obama has done on the issue of torture and Guantanamo), continuity with the foreign policy conduct of the prior administration is in important respects also conspicuous. For example, while the Obama administration made good on its campaign promises to expedite withdrawal from Iraq, it simultaneously focused more explicitly on Afghanistan, which was also a preoccupation of the prior Bush administration. Canada cannot fully and effectively craft a grand strategy for itself without taking into account, for example, how NATO and the United States will deal with Afghanistan, Islamist fundamentalist terrorism, and the security of energy supply lines and of Israel. Although not entirely independent of broader thinking on these matters, Canada has often in the past acted as a bellwether of change in international affairs. Canada's initiatives in its relations with Cuba and the opening to China, for example, come to mind.

Within these limits, the formulation of Canadian grand strategy can obtain meaning and show a unity of purpose within the Canadian polity and within NATO and United Nations mandates. Clarity and predictability of Canadian purpose will be of assistance to allies regardless of whether uncertainty has been reduced in international affairs, but even more so when that uncertainty is especially evident and problematic in international affairs. A coherent and predictable grand strategy can therefore enhance cooperation with and from allies.

Need for Willingness to Provide the Capability to Meet Objectives

A final guideline for grand strategy is that a polity must be willing to provide the capability necessary to achieve its asserted objectives. Nothing is more off-putting to allies than to hear pompous, moralistic assertions on policy, empty of any corresponding capability to achieve these objectives. Likewise, although soft power, to use Joseph Nye's apt term for prestige and reputation, is crucial to policymaking – and Canadian politicians have often seen soft power as a substitute for hard power – soft power in the absence of hard power is an oxymoron. As Nye has emphasized, hard power is what gives soft power its credibility and enables it to become smart power.

One of Canada's greatest assets in terms of soft power is its capacity to reach Washington. When coordination of policy is at its best between Ottawa and Washington, Canada is able to communicate with the United States not only on bilateral matters but also on multilateral matters in a fashion that perhaps no other government can. This coordination was evident regarding the Aristide matter in Haiti and in the more recent diplomatic decision to emphasize the G20 rather than the G8. That is an exercise of soft power in its highest form regarding the tough issues of statecraft. But Canada must back up its own grand strategy with evident willingness to spend on hard capability of the sort that will lend credibility to its own claims to a global foreign policy. To do this, it must specialize to some degree, in conjunction with its allies, so as to maximize its effectiveness. A grand strategy will presumably make sacrifice on the part of the Canadian polity more plausible and more generous.

Future Directions for Canadian Grand Strategy

In a world that suddenly changes, both in structural and in political terms, what type of grand strategy can assist in preserving these core values and national interests?

Perhaps the best way to answer this question is to draw inspiration from the grand strategy that has preserved these core values and national interests since 1945. The grand strategy envisioned here for the twenty-first century involves retaining cohesion among the democracies, with the United States in a position of leadership but not dominance, the NATO countries on one flank, and Japan, Australia, South Korea, and others in Asia on the other flank. When and if Russia and China are prepared to join this concert of powers more explicitly, they are welcome. But a grand strategy that unites the principal democracies remains imperative for the new century.

What kind of system exists at present? Albeit in a highly unequal context of power in which the United States is far more powerful than others, militarily and in important respects economically, the system is a quasi-five-actor system. The members are the United States, the European Union (EU), Japan, Russia, and China. Several factors make it a 'quasi-five-actor' system.

First, the EU is loosely formed. The EU constitutes an entity that is located somewhere between a very loose confederation and an empire without an emperor. But in economic matters such as regulation or trade negotiations, the EU has already made its mark. How much further it will institutionalize is one of the factors that remain highly speculative. An external shock of some sort could abruptly cause it to jell. Second, Russia is restive and torn between two realities. It possesses a diminutive economy, albeit driven by large energy sales, and a giant nuclear arsenal. This is an awkward combination. Third, the locations and trajectories of the United States, Japan, and China on their respective power cycles are crucial to an understanding of where this system is headed. Fourth, one other country is knocking on the door of the central system – India. India has the potential to transform this structure into a six-actor system, but that is far from certain.

Since the origin of bipolarity in 1945, global governance – initially for the West, but becoming truly global since the end of the Cold War – has been underpinned by an arrangement placing the United States at the centre, the Atlantic alliance on one flank, and crucial U.S. bilateral alliances in Asia, principally with Japan and with South Korea, on the other. This is the arrangement that has kept the peace for two-thirds of a century, in decisive contrast to the tumultuous first half of the twentieth century. What is the secret to the remarkable durability of this governance arrangement? Many factors contribute, including the willingness and capability of the United States to lead; the glue provided by the common values and democratic institutions of all member governments; the commitment to a liberal international trade and financial order from which all benefit, including the smallest countries; and an essentially open policy toward other governments, including Russia, China, and many developing countries who may want to associate themselves with this governance arrangement. This security relationship is at the same time both strong and flexible. It is strong because it relies on the power and cohesion of the great democracies. It is flexible because it holds open the possibility that others may join this coalition of states.

Another element of this governance arrangement is noteworthy. In a five-actor system, if three of the actors are associated and committed to stability, stability is likely to prevail. The equilibrium that results is stable; the system does not slide into major war. Tested by the systems transformation of 1989, this equilibrium did not falter. The reason that the systems transformation leading to the events of 1989–91 did not lead to major war, as had other systems transformations in the past, is that the equilibrium among the United States, the other NATO countries, Japan, and the other Asian democracies was strong enough to resist any 'break-out' designed by Soviet elites to attempt to save the Soviet Union through the use of force. Moreover, this equilibrium was flexible and sufficiently open toward Russia to welcome it and not aggrandize against it. Is this equilibrium strong enough, flexible enough, and durable enough to withstand future systems transformations as well? The most central question for Canadian grand strategy is what policies Canada supports to allow it to adapt to the most likely systems transformations that may take place so that it can survive and if possible thrive. Such a grand strategy presupposes an international equilibrium that is benign and reinforces this Canadian grand strategy.

For a variety of reasons, Canada has always been a reliable member of this governance arrangement. Canada is not an outsider. It has been a player from the beginning. Britain and Canada induced a then somewhat reluctant United States following the Second World War to once again become an institutionalized partner in transatlantic security affairs through the creation of NATO. Canada was an early supporter of the Bretton Woods Agreement and an advocate of the General Agreement on Tariffs and Trade, which laid the foundation for the new financial order. Canada, through its contacts in the British Commonwealth and the Francophonie, championed the kind of relations between democracies that are the foundation of the present alliance system and relations with crucial developing countries.

Canada also took a leading early role in extending a hand to prominent Russian officials like Mikhail Gorbachev, who would become central decision-makers during the Soviet transition. Sometimes hand-in-hand with the United States, sometimes at arm's length, Canada explored the 'opening to China,' helping to create a commercial and trading milieu that was welcoming to the former Maoist state. In North America, Canada and the United States formed NORAD, which became the bulwark of North American security through the Cold War. While not always agreeing with the United States or its other allies, Canada was an active participant in regional and international alliance in the context of security.

But the structure of the future international system is likely also to be quite different from that of the past system. Foreign policy roles of the various states are therefore likely to diverge from those in the past. In formulating its place in whatever new arrangements emerge and its corresponding grand strategy, Canada may discover both new challenges and new opportunities. In particular, the role of three central actors – Germany, Japan, and China – will increasingly be a focus on its statecraft.

Germany

Germany is a key member of the European Union because of its size, wealth, history, and geographic location linking Eastern and Western Europe. Germany is also, for similar reasons, a key member of the Atlantic alliance. Therefore, what Germany does affects the entire balance-of-power system. Insofar as the EU develops a single foreign and defence policy, all of Europe will replace Germany as a singly important actor. But until that decision to centralize is made, other governments, including Russia, will continue to see Germany as the lynchpin of European politics and therefore of how Europe relates to the United States and to Asia. Moreover, notwithstanding doubts regarding the German apparent willingness to use force (e.g., Afghanistan), in strategic matters Europe can do nothing of consequence without at least German acquiescence. Everyone accepts a passive Germany because a more active Germany (e.g., a Germany that doubled the size of its defence budget) would be an unpredictable and perhaps uncomfortable neighbour and member of the Western alliance. NATO cannot afford a Germany that is hostile to alliance aims.

Since 1945, in a supposed bargain with France over responsibilities, Germany has for the most part adopted a 'back seat' in foreign policy to France. France was to take the lead in foreign policy, Germany in economic policy. To compensate France for the financial cost of peacekeeping and related defence expenditures, Germany was to support subsidies to French agriculture through the Common Agricultural Policy, the terms of which were extended to at least 2013. But whatever the intra-European understanding about foreign policy initiative, the German foreign policy role, either implicit or explicit, remains key to the stability of Europe and to the global system.

That is why the German response to Russia is so relevant. Germany feels the dependency on Russia for natural gas. It is awed by the vast territorial expanse of Russia from the Baltic to the Pacific. It is conscious of Russian nuclear capability in contrast to its own absence of such capability and seeks to mollify Russia as a consequence. Since 1989, some of its constituents tend to draw Germany ideologically toward Russia and toward Russian politics in a kind of new *Ostpolitik*, thus complicating party politics and the formation of German governments. A temptation results to use foreign policy for German electoral purpose.

The net effect of these German predilections is to soften criticism of the Russian propensity toward military intervention inside Russia itself, such as in Chechnya, and in the Russian 'near-abroad,' such as regarding Georgia or Ukraine. Problematic would be the emergence of a German mentality of 'balance' that would divide the democracies in the vain hope of placating Russia. Ties to Britain and France inside Europe help put a brake on such propensities, as will the predilections of members of the former Eastern Bloc.

Japan

Strategically, as China rises, Japan ought to rely even more firmly on the bonds with the other democracies, especially those with the United States. But that logic is not necessarily the only logic that will appeal to some Japanese analysts and decision-makers. Historically, Japan has had something of an impulse to associate itself with the actor it construes as the most powerful. It did so towards Britain, for example, at the end of the nineteenth century and towards the United States at the end of the twentieth century. With what country will Japan ally at the end of the twenty-first century? This bandwagon approach for the Japanese is more plausible than balancing.

To the extent that the impulse to bandwagon prevails over the impulse to balance, Japan could respond to a more powerful China by seeking to associate itself with what it perceives as a hegemon, allowing its close ties to dissipate with other democracies, including Canada and the United States. While the object of grand strategy should never be to encircle a rising China (unless it shows aggressive intent) with a tight ring of actors perceived by China to be hostile to it,[15] it should likewise not be to abandon alliance among the democracies that so long has preserved equilibrium. As we engage China and accommodate its rise with constructive roles in the system, we must keep our defences strong.

For Japan, these two impulses – the one to preserve a strong security association with the other democracies largely through its links with the United States, the other to bandwagon with China – will preoccupy Japanese foreign-policy thought for a long time. History and cultural difference are on the side of those who will find uncompelling a Japanese bandwagon strategy toward China. On the other hand, politics inside Asia – for example, involving the Koreas or Taiwan – could drive Japan to adopt strategies that compromise the long-standing equilibrium of which Japan has traditionally been an important link.

Canada has historically identified with the logic of equilibrium that has prevailed since 1945 – the structural situation in which NATO and the Asian democracies flank the United States and deny any other powers the opportunity for aggression. The two countries that could be problematic in security terms are, of course, Russia and China. Consequently, Canadian grand strategy ought to be conscious of the need to keep both Germany and Japan inside the alliance framework. Canada has always aspired to a role of 'fixer,' even perhaps when the role was less feasible or less needed. In the future the role of fixer could become much more relevant. In a strongly hierarchic system such as existed after the Second World War, balancing is more difficult for small states, and the bandwagon approach was more common. As the world flattens, balancing attempts are likely to become more feasible and more commonly practised. Canadian grand strategy, while not exaggerating the capability to act as diplomatic fixer, should nonetheless be cognizant of where latent fractures may lie in the overall strategic framework and hence where the ointment of diplomatic suggestion and initiative can be most usefully applied.

Chinese Realities

Far more convincing than the tired argument of an inevitable and possibly military clash between a rising China and a declining United States is the reality that China will face a dilemma that it and others must manage. China has been growing at an astonishing rate for decades, pushed by globalization and its own hard work. Its relative power has increased correspondingly. Consequently, China's aspirations regarding its enhanced future foreign policy role and stature have matched its continued ascendancy in relative power. The problem is that at some point, the increasing rate of relative power growth is going to reverse itself and begin to decelerate. Based on the experience of other countries, it can be seen that the rate of Chinese relative growth will begin to fall off abruptly. All previous Chinese projections of sustained growth in future foreign-policy stature and role, place in the world, and corresponding capacity to make an ever greater mark for itself will be proven wrong. Precise prediction of the timing of this critical point is impossible, but that it will occur under well-defined conditions is certain; strategic assessment through simulations and other analytic approaches may also prove fruitful. Its timing depends essentially on the strength of absolute growth rate differentials involving multiple states of varying size. What is key is that the critical shift on the relative power trajectory can conflict with expectations based on the absolute trends.[16] But when the structural circumstances of systems transformation occur, governments will recognize this situation (as they did in 1989–91). Hopefully, they will act with as much strength, cohesion, and diplomatic skill.

Statistical evidence gathered across two centuries of statecraft has shown that such a critical point on a state's power cycle is an extremely unstable experience. For example, each of the major wars in which both Germany and Japan were involved was preceded by just such a critical point where structural change shifted from acceleration to deceleration. As the world changed massively and precipitously for each state, the governments were unwilling or unable to cope, and major war resulted. Governments that are not democratic are especially vulnerable to belligerency and overreaction at such points where the foreign policy stakes are enormous and fortunes turn against the state. If there are outstanding grievances such as those involving Taiwan, or border differences, or claims in the South China Sea, or differences over the Korean dispute, these are likely to become far more difficult to handle during an interval of abrupt structural change. Of course, war is not inevitable. All parties can manage such examples of systems transformation peacefully and without loss of security. But of the six major structural transformations since the origin of the modern state system, five have ended in major war. The odds are not good.

It is a mistake to believe that major war of the sort that plagued the first half of the twentieth century is inevitable, just as it is a mistake to assume that the twenty-first century will remain conflict-free. Any grand strategy must contain within it a capacity to surmount the possibility of a return to major instability in the twenty-first century, or, with equal importance, a contingency for managing with other well-intentioned governments a structural transformation in a fashion that is constrained and peaceful. Such crisis management, in the context of a dynamic structural equilibrium, is an essential component of grand strategy for every government, including Canada.

Conclusion

In shaping its own grand strategy, Canada must have foreign and defence policies and all the tools of statecraft and diplomacy that will allow it to play a constructive role in concert with other like-minded nations. But working closely with the United States will be especially critical. Canada's distinctly North American economic and security interests are such that Canada–U.S. relations will continue to figure prominently in Canadian grand strategy. Canadians and Americans share similar values, interests, and aspirations. But because of the asymmetry of their relationship, they can have different perspectives on the use of hard and soft power and how best to grapple with the power shifts and security issues we can expect as some countries decline and others rise.

It is always important to remember that, with rising states evincing no malign disposition, the objective is not to balance and oppose but to adapt and engage. Adapt and engage is what the United States, Canada, and other governments have done vis-à-vis China since the Deng reforms. But if the continuity in world order is to be preserved, the coalition of democracies must neither neglect its own security nor dissolve.

To the extent that the prevailing association among the leading democracies can be reinforced – come what may in structural terms – the prospects for international political equilibrium are quite good. Liberal idealists will call this governance arrangement a coalition of democracies. Conservative realists will call it a variant on the balance of power. Both are right. This arrangement has bolstered the stability of the global order for more than six decades. Its perpetuation would sustain world order well into the twenty-first century. In pursuit of its own national interests, Canada has a role to play in buttressing that equilibrium. Canadian grand strategy can help make this happen.

NOTES

1 See the thorough assessment of this question in David Pratt, *The 2007 Ross Ellis Memorial Lectures in Military and Strategic Studies: Is There a Grand Strategy in Canadian Foreign Policy?* (Calgary: Canadian Defence and Foreign Affairs Institute, 2008).

2 Charles F. Doran, ed., 'Power Cycle Theory and Global Politics,' special issue, *International Political Science Review* 24, no. 1 (2003); and Charles F. Doran, *Systems in Crisis: New Imperatives of High Politics at Century's End* (Cambridge: Cambridge University Press, 1991).

3 Paul Kennedy, 'Grand Strategies in War and Peace: Towards a Broader Definition,' in *Grand Strategies in War and Peace,* ed. Paul Kennedy (New Haven, CT: Yale University Press, 1992), 5 (emphasis in original).

4 Joseph S. Nye Jr, *Bound to Lead: The Changing Nature of American* Power (New York: Basic Books, 1990); and Joseph S. Nye Jr, *Soft Power: The Means to Success in World Politics* (Cambridge, MA: Perseus Books, 2004).

5 Charles F. Doran, 'Economics, Philosophy of History, and the "Single Dynamic" of Power Cycle Theory: Expectations, Competition, and Statecraft,' *International Political Science Review* 24, no. 1 (2003): 14.

6 John Bassett Moore, *American Diplomacy: Its Spirit and Achievements* (Whitefish, MT: Kessinger Publishing, 2005), 210.

7 As quoted in David G. Haglund, *The North Atlantic Triangle Revisited: Canadian Grand Strategy at Century's End* (Toronto: Irwin Publishing, 2000), 19.

8 David Haglund, 'The Parizeau-Chrétien Version: Ethnicity and Canadian Grand Strategy,' in *The World in Canada: Diaspora, Demography, and Domestic Politics,* ed. David Carment and David Bercuson (Montreal and Kingston: McGill-Queen's University Press, 2008), 7.

9 Haglund, *North Atlantic Triangle Revisited,* 15.

10 Joel Sokolsky, 'Guarding the Continental Coasts: United States Maritime Homeland Security and Canada,' *IRPP Policy Matters* (March 2005): 1–68.

11 Robert Gilpin, *War and Change in World Politics* (Cambridge, UK: Cambridge University Press, 1981); A.F.K. Organzki and Jacek Kugler, *The War Ledger* (Chicago: University of Chicago Press, 1980).

12 Charles F. Doran, *The Politics of Assimilation: Hegemony and Its Aftermath* (Baltimore, MD: Johns Hopkins University Press, 1971), introduced power cycle theory in the context of diplomatic history from the fifteenth to the nineteenth century. Doran, *Systems in Crisis,* assessed structural change in the nineteenth and twentieth centuries and recommended policy guidelines attuned to structural change. For a succinct summary, see Doran,

'Economics, Philosophy of History, and the "Single Dynamic" of Power Cycle Theory,' 13–49.

13 The members of the G20 are Argentina, Australia, Brazil, Canada, China, France, Germany, India, Indonesia, Italy, Japan, Mexico, Russia, Saudi Arabia, South Africa, South Korea, Turkey, the United Kingdom, the United States, and the European Union. Decision-making in the G20 is by consensus.

14 All empirical studies to date have strongly supported the key claims of power cycle theory regarding major war. See, for example, Daniel Chiu, 'International Alliances in Power Cycle Theory of State Behavior,' *International Political Science Review* 24, no. 1 (2003): 123–36; Charles F. Doran and Wes Parsons, 'War and the Cycle of Relative Power,' *American Political Science Review* 74, no. 4 (1980): 947–65; Jacob L. Heim, 'Tapping the Power of Structural Change: Power Cycle Theory as an Instrument in the Toolbox of National Security Thought,' *SAIS Review* 29, no. 2 (2009): 113–27; Henk Houweling and Jan G. Siccama, 'Power Transitions and Critical Points as Predictors of Great Power War: Towards a Synthesis,' *Journal of Conflict Resolution* 35, no. 4 (1991): 642–58; Patrick James and Lui Hebron, 'Great Powers, Cycles of Relative Capability, and Crises in World Politics, *International Interactions* 23, no. 2 (1997): 145–73; Brock F. Tessman and Steve Chan, 'Power Cycles, Risk Propensity, and Great-Power Deterrence,' *Journal of Conflict Resolution* 48, no. 2 (2004): 131–53.

15 The historical analogy is to a rising Germany in the decades before the outbreak of the First World War. By encircling Germany in the decades 1882–1912 and excluding it from colonial areas, the declining powers France and Britain only alienated Germany and confirmed in the German imagination that Europe was attempting to deny Germany a legitimate role and status in the system. Contrast the attitudes of pre–First World War Germany with the quite different belligerence of Hitler. Mistakes were made in each application of grand strategy.

16 See Doran, 'Economics, Philosophy of History, and the "Single Dynamic,"' 13–49; and Doran, *Systems in Crisis*, for a discussion of the conflicting messages that occur at such critical points and make adjustment so difficult. See also Heim, 'Tapping the Power of Structural Change,' 113–27.

2 Canada's National and International Security Interests

DON MACNAMARA

> We have no eternal allies and we have no perpetual enemies. Our interests are eternal and perpetual, and these interests it is our duty to follow.
>
> – Viscount Palmerston[1]

Whether cliché, truism, or political mantra, the first and most important obligation of government is the security of the country, its territory, its peoples, their assets, and their values.[2] As was so frequently stated by media commentators in shock over the World Trade Center and Pentagon attacks on 11 September 2001, 'Without security, nothing else matters.' But if security is so important, it should be seen to be so by all departments of the national government and the needs, ways, and means to ensure it clearly understood by the citizenry. For whatever reasons, it does not appear to be so in Canada.

A 'national security strategy,' a coherent set of policies dedicated to that first and most important obligation of government, would appear to be a legitimate response to a changed world, one changed in political, economic, socio-cultural, and military dimensions. This chapter aims to outline some first principles to achieve the development of a national security strategy for Canada.

What Is 'National Security'?

The question may not often be asked because many may think they already know the answer, though most likely only in narrow terms. Some may consider it 'internal security,' anti-espionage, or anti-terrorism police and counterintelligence, or 'security intelligence.' Others may assume it entails military security, both domestic and international. Few will think of it in the more comprehensive terms that we now use.

Captain Bernard Thillaye, Royal Canadian Navy (ret'd), coined a succinct definition: 'National security is the matter of guarding national values and interests from internal and external dangers.'[3] That definition is short and clear – but implies a scope of national security beyond a military dimension. In 1980, the National Defence College of Canada adopted a definition that went beyond the military dimension: 'National security is the preservation of a way of life acceptable to the Canadian people and compatible with the needs and legitimate aspirations of others. It includes freedom from military attack or coercion, freedom from internal subversion, and freedom from the erosion of the political, economic, and social values which are essential to the quality of life in Canada.'[4] Then in 2004, the Paul Martin government published *Securing an Open Society: Canada's National Security Policy*, within which the scope of the first National Security Policy was described, though importantly not defined:

> National security deals with threats that have the potential to undermine the security of the state or society. These threats generally require a national response, as they are beyond the capacity of individuals, communities or provinces to address alone.
>
> National security is closely linked to both personal and international security. While most criminal offences, for example, may threaten personal security, they do not generally have the same capacity to undermine the security of the state or society as do activities such as terrorism or some forms of organized crime.
>
> Given the international nature of many of the threats affecting Canadians, national security also intersects with international security.[5]

Expanding and consolidating these definitions to include both the central responsibility of government and the fundamental values of Canada, the following composite definition of national security is proposed for use in developing Canada's national security strategy:

> National security is the first and most important obligation of government. It involves not just the safety and security of the country and its citizens. It is a matter of guarding national values and interests against both internal and external dangers – threats that have the potential to undermine the security of the state, society, and citizens. It must include

not just freedom from fear of attack against themselves, their property, community, or national sovereignty, but also the preservation of the political, economic, and social values – respect for democracy, the rule of law, individual freedom, and human rights – that are central to the quality of life in a modern state.

National Interests and National Security Strategy

Although there are many different models for developing a strategy or for 'strategic planning,' the common starting place is the identification of the values and goals of an organization or nation. The values and goals together constitute national interests. The next step is to assess the operating environment – internal and external – to identify the events, issues, trends, and risks or threats that may affect the nation's interests, and then to determine what effects or impacts they may have. It is then necessary to determine how the nation's interests can be protected or advanced and analyse the nation's capabilities to determine the resources available and what limitations or constraints may exist. The final step is the development of the strategy itself – an integrated set of coherent policies and plans to chart the path through the challenges of perceived issues, trends, risks, or threats and their effects on national interests; this includes identifying constraints, the means both necessary and available, and the risks in making choices for the ends of minimizing their effects on and maximizing the benefits for the nation and its people.

So, a national security strategy for Canada must ask and answer six questions:

1   What are our interests – our values and goals?
2   What events, issues, trends, risks, or threats are developing in our domestic and international environments?
3   What impact may they have on our interests?
4   What are the ways we can protect and advance our interests?
5   What are the available means – resources and constraints?
6   What is the strategy – the policies and plans?

The rest of this chapter will address the first two steps and start to address the third, while the other chapters of this volume touch upon the other questions.

Canada's National Interests

What are Canada's national interests? What are the values and goals of which we commonly speak? Various constitutional, policy, and ministerial documents address these questions, but often less directly than desired and without the clarity and understanding necessary for the citizenry. Canada's fundamental values, simply stated, are *democracy, including the rule of law, individual freedom,* and *human rights.* And second- and third-order derivatives of those would lead us to others, such as tolerance, compassion, health care, education, and others so often mentioned in the same breath. But it must be clear that the values for which Canadians would fight to defend are those fundamental values, and not their derivatives.

The concept of national interests also needs clarification. The term *national interests* or *in the national interest* is often used in a noble or stirring way to support some government action or policy, but seldom is 'the interest' specifically identified or even the meaning and context explained. Some political leaders and government officials prefer to keep such statements unexplained and wish to avoid being clear about what 'interests' may be in aggregate, lest they themselves become constrained. However, the concept of national interests can be a useful analytical tool as well as a means to communicate with citizens when determining the potential impact of issues and events on a nation.

But while the use of the term is common, it has been used without precision and is therefore unpopular in some quarters. Elmer Plischke, in an exhaustive study, stated, 'Much of the difficulty of comprehension and objection to its application in the conduct flows from its careless and equivocal use by political leaders and the biased and parochial interpretations of some of its analysts. But, these are scarcely valid reasons for justifying the invalidation of a concept as prevailing and important as national interests in managing and understanding the foreign policy process.'[6]

Donald Nuechterlein, a prolific writer on U.S. national interests as a tool in determining policy responses to issues, also described national interests as the aspirations and goals of sovereign entities in the international arena – the perceived needs and desires of one sovereign state in relation to the sovereign states comprising its external environment. He has identified four basic national interests that can usefully guide the policymakers of great powers in formulating foreign and national security policies: defence interests, referring to the defence of the home-land; economic interests, or the enhancement of the nation's economic well-being; world order interests, referring to the maintenance of a sta-ble international political and economic system; and ideological inter-ests, including the protection and promotion of shared values.[7]

For the sake of comparative analysis and assessment of the impor-tance of issues, simply identifying or connecting an event, trend, issue, or threat is insufficient. Further analysis is necessary to identify the intensity of the impact and thus the nature of response to circumstances affecting an interest. Typical levels or intensity can be classified as

- *vital interest,* meaning an impact on the survival or physical secu-rity of the country and its citizens, which may demand a military response;
- *major interest,* which may have a substantial impact, serious but not affecting the safety or survival of the state or citizens, but still demanding a major diplomatic or policy response;
- *humanitarian interest* demanding a response to disasters – natural or otherwise – because our values demand it; and
- *peripheral interest,* which is at a more individual or commercial (consular) level not affecting the state.

Canada's national interests, commonly stated in foreign policy docu-ments as national objectives, have been very consistent over the years, although sometimes stated in a different order and also sometimes clouded by elegant descriptors. For analytical purposes, however, they can be used as lenses through which we can view the domestic and international world to clarify and determine just what issues, trends, risks, or threats are important to us and to what degree. Consistent with Nuechterlein's approach and our own policy documents, Canada's fundamental national interests can be divided into four components. First, there is the question of *security,* which refers to the protection of Canadian territory, the security and unity of its people, and the pro-tection and enhancement of the country's independence. *Prosperity,* to promote economic growth and support the prosperity and welfare of the Canadian people, is the second national interest. The third interest is in a *stable world order,* which reflects a broader concern to contribute to international order and stability in the interest of security and pros-perity. Lastly, it is important to recognize that the *projection of values,* to work with like-minded states in and outside international forums for the protection and enhancement of democracy and freedom, is equally a national interest.[8]

These fundamental national interests (security, prosperity, stable world order, and projection of values) together with our fundamental values (democracy, rule of law, individual freedom, and human rights) can be used as the filters through which the world is viewed to determine what are and will be Canada's national security concerns, and assessed in terms of the intensity of their impact on our interests.

Strategic Culture

The response to the perceived impacts of issues, trends, or risks on Canada's interests will, of necessity, depend on the intensity of the impact and the capabilities and available resources to respond. However, the nature of the response could also be affected by Canada's 'strategic culture.' While it is beyond the scope of this chapter to address this concept in detail, for the purposes of this discussion, the definition of strategic culture provided by Colin Gray will be used: 'Strategic culture is the world of mind, feeling and *habit in behavior.*'[9] As Alan Bloomfield and Kim Richard Nossal state, 'The real utility of the concept of strategic culture is its ability to deepen our "explicative understanding" of the patterns of security behaviour of states.'[10]

Nossal has demonstrated its utility in explaining Canada's strategic culture history in terms of 'defence of the realm,' which denotes the fact that Canada has sought 'to defend a broader definition of political community than just "Canada."'[11] Different 'realms' included the British Empire (1898–1918), a 'shrunken realm' through isolationism (1919–39), a North Atlantic Treaty Organization–North American Aerospace Defence Command realm (1945–91), a shrunken Atlantic alliance–United Nations realm (1991–2001), followed by uncertainty in the 'hyperpower era' since 2001.

Canada indeed has a strategic culture of 'forward defence' of its interests, as reflected in the expeditionary deployment of armed forces from the Boer War to Afghanistan, and in both bilateral (historically first with the British, then with both the United Kingdom and United States), and multilateral alliances or coalitions. Indeed, unlike European countries and many Asian countries, Canada, the United States, Australia, and the United Kingdom (except for the Blitz) have not had war brought to their homelands. But international political, economic, and socio-cultural factors have affected Canada's vital, major, and humanitarian interests and have led to such deployments, protecting Canada's interests abroad to reduce the risk of having to defend them at home.

The prevention of nuclear war was a vital interest that led Canada to deploy troops in peacekeeping operations in widely different parts of the world, to prevent the escalation of regional conflicts into an East-West nuclear exchange that could destroy Canada. Equally, it is the prevention of major instability in Southwest Asia that could result in further mass casualty terrorist attacks against Western targets that led to the most recent expeditionary deployment to Afghanistan.

This strategic culture is stated in military terms and may not match the cultures of other government departments and agencies that have been added to the 'national security' dimension through the 2004 *National Security Policy,* as reflected in the 3-D (defence, diplomacy, and development) or 'whole-of-government' approach, and may account for the lack of coordination and cohesion in the Afghanistan mission (discussed at greater length in Ann Fitz-Gerald's chapter in this volume). Common goals across government reflecting an understanding of the cultures and the lenses through which those goals are viewed and articulated will be an important element of any coherent national security strategy.

The Responsibility to Protect

It is also likely that Canada's 'expeditionary' strategic culture contributed to its leadership in the International Commission on Intervention and State Sovereignty in 2001 and its subsequent report, *The Responsibility to Protect* (R2P), which effectively justified the humanitarian right to intervention and was issued only on 30 September 2001, less than three weeks after the World Trade Center and Pentagon terrorist attacks.[12] And as idealistic as the 'R2P doctrine' may be, it was adopted at the UN World Summit Outcome in September 2005 – a clear and unambiguous acceptance by all governments of the collective international responsibility to protect populations from genocide, war crimes, ethnic cleansing, and crimes against humanity.

Notwithstanding its adoption, the realistic application of this doctrine has become problematic. In it, sovereign states are said to have 'a responsibility to protect their own citizens from avoidable catastrophe – from mass murder and rape, from starvation – but that when they are unwilling or unable to do so, that responsibility must be borne by the broader community of states.'[13] In order to justify any form of intervention, all courses of preventive action must be exhausted. These include preventive diplomacy, preventive deployment (Macedonia), peacekeeping (chapter 6 of the UN Charter), or the use of sanctions (Iraq, South Africa).

When preventive measures fail to resolve the situation, then intervention by members of the international community may be required. These coercive measures may include political, economic, or judicial measures, and in extreme cases may also include military action. But what is an extreme case? Where do we draw the line in determining when military intervention is defensible? In the commission's judgment the relevant decision making criteria are right authority, just cause, right intention, last resort, proportional means and reasonable prospects of success.

There remain, however, some serious questions that require clear answers if this doctrine is ever to be applied by the international community. Who decides to intervene? Who acts? With what and whose resources? To what defined end-state? For Canada in particular, there should also be a component of the national security strategy that demands clear answers to related and equally important questions. What are Canada's interests in any situation invoking R2P? At what level or intensity of interest? What military and non-military resources would be relevant and capable for 'deployment'? And finally, what is the aim/'end-state' and what are the criteria for success? The decades-long Afghanistan mission might not be openly guided by the R2P doctrine, but these questions are equally applicable to these sorts of stabilization missions and in urgent need of answers. Sadly, despite an extensive public and political debate on the merits of the current mission, there has been remarkably little analysis of these issues – though several chapters in this volume (see the essays by Bercuson and Granatstein, Fitz-Gerald, and Bland and MacDonald) do an admirable job in addressing some of these questions.

Conclusion

The broad definition of national security, the need to understand whole-of-government responses to challenges to Canada's national security interests, and the recognition of Canada's strategic culture will place increased demands on the research and analysis communities to identify the issues, trends, risks, and threats to Canada. Indeed, a number of domestic and international agencies have recently undertaken and published reports on these topics.[14] It should be noted that all such studies emphasize that they are forecasting – or attempting to address and understand the future. But the future remains unknowable and the conclusions are at best attempts to understand and be prepared for a future full of both change and surprise – in other words, the purpose of a national security strategy.

A distillation of the topics identified and their challenging scope and scale should remind Canadians of the complexity of the current and future security environment. Challenges affecting Canada's fundamental interests include a number of issues:

- the international economy, including debt, credit and investment capital;
- terrorism, such as cyber-terrorism/warfare and the use of weapons of mass destruction (WMD, including nuclear, biological, and chemical);
- world order, in particular the political/economic restructuring in North America and the EU, Eastern Europe and Russia, the Middle East and Southwest Asia (Iraq, Iran), Central and East Asia (China, India, North Korea), Latin America (Brazil, Venezuela), and Africa;
- regional conflict and failed states, in particular in Africa (Sudan, Congo, Liberal, Sierra Leone, Cote d'Ivoire), Southwest Asia (Afghanistan, Iraq, Pakistan, Palestine), Latin America and the Caribbean (Haiti), and Eastern Europe (the Balkans);
- weapons proliferation, including WMD (North Korea, Iran);
- natural resources, such as energy, oil and water (the Middle East and Russia);
- the environment, ranging from climate change to natural disasters;
- disease, including old threats like HIV/AIDS (especially in Africa) and newer pandemics like the H1N1 flu;
- refugees, population migration, human trafficking (Asia, Latin America, Eastern Europe, North America); and
- drugs, organized crime, money laundering, which is a virtually global problem but is especially a concern in South America, Southwest and South Asia, Eastern Europe, Southern Europe, Mexico, the United States, and Canada.

These international issues can also be usefully classified by geographic area and its relative impact on specific interests. For instance, the international economy actually represents a domestic issue as much as an international one, insofar as it affects Canadian national interest in economic prosperity, on one hand, and a stable world order on the other. Militant Islam and WMD is an issue that largely originates in Southwest Asia, though it certainly has an international dimension in today's globalized world and represents a direct challenge to both the non-proliferation regime and the broader American-led institutional order. It therefore affects Canada's interest in security and a stable world order. The United States, with its strategically vital relationship with Canada, undoubtedly has a strong impact on all four of our national interests – security, prosperity, world order, and values. Other important countries may in turn affect different interests. For example, Mexico is a concern primarily for security, prosperity, and values; Russia and India concern security, prosperity, and world order; Brazil affects prosperity and world order. Importantly, much like the United States, China also concerns all four major Canadian national interests – and its importance to Canadian interest in security, prosperity, world order, and values is likely only to grow in the years ahead.

Canada lives in a turbulent world and is vulnerable in physical, political, economic, socio-cultural, and military terms. The country's strategic culture is rooted in the forward defence of its interests, with deployed expeditionary forces in an alliance/coalition context. Yet Canada still needs a clear and comprehensive statement of national interests, not just generalities, and this statement must be mindful of American national security interests and policy. Canada also needs a clear and coherent national security strategy involving all of government, and one that is aware that the country's security capabilities have been seriously underfunded and understaffed and the Canadian Forces, police, intelligence, and diplomatic services over-committed. The subsequent chapters in this volume will shed light on how Canada has traditionally approached these matters, and offer some thought on key elements for any Canadian national security strategy – or grand strategy, to use the term favoured in the preceding chapter.

NOTES

1 Henry John Temple, Viscount Palmerston, speech on the Polish Question, House of Commons, 1 March 1848.
2 This point is reiterated in Canada's 2004 *National Security Policy* document: 'There can be no greater role, no more important obligation for a government,

than the protection and safety of its citizens.' Canada, Privy Council Office, *Securing an Open Society: Canada's National Security Policy* (Ottawa: Privy Council Office, April 2004), vii. Also, 'It is customary in the democratic countries to deplore expenditures on armaments as conflicting with the requirements of social services. There is a tendency to forget that the most important social service a government can do for its people is to keep them alive and free.' John Slessor, *Strategy for the West* (New York: William Morrow, 1954), 68.

3 Bernard Thillaye, 'Politico-Strategic Forecasting' (MA thesis, Royal Military College of Canada, 1972), 79.

4 This definition was coined by L.V. Johnson, commandant, National Defence College of Canada, 1980–3.

5 Canada, *Securing an Open Society*, 3.

6 Elmer Plischke, *Foreign Relations: Analysis of Its Anatomy* (New York: Greenwood, 1988), 37.

7 See Donald Nuechterlein, *America Recommitted: A Superpower Assesses Its Role in a Turbulent World*, 2nd ed. (Lexington: University Press of Kentucky, 2001).

8 These interests have been distilled from Canadian foreign and defence policy white papers and statements, 1995–2007.

9 Colin Gray, 'Strategic Culture as Context: The First Generation of Theory Strikes Back,' *Review of International Studies* 25, no. 1 (Jan. 1999): 58 (emphasis in original), as qtd in David Haglund 'What Good Is Strategic Culture,' *International Journal* 59, no. 3 (Summer 2004): 479–503. A comprehensive discussion of strategic culture may be found in other articles in that same issue of *International Journal*.

10 Alan Bloomfield and Kim Richard Nossal, 'Towards an *Explicative Understanding* of Strategic Culture: The Cases of Australia and Canada,' *Contemporary Security Policy* 28, no. 2 (Aug. 2007): 286.

11 Kim Richard Nossal, 'Defending the "Realm": Canada's Strategic Culture Revisited,' *International Journal* 59, no. 3 (Summer 2004): 504.

12 International Commission on Intervention and State Sovereignty, *The Responsibility to Protect* (Ottawa: International Development Research Centre, 2001).

13 Ibid., viii.

14 The following sources identify the future global security challenges: Allied Command Transformation, *Multiple Futures Project: Navigating to 2030* (Norfolk, VA: Allied Command Transformation, April 2009); Peter J. Gizewski, 'The Global Security Environment: Emerging Trends and Potential Challenges' (paper prepared for the annual meeting of the

Canadian Political Science Association, Carleton University, Ottawa, 27 May 2009); Leger Marketing, *Voice of the People 2006: What the World Thinks on Today's Global Issues* (Montreal: Transcontinental: 2006); Secretary-General's High-Level Panel on Threats, Challenges and Change, *Securing an Open Society; A More Secure World: Our Shared Responsibility* (New York: United Nations, 2004); United Kingdom, *The National Security Strategy of the United Kingdom: Security in an Interdependent World* (London: Cabinet Office, March 2008); and United Kingdom, *The National Security Strategy of the United Kingdom: Update 2009 Security for the Next Generation* (London: Cabinet Office, June 2009); United States, Joint Forces Command, *The Joint Operating Environment 2008: Challenges and Implications for the Future Joint Force* (Norfolk, VA: JFC, 2008); United States, White House, *National Security Strategy of the United States* (Washington, DC: White House, 2006).

3   The Balance of Freedoms: A Fresh Strategic Framework

The end of the Cold War, the end of the unipolar Pax Americana era that followed, the end of the 'protection of distance' heralded by 9/11, and the end of the 'presumption of financial competence' experienced in 2008–9 – all speak to what is an unavoidable new beginning. That 'new beginning' embraces nothing less than the recognition that integrated military, strategic, and economic security are the only joint instruments by which the world can move on. So generals and other flag officers who claim little if any interest in social or economic matters in target countries, allied countries, or countries at risk will need to acquire an interest and retain expertise quickly. And social planners, local politicians, diplomats, and advocacy groups from business, labour, the poor, and the middle class will also have to add security and international stability to their narrow focus. The compartmentalized geopolitical, economic, or strategic plan is very much a thing of the past.

In simple terms, the core freedoms required so people can live productive, happy, and decent lives are the *freedom from fear* and the *freedom from want*. These two freedoms, which are admittedly borrowed from what U.S. President Franklin Roosevelt has termed the Four Freedoms in a 1941 speech, require supporting pillars of investment and commitment.[1] The first freedom can be sustained only when there is a robust pillar of national and international security capacity, deployable quickly to contain aggression, arrest criminals, and eliminate terrorist assets and agents. The second freedom requires nothing less than an all-out attack on absolute poverty – the kind of poverty that creates jealousy, hatred, and fecund ground for violent and terrorist prescription among the millions worldwide – in Africa, South America, the Middle East, and in some parts of Eastern Europe – who have literally nothing to lose from violent choices directed against those who do have something to protect and something to lose. Robert Zoellick said it well: 'This is not security as usual or development as usual ... This is about *securing development.*'[2]

The two pillars of investment in support of the two core freedoms are inexorably linked. In terms of global security, the trade-off between guns and butter is the ultimate false dichotomy. Without investment in pillar two (economic and social opportunity), one will need to invest far more in pillar one to cope with the poverty-driven insurgencies, coups, invasions, and power and resource struggles that will ensue. Indeed, while poverty may not be the only driving force, it is a vital fuel to the insurgency and terrorism that increasingly plagues the post-9/11 world. Without pillar one being sustained at robust levels of deployable military, police, special force, naval, and air capacity, there may well not be enough time to engage fully on pillar two. The 'balance of freedoms,' in which effort is given equally to global poverty reduction and international security (including military) capacity, has never been more apparent, dynamic, or salient. The critical challenge democratic societies face, especially those where there are healthy competitive forces arguing over resource allocation, is how to manage this balance at home and abroad. Failure to do so can be politically and economically lethal. Managing the balance has never been more critical a role for political, military, and economic leadership.

Canadian Interests and the Balance of Freedoms

Much of Canada's social and fiscal infrastructure, however imperfect, has been designed explicitly, or been modified, to reflect our regional and multinational realities in a way that seeks to promote not just a civil society but more importantly, a society that is truly civil. That civility – which is reflected in everything from refugee policy and student loan programs to the Charter of Rights and Freedoms and official languages laws, and so much more – is what helps make Canada's quality of life among the best in the world.

Canada's brands of democracy and economic opportunity are mutually dependent. They also protect the core freedoms and rights that are so vital to the life Canadians have built for themselves at home and hold up as an example for others less fortunate abroad. Some call it hopelessly naive and unsophisticated, but Canadians do believe that Arab women should have the right to vote and drive, that Muslims in

Bosnia deserve human rights, and that Israeli children should be able to go to school without being blown up. Canadians do believe that 800,000 Rwandans should not have been butchered and that girls in Afghanistan have the right to be educated. And while the redoubt of the isolationist is to ask just how much Canadians are prepared to contribute or sacrifice – from their own taxes or the money that could otherwise be allocated to health care – for any of the positive outcomes, the answer can be given only in the context of a democratic framework that reflects our mix of core values and vital interests. In the beginning and in the end, civility at home is demonstrated by successfully defending or promoting civility and security abroad.

Canada pursued its vital interests when it proposed, through the Louis St Laurent government and Secretary of State for External Affairs Lester Pearson, a United Nations Emergency Force at Suez to find a way for the British, French, and Israelis to stand down from a confrontation with Egypt and perhaps Russia. Our vital interest there, beyond the free movement for world shipping through the Suez Canal, was keeping the Cold War between East and West from producing a proximate thermonuclear risk. Not all of those things that violate our core values necessarily affect our vital interests. But the first rule of defence and national security is that threats should be addressed as far away from one's own population and territory as possible. We share this vital interest with Americans, whether our government is to the left or right of theirs, whether we approve of their approach to gun control or they disagree with our approach to the medical use of marijuana. We also share common economic and geographic space with America, and our respective vital interests embrace the safety and security of the citizens of both countries of that space.

Thus a clear foreign policy strategic framework should not begin with platitudes about international development or peaceful co-existence. A framework that reflects Canadian leadership would stipulate those activities or deprivations abroad that Canada will not tolerate, the values and vital interests it thinks are at stake, and the prerogatives Canada is prepared to assert in defence of those values and vital interests. Threats to our national security, efforts at ethnic cleansing or genocide, destructive levels of poverty, state or non-state commitments to eradicate nations or cultures or other religious or cultural groups, the threat of weapons of mass destruction and violence against civilian populations all need to be factored into a Canadian framework for foreign policy engagement. And while the military capacity to enable

Canadian reach and impact is vital, also vital are the abilities to disarm post-conflict factions, to rebuild societies' infrastructures, to promote democracy, and to enhance social and economic self-sufficiency.

When close allies are threatened or attacked, Canadian engagement cannot be equivocal. When Canadians are at risk at home or abroad, we must have the capacity to respond without dependence on others. Geopolitical integrity in the new post-2010 framework requires that we practise abroad what we say and believe at home regarding our core values and vital interests, with both our diplomacy and our military, our development and security capacity locally. The extent to which a country allows that gap to grow – between what it says and believes and what it is prepared to do – determines the degree of international influence that country deserves. The dilution of impact reduces a country's leverage, which is essential to its vital interests on trade, economy, environment, and the general world order.

We know, for example, that the cycle of deep recession, public anxiety driven by rising unemployment, and a broadening gap between rich and poor can wreak havoc with international stability and the political moderation of most countries. We know where that post-1929 cycle led in mid-Depression Europe; we know how fiscally and economically hard times lead irrevocably to reducing military capacity in the democracies as governments re-allocate spending priorities and, certainly in the past, let military preparedness fall by the wayside. That is what Prime Minister Neville Chamberlain and others did during the Depression in the United Kingdom in the 1930s; it is what happened in the United States under the pre–Pearl Harbor stewardship of President Franklin Roosevelt and in Canada under the toxic complacency of Prime Minister Mackenzie King.

We know, too, that the mix of denial relative to the real trajectory for the fascist and Axis powers in the 1930s and the economic pressures associated with the Depression produced a passivity that looked the other way as fascist powers moved on Eastern Europe, in Czechoslovakia, in Abyssinia, or in Asia. A war that could have been stopped with relatively little risk in the latter half of the 1930s was allowed, through weakness, denial, lack of preparation, and lack of will, to proliferate to almost every continent, kill fifty million people, and perpetuate some of the worst atrocities and attacks on the human condition ever seen. There is a price for the politics of denial. There are consequences to the twin scourge of growing poverty and military incapacity.

A gargantuan effort – involving huge sacrifices by allies like Canada, the United Kingdom, the other dominions, and, after awhile, the United States, including millions of soldiers, airmen, and sailors, huge economic re-tooling and military production – was required to withstand total domination of the world by despots who cared little for democracy, freedom, diversity, or equality of opportunity. That raises the question of where we are now, in the midst of a new American presidency, at a time of continued economic uncertainly, and far from complete rebuilding and re-investing in our own armed forces – forces that have been stressed to the hilt by the Afghanistan commitment. We can, without much division, surely agree on a few fundamentals of realistic contextual awareness:

- The triumphalism at the end of the Cold War was excessive and ultimately destructive of our core economic and geopolitical interests. It has yet to do as much damage as the triumphalism that produced the Treaty of Versailles, which, despite some protracted negotiations amongst the participants, still resulted in such harsh conditions being imposed on Germany. But the multi-polar instability, broad global insurgency, and emergence of aggressive and nihilist non-state actors around the world in some measure emerged as we let post–Berlin Wall triumphalism obscure our judgment in the West and elsewhere. It also produced a strategic void in the likely outcome of the collapse of the Soviet 'client state' system and the forces that would unleash.
- Part of that triumphalism led to the mistaken conclusion that the collapse of Communism meant the success and flawless reality of capitalism – perhaps the most illogical of conclusions. That collapse for structural reasons, combined with poor maintenance and bad management of one building in one part of town, does not mean that your own building is perfect. In the 2008–9 recession, in the unravelling of the massive and engineered credit overhang, we see the wages of such triumphalism writ large.
- At a time of explosive threats in the Middle East, continued existential threats in the Pakistan/Afghanistan region, and the relentless expansion of nuclear capacity in unstable regions, our margin of manoeuvre is becoming constrained. And we face all this at a point when economic realities will dilute America's ability to finance the old exceptionalist view of global military dominance at the same levels we have seen in the past.

As the current U.S. administration continues to re-engage Afghanistan and re-calibrates its world stance, the global recession and the pressure produced by poverty and concurrent unrest will be real and demanding.

Revitalizing Canadian Leadership: A New Framework

The key question we face in Canada at this time is very clear: how do we prevent global recession from turning to global depression, and depression from once again turning to war? We face that question as women and men who are part of a larger world and who understand that the core purpose of robust statecraft and defence capacity is to prevent war and the indiscriminate tragedy it imposes on so many. The second but equally vital question we face as Canadians is equally compelling: what can Canada do with our existing resources to keep the present global context from worsening? The good news is that with some determination, some focus and vision, we can make a difference.

It is vital too in Afghanistan and elsewhere that we do not confuse the trappings of nascent democracy with action on the core issue of the poverty divide. As Richard Sandbrook has reflected, 'The initial euphoria occasioned by democratic breakthroughs in developing countries is typically followed by disillusionment as democracy fails to bring the anticipated improvements. Persistent or deepening social inequalities, economic security arising from volatile global markets, continuing mass poverty, and anemic and remote governance are the usual culprits.' As he goes on to note, 'People in poor countries overwhelmingly conceive of real democracy as a system that tackles poverty, inequality and powerlessness. Such challenges often involve confronting entrenched power structures.'[3] A genuine foreign policy framework must separate local reality from apparent democracy that offers no hope of social justice.

This is not a time to let recession dilute the rebuilding of our Canadian armed forces – as some in the Treasury Board, Privy Council Office, and Finance Canada would love to let happen. An Asia-Pacific strategy and the new focus on the Americas all speak to enhanced military and especially naval deployability. Increasing our armed forces reserves, expanding our regular force, engaging with the next critical tasks in shipbuilding and the new technologies that enhance force protection, multiply force impact, and enhance deployability and flexibility, have never mattered more. Those in the civil service who oppose this should be encouraged to serve their country outside of government. Employment-enhancing Reserves and Regular force recruitment should be expanded, in communities, high schools, universities, and colleges; and programs to advance citizenship status to those who volunteer for combat-ready and overseas roles should be considered. Building our real, deployable defensive capacity will increase our ability to engage with diplomatic intensity and creativity in the pursuit of the kind of understandings that reduce the risk of war. As an example, between the Canadian Coast Guard, navy, and fisheries there are now roughly eighty-five hulls that need to be constructed in the coming decade. We must also commit to a sixty-ship, fighting, three-ocean navy, the jobs and infrastructure that would produce it, and its vital role in discharging alliance duties in the Atlantic and Gulf zones, in the Asia-Pacific and our country's new commitment to the Americas.

On the issue of poverty at home and abroad – the other great destabilizer and source of conflict – Canada can and should lead the Group of Eight (G8) and Group of Twenty (G20) in making its eradication a core objective – and to do so by offering a significant Canadian contribution, both political and financial, to a tightly monitored program for global poverty reduction, and convincing other countries to follow our lead.

In Afghanistan, poverty is grinding and wildly supportive of Taliban recruitment against our forces, against the North Atlantic Treaty Organization (NATO) in general, and against the Karzai administration. If Canada were to add poverty reduction to our present military role in Afghanistan, which currently includes military training and possibly appropriate intelligence, sea interdiction, and special force support for the allied effort, that would be a project into which we could recruit financial and people support from other NATO and supportive partners. In this we would be confirming what Canadian and other NATO commanders in the field have said for years – Afghanistan needs more than a military presence to be stabilized and made secure. Most importantly, we would be making it clear that we will not walk away from a people and nation in whose interest and support so much Canadian blood and treasure has been given, and so much is at risk in the years ahead if equilibrium is not attained.

Robust military capacity, expeditionary deployability, global leadership on poverty, and a fresh focus on Afghanistan in the years ahead will say to the world that Canada will not turn inward, will not be subsumed by small-time partisan excess or the vicissitudes of domestic politics, but will face the exigencies of a new world order with courage, creativity, and political will. There could be no greater signal of who we are, what we believe in, and what Canadians can do and have done for our American and NATO allies. There could be no greater Canadian prophylactic measure to contribute to keeping the world from falling over the edge.

Managing Risk amidst Global Insecurity

A core mission for any democratic government in its foreign policy framework is long- and short-term risk management – managing those security and economic risks that no citizen or family or small town or large city could ever manage on its own.

Risk management is not a new idea. It has been part of the auditing, emergency planning, homeland security, actuarial, and deposit and loan matching worlds of banks, insurance companies, governments, and financial planners for years. The SARS outbreak a few years ago taught us about some of what we needed to improve in aspects of public health. Y2K at the century's turn taught us about what can go right when planning, implementation, and investment levels are robust and risk is well managed. Public risk management today for Canada does not entail only the military.

A critical question facing Canadian public policy is clear: what does public risk management on a global basis mean for Canadians? What are the processes by which public risk priorities must be assessed, and what are the vital instruments we need to procure to manage risks before they expand and perhaps overflow? It is in that context that procurement – as an instrument in managing public risk – must be assessed. The cost risk of any procurement must be compared to the larger cost risk any procurement is meant to manage.

The lack of a coherent integrated national security analysis and planning structure beyond the Privy Council Office means that while the Canadian Security Intelligence Service, Canadian International Development Agency (CIDA), the Royal Canadian Mounted Police, the Canadian Border Services Agency, Military Intelligence, and Privy Council Office officials may all do great work, its coordinated and integrated availability for planning, scenario training, deployment ability, or logistics capacity enhancement is, at best, unstructured and at worst, only compartmentally available. That is not good enough but that is where we are. Bright, able, good, and patriotic people of relevant experience in all of these areas work hard, but there is no fully integrated product. A brief synopsis to the prime minister from the clerk of the

Privy Council on an issue may be succinct. But succinct and fully informed or integrated are different things entirely. And that lack of optimal coherence diminishes a government's ability, any government's ability, to embrace the urgency necessary to make purpose-driven and timely procurement decisions. The real public risk – of sea lanes being interrupted, of a massive increase in the Chinese navy, of growing pre-nuclear capacity in Iran, and the likelihood of nuclear proliferation in the Middle East, including an arms build-up amongst the Sunni nations, in response – are dynamic parts of the changing public risk profile for Canada. Back in 2009, the normally left-of-centre Manchester *Guardian* reported that Russia's new security strategy focuses on potential clashes with other countries over energy resources, in which the Arctic region is clearly highlighted in the document.[4] This speaks clearly to the serious sovereignty, capacity, and logistic risks we are not now adequately able to handle.

A similar area of concern with respect to the Sunni nuclear proliferation challenge, involving many of the states in the Middle East with which Canada has cordial and constructive relations, was highlighted by Mohamed El Baradei, then head of the International Atomic Energy Agency. The anti-proliferation regimes we have relied on are in danger of collapse, he believes.[5] Canada's entire risk management strategy in the 1950s and 1960s was tied to engaging against proliferation and having the deployable expeditionary capability (land, sea, and air) to engage with other allies to prevent thermonuclear escalation – as was the case in Sinai in the 1950s. Our ability to engage with the same capacity, as we speak today, is minimal at best.

A wonderful brigadier general friend once commented that a 'nano-second' could be defined as the time between the eruption of an international crisis and the appearance on our streets of hundreds or thousands of nationals or diaspora from the region demanding Canadian action. With the decision of some Tamil demonstrators to illegally block traffic or occupy thoroughfares, waving flags emblematic of a banned terrorist group, in one case in a multi-hospital zone, we now have an additional local definition of public risk.

The non-partisan question that governments and political parties that want to form or stay in government must answer is very clear cut. And thankfully, there is little core distinction here between what governments of the left, right, or centre must address on the capability side regarding public risk. Will we have, at a bare minimum, the ability to patrol our own territory, respond to a crashed passenger airliner, or deal with an environmental emergency in our own north, or is that a public risk we leave to others to manage? When our 'helpful' Russian friends expand their claims, their patrols, their nuclear capacity on and beneath the sea, is that sovereignty risk we care about, or one we ignore? Can we deal with an international crisis that threatens stability, economic continuity, and the freedom from intimidation and fear that governments in Canada owe our population?

Are we able to support, extricate, and reinforce our troops? Is a failed Caribbean state something we need to plan for and be able to deploy towards relatively quickly? When Canadians are at risk at home or abroad, do we have the air, sea, special force capacity, with force-multiplying technology to respond? When does relative incapacity or the refusal to build capacity actually increase public risk? We know what the costs of procurements are and can be – and we understand how bureaucratic delays can increase those costs. The question we must ask, as Canadians and taxpayers, should be pointed: how much does the increase in public risk, produced by delay, cost in both dollars and lives? It is an unpleasant question but it cannot be avoided. When any group of bureaucrats want contractors to shoulder more of the cost risk than the state, what does that mean about the democratic management of large public risk itself?

And while the numbers associated with kit modernization, new optronic, avionic, or weapons capacity are large, while an integrated multi-hull commitment to meet the collective new hull needs of the Coast Guard, fisheries, Arctic operations, and naval forces are also large, they are dwarfed by dollars spent just in the last few months to bolster financial liquidity. Hundreds of billions committed to let the Canada Mortgage and Housing Corporation repatriate sound mortgages from financial institutions, multi-billion-dollar commitments to infrastructure including myriad hockey rinks, car companies, pension plans, and the rest have emerged with remarkable speed. I do not differ with any of these as short-term responses to a massive liquidity risk engendered elsewhere and that caused potential and real economic risk here at home. But all of this presents the larger public risk management challenge – relative to defence, international instability, natural disasters, and aid to the civil power. If we are not investing now to dilute the un-manageability of that risk, we are in fact contributing to that risk through acts of omission and delay. So reforming the way Canada executes its military procurement is not just a 'wouldn't it be nice' process improvement, where the explicit tactic of structured delay is done away with. Its absence makes public risk less manageable and substantially more acute. That risk may be off the coast of Somalia, in downtown Toronto, over Canadian Arctic airspace, or at a Canadian airport. That risk may be enhanced for Canadians on a Mediterranean cruise on a large charter ship, or for Canadian residents in Mexico, or holidaying in the Dominican Republic, or for large expatriate Canadian populations in diverse areas of the world.

Government's primary role, whether it is left, right, or centre, is to manage those risks that citizens and communities and businesses cannot possible manage on their own. That is what armed military deployability is about. That is what submarines, new combat and transport aircraft, Joint Support Ships, and new land troop transport and force protection measures are about. That is what unmanned air surveillance and related kit help a civil society to do. And that is why 'process *über alles*–generated delays' must be confronted for what they are – direct attacks on any government's capacity, or the resilience of that capacity when the threat is enhanced or experienced, at home or abroad. This is not a priority just like any other. It is not on par with new roads, or small craft wharfs and harbours. It should not compete with bank liquidity measures or enhanced computer capacity.

Next to the Americans, we probably had the best equipped front line combat force in Afghanistan. The present government deserves immense credit for that, as does the former and present chief of defence staff, present and former defence ministers, and the prime minister himself. The continued ability of our forces to diminish public risk and sustain governments' capacities to manage that risk at home or abroad must not be allowed to weaken, because process overshadows results. And an Ottawa obsessed with inputs quickly loses the capacity to influence outcomes.

Doing things like procurement or social policy, in the same endless, insensitive way, falls into what political science theorists have referred to as 'path dependency' – where it is easier to go back and forth, at varying speeds, ever deeper, in the same rut, than summoning the courage or energy to propel oneself out of the rut to start a new furrow in a new direction. Path dependency is a comforting process rather than a courageous result. And in today's Canadian bureaucracy, comforting process outweighs courageous outcomes most of the time. The range and nature of public risk is such that what is comforting today can be deeply disastrous tomorrow – reflect for a moment on the years during which the Chalk River challenge was un-remediated meaningfully over the last two decades. Choosing comfort over courage has consequences.

Conclusion

Failure in pursuing the balance of freedoms with the strategic tools vital to both the security and economic side of freedom constitutes the most salient risk to short-term security at home and abroad and medium-term global survival. Climate change cited by many as the most urgent existential risks for the entire planet is not an isolated climactic danger disconnected from economic and security cycles. Its interconnected reality with the economic and security risk spectrum is what makes its dynamics a part of that spectrum so challenging for existing economic, political, and institutional structures.

Facing up to the institutional issues here by organizations and agencies like NATO, the European Union, CIDA, the United Nations, the Commonwealth, the Association of Southeast Asian Nations, and others is long overdue and strategically vital. Organizations built in the days when military and economic threats to security were seen as separate and distinct have served us reasonably well. But those days have gone. And so has the discrete separation of threats and freedom-destroying forces.

Our responsibility as a free country devoted to democracy, the rule of law, freedom from fear and from unreasonable want is clear and precise. We must invest in the two pillars of rapid deployable military and security capacity and focused global poverty reduction in the interest of a new and robust foreign policy framework. The balance of freedoms has never mattered more. Continued imbalance has never been more dangerous.

NOTES

1 Franklin Roosevelt's Four Freedoms speech offered four fundamental freedoms: freedom of speech, freedom of worship, freedom from want, and freedom from fear. I focus on freedom from fear and freedom from want, simply because I believe these two freedoms are more fundamental; it is upon these latter two freedoms that freedom of speech and worship largely depend.

2 Robert Zoellick, 'Fragile States: Securing Development,' address to the International Institute for Strategic Studies, London, UK, 12 Sept. 2008, http://www.cfr.org/poverty/zoellicks-speech-international-institute-strategic-studies-fragile-states-securing-development/p17228. Emphasis in original.

3 Richard Sandbrook, 'Astute Governance Promotion versus Historical Conditions in Explaining Good Governance: The Case of Mauritius,' in *Exporting Good Governance: Temptations and Challenges in Canada's Aid Program*, ed. Jennifer Welsh and Ngaire Woods (Waterloo, ON: Wilfrid Laurier University Press, 2007), 219.

4 Luke Harding, 'Energy Conflicts Could Bring Military Clashes, Russian Security Strategy Warns,' guardian.co.uk, 13 May 2009, http://www.guardian.co.uk/world/2009/may/13/russia-security-strategy-energy-warning.

5 See Julian Borger, 'Mohamed ElBaradei Warns of New Nuclear Age,' guardian.co.uk, 14 May 2009, http://www.guardian.co.uk/world/2009/may/14/elbaradei-nuclear-weapons-states-un.

PART TWO

The Home Front

4 Defence Procurement and Industry

CRAIG STONE

> The government has determined that its procurement activities should also be consistent with and supportive of such national objectives as industrial and regional development, aboriginal economic development, the environment and other approved socio-economic objectives.[1]

This statement by the Treasury Board makes it clear that the Canadian government believes that there needs to be a connection between procurement and the nation's industry. More importantly, the statement implies that this connection needs to be consistent and supportive of the government's development and economic objectives. Framed in the language of this book, it implies that procurement should meet national interests and advance those interests. For example, economic development helps to promote economic security of Canadians, which is part of the Personal Security domain articulated in the 2004 *National Security Policy*, and that is in the national interest.[2]

This chapter discusses this issue and frames the discussion around how linking procurement and industry is in our national interest and actually promotes national security. In order to accomplish this task, the chapter will first discuss defence procurement in Canada and the need for procurement reform. Next the chapter will discuss the defence industry in Canada and the need to connect industrial regional benefits (IRBs) to an industrial strategy. Finally the chapter will conclude by connecting procurement and industry to the *Canada First Defence Strategy* (CFDS) and the need to ensure that the planned $490 billion of spending needs to be executed within a broader industrial framework that promotes Canada's national interest and contributes to the strengthening of Canada's economy.

The starting point for this discussion is to deal with the more common arguments and assumptions that are put forward when discussing the validity to the underlying premise that procurement should be connected to industry. Since these assumptions may not be shared by everyone, a few words of justification are appropriate. First, the procurement policy statement at the beginning of the chapter indicates it is government policy that the two activities should be connected. The policy is also articulated by Industry Canada through its IRB policy, which 'provides the framework for using federal procurement as a lever to promote industrial and regional development objectives.'[3] Challenging the policy would require sufficient evidence and enough support by politicians and the bureaucracy to make the case to change the policy. This has not occurred.

Second, the argument that the government bears no responsibility for ensuring the viability or continued existence of an industry may be appropriate for some commercial activities but ignores the reality of military procurement. In military procurement, the government is the sole buyer and 'determines technical progress through its choice of equipment ... can determine the size of the domestic defense industry, its structure, entry and exit, prices, exports, profits, efficiency and ownership.'[4] In addition, there must be some level of capability within the domestic defence industry in order for the military to repair and overhaul its major equipments, provide guaranteed sources of supply for strategically significant items of national interest, and meet national emergencies.

Third, and perhaps most important in the long run, is the expectation of the Canadian taxpaying public. Taxpayers have every right to expect that the government will spend public money in a manner that promotes the long-term well-being of the nation. This would not be achieved if the government completed all of its procurement abroad without any regard to its own future development. This is an important notion, because the economic argument about using taxpayer's money most efficiently would not necessarily support spending money in Canada. Using military procurement as an example, and accepting that the most important requirement is to ensure that whatever is purchased meets military operational requirements, a specific amount of money may buy more from a foreign supplier than a Canadian supplier. This would lead to more capability being acquired for the same amount of money or a similar capability for less money when comparing the two suppliers. Economically, while a more efficient use of resources, it ignores the politics associated with any large public expenditure with government money and does not promote long-term Canadian industrial competitiveness and would therefore not be in the national interest.

Although all of the examples provided above could be challenged, there is insufficient evidence that there is enough political support to make the government behave differently. Therefore, the underlying assumption that procurement and industry should be connected appears to be valid. Consequently, a review of the defence procurement and the state of the industry is needed before addressing the broader national interest requirement.

Defence Procurement in Canada[5]

John Read argues that procurement within government 'is a complex process that requires careful planning, constant oversight, and a highly sophisticated set of professional skills. Government procurement is a delicate balancing act that must meet the operational requirements of government while at the same time seek to leverage the purchase to achieve broader government socio-economic benefits.'[6] This includes ensuring that the acquisition is conducted openly and transparently, with fairness to all possible contenders and ensuring that taxpayers receive full value for every dollar spent. As the largest purchaser within government, this is particularly true for the Department of National Defence (DND).

Table 4.1 shows that three government departments or agencies (National Defence, Public Works, and Public Safety) represented 79 per cent of spending on the acquisition of buildings and equipment and 78 per cent of spending on the acquisition of machinery and equipment, with DND the largest of the three in both categories, at 34 per cent and 68 per cent respectively.

In the past, Dan Middlemiss argued that defence procurement was a vital component of Canadian defence policy. 'It is what puts the "arms" into the armed forces and because of the many (sometimes very large) contracts and jobs involved, it is also "big business" in Canada.'[7] Despite this argument, the overall impact of defence procurement as a factor in the Canadian economy is marginal at best: 'Total defence production accounts for considerably less than 1 per cent of both Gross Domestic Product ... and total employment.'[8] Fundamentally, both arguments are valid; it is the context that is important. Although defence spending is only a very small part of the overall economic activity of the nation,

Table 4.1.   Expenditures on capital items for selected departments 2007–8 (000s$)

	Acquisition of buildings and works ($)	% of total	Acquisition of machinery and equipment ($)	% of total
National Defence	246,581	34	3,316,336	68
Public Safety and Emergency Preparedness	175,845	24	348,760	7
Public Works and Government Services	150,042	21	126,635	3
Foreign Affairs and International Trade	45,310	6	175,820	4
Veterans Affairs	30,457	4	10,898	0
Canada Revenue Agency		0	107,720	2
Health	5,612	1	101,587	2
Industry	15,393	2	173,694	4
Fisheries and Oceans	19,544	3	87,777	2
Total	727,552		4,893,442	

Source: Canada, Department of Finance, Public Accounts 2007–8.

procurement remains an important aspect of our defence policy, especially when major capital equipment is being considered.

For example, the government announced $15 billion in military equipment purchases in June 2006 that included ships, trucks, helicopters, and transport planes. The last time such an ambitious equipment acquisition plan was undertaken was in the late 1970s and early 1980s, when new fighter aircraft, ships, maritime patrol aircraft, and an air defence weapon system were purchased. More importantly, the government's 2009 CFDS indicates that 'over the next 20 years, these increases will expand National Defence's annual budget from approximately $18 billion in 2008–9, to over $30 billion in 2027–8. In total, the Government plans to invest close to $490 billion in defence over this period.'[9]

Investment in the future is the important issue, because the $15 billion in procurement projects announced in 2006 already include agreed upon industrial regional benefits, most of which will accrue to American prime contractors rather than Canadian companies based on the nature of the acquisitions and type of purchase. Since the Canadian Forces (CF) has significant additional capital investment requirements (equipment and infrastructure), a defence industrial strategy can help ensure that the money is spent in a manner that promotes both national security and economic prosperity.

Defence procurement is the demand side of the defence equipment market and requires militaries and governments to make choices between defence contractors and services. When choosing contracts and services, the national security requirements should dictate who gets what. As well, the selection of the actual defence contractor is a complicated and lengthy process. Decisions are required on whether or not to source the equipment from a domestic supplier or a foreign supplier. Any decision to open the contract to foreign companies will likely be opposed by domestic suppliers and those who advocate the use of defence purchases for other economic and political goals. Both the type of contract to be awarded and how the choice will be made must be decided. Although beyond the scope of this chapter, there are significant differences between the types of contracts.[10] There are a number of variations, and each contract will be designed to meet the needs of both the defence firm and the purchaser. In Canada, versions of all of these methods have been utilized, though procurement in the late 1990s and early 2000s is generally connected to the notion of *best value*.

However, there are difficulties with defining the notion of best value. How, precisely, can best value be defined, and how does a nation actually evaluate a proposal? The examination by former assistant deputy minister (materiel) Alan Williams of Canadian defence procurement looks at these issues and suggests that best value should be achieved through a compliant, lowest-cost methodology.[11] Under this method, some argue that the actual requirements of the military are being met at the lowest cost and that is therefore the best value. Unfortunately, the lowest cost may also be the most expensive to maintain, which would cost more over the long term to keep in service. Under these circumstances, it would not be best value over the long term. This argument misrepresents the notion of best value that is intended by Treasury Board and others like Alan Williams.

There are many views and opinions on this issue, but Treasury Board defines *best value* as 'the combination of price, technical merit, and quality, as determined by the contracting authority prior to the bid solicitation and set out in the bid solicitation evaluation criteria, and which forms the basis of evaluation and negotiation between buyers and sellers to arrive at an acceptable basis for a purchase and sale.'[12] In this context, Treasury Board notes that achieving best value is not to be limited and confined to just the actual procurement. It should include all aspects of the process, including such activities as the planning and appraisal of alternatives, the definition of requirements, evaluation of sources, selection of contractor, and contract administration.[13] This would be consistent with the intent of Williams's notion of compliant, lowest-cost methodology.

Regardless of what method is chosen, there is a process for procuring military equipment in Canada. Not surprisingly, there has been significant criticism about how long this process takes and whether or not it is possible to improve it. More significant is that the criticism has been a long-term problem for the government and the military. For example, as far back as 1982, the auditor general noted, 'In light of our assessment of the Defence Program Management System, a brief discussion is in order about the long period of time sometimes required between the needs identification phase and the delivery of the equipment.'[14] More recently, in 2003, the Ministers Advisory Committee on Administrative Efficiency made several observations:

Procurement. Procurement is universally viewed as being a slow and cumbersome process that does not fully respond to Defence's needs:

- acquisition of major military systems takes too long, with the average being over 15 years for major capital equipment procurement;
- there is substantial duplication of effort or functional overlap between DND and the Public Works and Government Services Canada (PWGSC);
- DND's internal approval process involves excessive non-value-added review and an undifferentiated approach to risk management; capital projects are not always closed in a timely fashion;
- excess inventories of contractor-held spare parts result in unnecessary management and holding fees;
- there is no senior management visibility of the costs associated with supporting surplus systems and no systematic review of the disposal process;
- Defence often pays more than necessary and buys information technology and software without full visibility of its total requirements; and
- the total value of projects approved for inclusion in the long-term capital plan far exceeds available funding, yet projects included in the plan with little or no likelihood of approval consume staff resources and administrative overhead.[15]

Discussions on how to improve and remedy the concerns use language that is framed around trying to reduce the average acquisition time to less than fifteen years. Figure 4.1 shows the historical and target cycle time lengths for procurement.[16]

Figure 4.1. Historical and target cycle times in defence procurement process

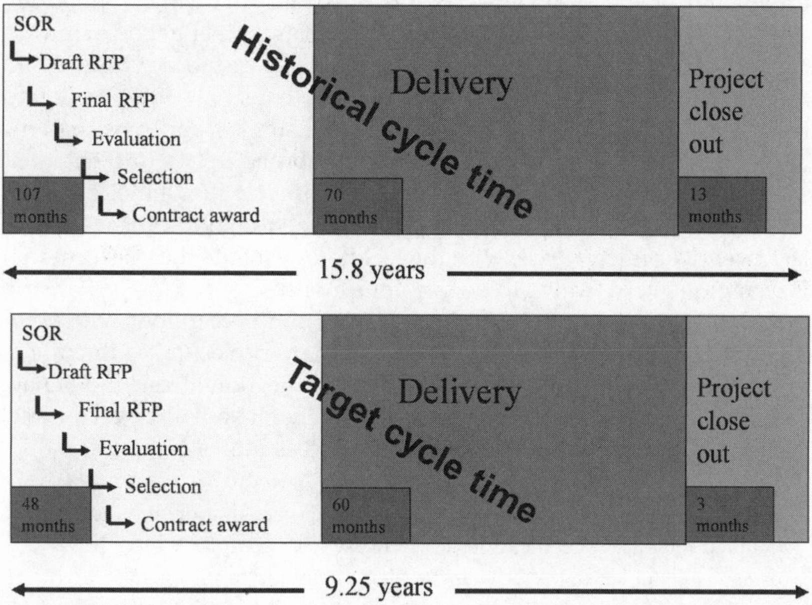

SOR
↳ Draft RFP
  ↳ Final RFP
    ↳ Evaluation
      ↳ Selection
        ↳ Contract award

Historical cycle time

Delivery

Project close out

107 months   70 months   13 months

◄——————— 15.8 years ———————►

SOR
↳ Draft RFP
  ↳ Final RFP
    ↳ Evaluation
      ↳ Selection
        ↳ Contract award

Target cycle time

Delivery

Project close out

48 months   60 months   3 months

◄——————— 9.25 years ———————►

Adapted from Alan S. Williams, *Reinventing Canadian Defence Procurement: A View from Inside* (Montreal and Kingston: Breakout Education, 2006), 96–7. Reprinted by permission of the publisher.

A related but separate issue that is often raised about the length of the procurement process is whether or not the contracting functions that are completed by PWGSC should be integrated directly into DND. For many this seems to be a very logical recommendation, and there would seem to be both positive and negative aspects to such an action.[17] However, in his testimony to the Standing Committee on National Defence, Michael Fortier, the minister of public works and government services Canada, observed that although Canada was one of only a few countries where the military was not responsible for its own procurement, 'this separation has existed for nearly 70 years. We believe that it is crucial to help ensure not only that the process is fair, but also that it is seen to be fair. By keeping the needs identification and contracting functions separate, the Canadian approach allows for civilian oversight throughout the procurement process. This is key to the way we do business in Canada.'[18]

It must be emphasized that the need for procurement reform is not unique to Canada. The United States, Australia, the United Kingdom, and many other nations with modern militaries have engaged in reform exercises. Like Canada, these countries also have those who want to reform their system because it takes too long to get new equipment into the hands of the military. The problems are similar, and most nations are learning from each other as different approaches are implemented in order to address the concern. The real challenge for all modern militaries is to strike a balance between weapon system platforms, which last twenty or thirty years, with the technology inside the platform that is changing every twelve to twenty-four months.

And it is important not to confuse myths and perceptions with what is actually happening. Not every procurement project takes the fifteen years shown in figure 4.1. Responding to questions from the Senate Committee on National Security and Defence about this very issue, Assistant Deputy Minister (Materiel) Dan Ross indicated,

> When I took over this job four years ago, we were in a business of very detailed technical specifications and lowest price compliant bids. It was a process that took four or five years to release a request for proposals, ... with an average of eight to nine years to get to the contract-award stage.
>
> Our recent experience has reduced this to one to three years. We have gone to performance-based procurement, as other NATO nations do. We state high-level performance requirements except for the simplest things. We are pursuing a best-value solution that takes into account the total cost of ownership of an asset, not only the cheapest price, which then perhaps has an expensive ownership situation. We are minimizing the risk and cost of development and taking commercial off-the-shelf solutions.[19]

The inclusion of figure 4.1 also raises the issue of what the procurement process actually is. It is clear from examining the figure that significant activity occurs before the military even takes delivery of the equipment. Here again, there are varying views on what the process, is but the differences are not significant. They all deal with basic tenets for any procurement process in Canada – fairness, openness, and transparency.

To demonstrate this, figure 4.2 and table 4.2 provide two variations of a procurement process. Figure 4.2 provides the version utilized in 2006 within National Defence and is based on the DND Defence Management System, while table 4.2 provides a process described in a 2008 report by the Standing Committee on National Defence.[20] The Defence

Figure 4.2. Major steps in the procurement process, 2006

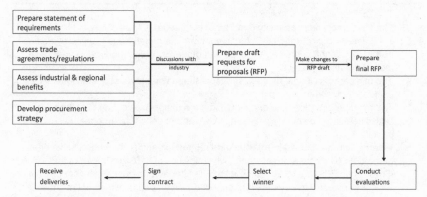

Source: Williams, *Reinventing Canadian Defence Procurement*, 38. Reprinted by permission of the publisher.

Management System is used within DND to establish requirements and obtain the military capabilities needed by the CF to meet government roles and tasks. Since 2000, this management system has provided a linkage between defence policy and departmental planning; an overall strategic resource-management framework; a department-wide process for performance measurement; and a detailed framework for reporting to government in accordance with Treasury Board policies and procedures.[21]

The process articulated in table 4.2 is essentially the same but is articulated using words rather than a process chart. Depending on how figure 4.2 is interpreted, it has seven steps, with step 1 containing four items, nine steps with 'discussions with industry' and making changes to request for proposal draft counting as steps in addition to those articulated inside the boxes, or thirteen steps if each of the four items in step 1 is considered an individual step rather than combined. Regardless of how the figure is assessed, there are no substantial differences between the steps in figure 4.2 and the process outlined in table 4.2.

The difference between the two lies in focus and intent. The process in table 4.2 is focused on the departmental connections to the broader government checks and balances and the role of the minister, Treasury Board, and Cabinet, while the DND version in figure 4.2 is focused on the process outside the government machinery. Of note for both variants, neither provides much detail on what happens after the winning bid is

Table 4.2.   The twelve steps of procurement

1	The CF identifies a capability deficiency.
2	The CF establishes capability requirements to address the deficiency.
3	The Department of National Defence confirms the capability is justified by defence policy and identifies the capital funds and other resources required to undertake the major Crown project.
4	The minister of national defence sponsors the major Crown project in Cabinet, seeking approval-in-principle.
5	The minister of national defence sponsors the major Crown project at Treasury Board seeking preliminary project approval and expenditure authority to begin the project.
6	When Cabinet approval-in-principle and related expenditure authority have been granted, DND forms a project team, which includes DND, Public Works and Government Services Canada, and Industry Canada personnel who cooperatively work with industry to complete the project definition phase, which defines the number, location, and type of equipment, how it will be operated, personnel, operating and support costs, contractual terms and conditions and IRBs, etc.
7	When the project definition for the major Crown project is complete, the minister of national defence returns to Cabinet for effective project approval for the implementation phase.
8	The minister of national defence then returns to Treasury Board for further expenditure authority to continue with the project and tender a request for proposal to industry.
9	When both effective project approval and expenditure authority are granted, PWGSC proceeds with formally releasing the RFP and, once bids are received after a specified time, with bid evaluation.
10	Bids are evaluated against evaluation criteria and done in three separate parts – technical (by DND), contractual terms and conditions (by PWGSC), and IRBs by Industry Canada. A bid roll-up of all parts for each bidder determines the overall winner.
11	Approval for contract award from Cabinet is sought and, once granted, PWGSC awards a contract on behalf of the government.
12	Thereafter, DND takes on overall responsibility for managing project implementation (aided by PWGSC and Industry Canada staff) until project completion.

Adapted from: Canada, House of Commons, *Procurement and Associated Processes,* Report of the Standing Committee on National Defence, Rick Casson, Chair, 39th Parliament, 2nd Session (Ottawa: House of Commons, February 2008), 4.

selected and a contract is awarded. More importantly for the focus of this chapter, both processes recognize the need to include industry and industrial benefits as part of the decision-making process. The question that comes to mind within this framework is how Canadian industry should be engaged in this process.

Canada's Defence Industry

Canada has had a unique experience compared to most nations with industrial preparedness and maintaining a defence industrial base. The defence industrial base in Canada since the Second World War has been characterized by two main trends: a closer cooperation and integration with the U.S. defence industry, and a shift away from major platforms to subsystems and components.[22] Canada enjoys a unique relationship with the United States that dates back to the Ogdensburg declaration signed on 18 August 1940. At that time, Prime Minister King and President Roosevelt agreed to coordinate defence production and established the permanent joint board on defence. Subsequently, the two leaders formalized Canada-U.S. collaboration in defence production with the Hyde Park agreement on 20 April 1941.

In the early years, the agreements for the first time linked the military and economic defence requirements of North America.[23] Throughout most of the latter part of the twentieth century, our nations worked under the framework of the Defence Production Sharing Arrangement. Through this arrangement, 'Canada agreed to purchase integrated weapons platforms from the US in return for privileged access to American defence markets. . . . Canadian firms are treated as American firms in Department of Defence . . . procurement.'[24] In essence, the agreement provides Canadian companies the opportunity to supply the U.S. armed forces with a wide range of goods and services in competition with other U.S. companies. Canada's defence industry is considered part of the North American defence industrial base, Canadian companies can be U.S. planned producers, and in many areas Canadian companies are considered by U.S. military equipment buyers as if they were U.S. domestic sources. Therefore it is difficult to make any meaningful assessment of the Canadian defence industrial base outside of the broader North American context.

However, despite the success of this unique relationship, there are many shortcomings to Canada's defence industrial base. In general, our indigenous defence industrial base is not structured for wartime sustainment, the military is highly dependent on non-domestic sources of supply, and since defence industrial preparedness is primarily a national security consideration, there are few political or economic reasons to support implementing a defence industrial preparedness plan.[25] Since 1999, the Canada–U.S. defence industrial relationship has been complicated by the U.S. decision to revoke Canada's exemption and special status in the International Traffic in Arms Regulation. The impact of this U.S. decision was the unilateral rescinding of many defence economic agreements and arrangements developed and nurtured since the Second World War. The Canadian Defence Industries Association estimated at that time that access to the U.S. market accounted for over half of defence exports – a value of $1 billion and as many as 10,000 well-paying high-tech jobs.[26] Since 1999, officials on both sides of the border have worked diligently to restore most of the exemptions that existed prior to 1991. There remain minor areas where U.S. security concerns and Canadian Charter of Rights obligations continue to be a source of friction for Canadian defence industries. In 2011, these are managed case by case, in order to find acceptable solutions for all parties.

The connection to the International Traffic in Arms Regulation and the U.S. / North American market is important because of the significant dependence of Canadian defence firms on the American market. Binyam Solomon notes that the defence industry in Canada today is largely foreign-owned or a subsidiary of large European and U.S. aerospace and defence corporations.[27] The few exceptions are in very specific areas such as the shipbuilding sector, now owned by the Irving Group of companies, a Canadian privately owned business; Bombardier, a diversified transportation company; and CAE, provider of simulators and integrated training services. Canada's military vehicle sector used to be dominated by the Canadian-based General Motors Canada Diesel Division, but this subsidiary of the American automotive company was sold to General Dynamics Land Systems. As well, Bernie Grover notes that Canada is competitive in flight simulation, space robotics, satellite communication subsystems and components, and surveillance and detection products.[28]

The important issue for Canada is that a very limited number of Canadian companies manufacture large defence and space systems to meet domestic requirements; most companies often serve as subcontractors for large foreign defence and space programs. Consequently, inter- and intra-firm investment and trade are important for Canadian companies.[29] As well, Solomon argues that there is anecdotal evidence that suggests the Canadian defence industrial base 'labour force is highly educated and specialized in fields of study that are considered crucial for the new knowledge economy.'[30] Statements like this that make the connection between the defence industry and its value to Canada are also supported by others involved in the defence industry, such as analysts like Bernie

Grover, trade associations like the Aerospace Industries Association of Canada or the Canadian Association of Defence and Security Industries, and trade magazines like *Frontline Defence* or *Canadian Defence Industry*. For example, Tim Page, president of the association, indicates that defence and security industries in Canada are 'contributors to the Canadian economy (70,000 jobs producing $7 billion in annual revenues, roughly half of which is earned internationally); generators of technologies and innovation for global commercial, military and security markets; partners to the government's national security objectives and sovereignty; and, providers of competitive, world-class military and security assets of strategic importance to Canada and available when they are needed.'[31]

Although the views of industry and its advocates are important, such perspectives should be balanced against actual national security issues instead of economic survivability for a particular company. In the context of this chapter, the impact of procurement and industry on our national interests is more than just protecting jobs and companies. At the same time, however, government policies and decisions must be implemented in ways that promote long-term economic prosperity and competitiveness. Remaining competitive and promoting economic prosperity is clearly in our national interest, and it appears that Canadian governments are finally recognizing the need to connect defence procurement with a broader defence industrial strategy that looks beyond the next general election. Unfortunately, the best policy instrument for the government to achieve this intent is the same policy instrument that has been criticized in the past – industrial regional benefits and economic offsets. Like most policy instruments, the problem is not necessarily the policy itself but rather its implementation, and that has been the problem in Canada.

Industrial Regional Benefits, Offsets, and the Need for a Strategy

Although DND establishes major equipment requirements, there are many other government agencies involved. PWGSC tenders contracts and is the government department responsible for ensuring the integrity of the purchasing process. In addition, Treasury Board approves expenditures, Industry Canada is tasked with IRBs and reviewing, evaluating, and advising industry on proposals, the Department of Foreign Affairs and International Trade is involved with foreign relations and exports, and Cabinet must also recommend all major capital procurement. With the $490 billion of planned expenditure over the next twenty years, policy and implementation need to be correct.

As indicated at the outset of this chapter, Canada does have an IRB policy, which has evolved over time in response to trade liberalization and Canada's strategic need to meet industrial development in high technology. The policy 'provides the framework for using federal procurement as a lever to promote industrial and regional development objectives' and 'seeks to promote Canada's international competitiveness through a strong continuing integration of scientific, technological, industrial and regional strategies and activities in all parts of Canada.'[32] It goes on to articulate that Canada's fundamental reason for having an IRB policy is to focus on five key strategic objectives:

1 innovation – improve Canada's innovation performance through new technologies, processes, services, etc. that are not available in Canada;
2 connectedness – development, promotion, and use of electronic commerce and online digital applications that promote business;
3 marketplace – promotion of Canadian capabilities and expertise in a fair, efficient, and competitive marketplace;
4 investment – improve Canada's position as a preferred location for domestic and foreign investment; and
5 trade – work with Canadian firms to increase Canada's share of global trade markets.

However, just as important is that procurement has always been a vehicle for promoting non-defence interests. As James Fergusson has argued,

> For the political elite in Canada, capital spending in defence is perceived as a major vehicle for promoting a variety of non-defence interests. It represents the largest single area of discretionary spending available to the federal government. As a result, capital spending is used to promote political interests and support a wide range of socio-economic interests in the areas of industrial and regional development. Politically, spending is used as a means to funnel federal dollars into key political regions and ridings. Industrially, capital spending is used to support the establishment of new industries, sustain existing industry and enhance Canada's industrial competitiveness. Regionally, defence capital dollars are a means to re-direct federal monies to disadvantaged areas.[33]

Another perspective to be aware of in any debate on Canada's IRB policy is that few companies rely heavily on Canadian defence purchases for survivability and even fewer build complete weapon systems. The realities of the market are that Canada's defence requirements are too small for a company to be in business just for DND; this has led most Canadian companies to seek other markets and to specialize in such well-defined areas as communications, displays, instruments, and simulation.[34] This implies that Canadian companies are competitive enough to be successful in the global marketplace. The question, therefore, is whether a government should be using public money to promote an already successful commercial enterprise, or use public money to promote new capabilities. By what criteria should these decisions and trade-offs be made? The government's IRB policy provides some guidance, as does the defence industry association.

Tim Page articulates seven criteria for industry to measure whether or not meaningful and sustainable industrial, economic, and trade benefits are achieved through defence and security procurements. He argues that achieving these criteria 'will strengthen the government's ability to address Canada's national defence and security priorities now and into the future and build a stronger, internationally-competitive economy built around highly valued knowledge-based jobs.'[35] Page frames the criteria as questions and deals with a wide range of important issues that need coherent and consistent application across government if they are to be successful. In reality, his seven criteria are framed around two broad themes.

How should government leverage procurements to promote the defence industrial base and existing and future company competitiveness and capabilities? Page argues that since Canada does possess world-class capabilities in defence and security, 'where competitive Canadian-based capabilities exist and can respond to the defined operational requirements, the Canadian Association of Defence and Security Industries believes that those Canadian-based companies should be the preferred suppliers.'[36] Alternatively, if there are no competitive Canadian suppliers, the government should target areas that are of strategic long-term importance to the country and that allow Canadian industry to become knowledge leaders in that area. Making decisions in the longer term leads to the second broad theme within Page's seven criteria.

The government needs to make procurement decisions that are connected to a broader strategy that promotes long-term competitiveness and viability of existing Canadian industry and those sectors that Canada wishes to promote for future prosperity. In this context, Page argues that the industry is really seeking commitment from government that reflects meaningful IRB obligations that connect the strategy to industry capabilities and promotes and integrates research and development requirements now and into the future.[37] As the government begins to implement the CFDS, taxpayers will expect that the expenditure of $490 billion meets many of these criteria.

The challenge to all of this will be the trade agreements that Canada has with other nations and the provinces. Although the North American Free Trade Agreement and the World Trade Organization allow defence to be excluded, the Canadian Agreement on Internal Trade is much more problematic. The internal trade agreement requires all defence procurement to be tendered for competition unless the government declares a national security exemption. As well, the internal agreement allows companies and organizations to appeal the decision on a winning proposal, and this creates additional delay.

Implementing the *Canada First Defence Strategy*

In his opening remarks for the *Canada First Defence Strategy*, Minister of National Defence Peter McKay states,

> Building on the significant investments made in our armed forces over the last two years, this document sets out a detailed plan to modernize the Canadian Forces. Providing balanced investments across the four pillars upon which military capabilities are built – personnel, equipment, readiness and infrastructure – our plan will increase the size of the Forces and replace their core capabilities. The implementation of this 20-year plan will provide Canada with a strengthened, state-of-the-art military and the predictable funding that Canadian industry needs to position itself effectively to meet the Forces' equipment and technology requirements over the long haul.[38]

It is clear from this statement that the government is looking at the longer-term requirements of the military and expects industry to be an active participant in meeting the needs of the military. However, the statement also clearly limits the ambition of government and, to some degree, reflects a lack of vision for the future. In the first instance, the intent is to modernize and replace core capabilities. This will reverse more than a decade of underfunding and a paucity of decision-making by past governments (Conservative and Liberal), but does nothing to indicate what new capabilities the government wants to establish to meet expected future security challenges and what current capabilities it wants to remove because the capabilities are not required for the expected future security challenges.

The statement also implies that with predictable funding, industry will be capable of meeting those future needs. The notion of Canadian industry reversing decades of being experts in specific areas and being unable to meet most the military's needs is perhaps unrealistic, but it is an acknowledgment that industry needs a longer-term plan. A more detailed review of the strategy beyond the minister's introduction reveals a more realistic expectation of industry, with statements such as 'The infusion of long-term stable funding ... will enable industry to reach for global excellence and to be better positioned to compete for defence contracts at home and abroad, thus enabling a pro-active investment in research and development and opportunities for domestic and international spin-offs as well as potential commercial applications.'[39]

More importantly for the focus of this chapter, the government has for the first time articulated a connection among defence spending, industry, and national interest, although it is necessary to imply the national interest connection. The government argues that its articulation of long-term funding sets the stage for a renewed relationship with Canadian defence industry and that 'Canadians will profit from the development of high-tech, high-value sustainable jobs in all regions – directly through the development of military capabilities and indirectly through technological spinoffs and commercial applications. This will put Canadians to work protecting Canadians. Universities and colleges will also benefit through increased opportunities to undertake cutting-edge research.'[40]

When discussing long-term funding, the government does make connections among funding, procurement, new industrial capabilities, research and development, economic prosperity, and jobs for Canadians in order to meet defence needs.[41] This will be beneficial for national security, promote economic development, and therefore be in our national interest. The difficulty for industry will be deciding how much of this they are prepared to accept as a basis for long-term business-investment decisions, especially when a new government might not necessarily live up to a previous government's decision. Industry has not forgotten that the Liberal government cancelled the Conservative government's EH-101 helicopter project after returning to power in 1993. Even with a stable majority government, there will always be some caution in accepting the promises and in assessing the long-term viability of the CFDS.

Nevertheless, there should be some optimism in the notion of expecting governments to recognize the need to connect procurement and industry. There has been no significant opposition to the government's plan to invest in the military. More importantly, the Conservatives are actually continuing the process that was started by the previous Liberal government under Paul Martin. Therefore, barring a significant change in the security environment, a change in government back to the Liberals should not have any major impact to funding and priorities – the Arctic and defending Canadian sovereignty will remain an issue, working with the United States in defending North America will remain an issue, and contributing to peace and security abroad will remain an issue.

Table 4.3 provides an indication of where the government plans to invest in defence in the next twenty years. What is important is that $265 billion of the $490 billion is for personnel or projects already announced. There will be little opportunity for industry to benefit from this spending beyond what already exists in the announced contract awards. Meanwhile, $205 billion is to go to infrastructure, readiness, and other capital. Most of this spending should be available to Canadian industries that are competitive bidders or simply because they are local workers. For example, infrastructure spending generally requires industry and workers from the area where the construction is being completed. The majority of $40 billion of infrastructure spending should be awarded to Canadian companies. On the other hand, readiness spending, logically a Canadian industry provider for most activities, raises the issue of whether or not the supply and maintenance of weapons systems should be completed by Canadian industry in order to protect intellectual property and guarantee access.

The remaining $20 billion for new equipment will be the most controversial and will require foreign defence industries to provide complete weapon systems and the government to deal with the issues discussed in this chapter – how to connect defence procurement and defence industry in a way that promotes long-term economic development and Canadian national interests.

This planned spending should result in the government making decisions that deal with issues like whether or not to revise its shipbuilding

Table 4.3. Canada First Defence Strategy: Total defence spending 2008–9 to 2027–8 (accrual numbers)

Pillar	Amount ($B)	% of total	Remarks
Personnel	250	51	70,000 Regular and 30,000 Reserve personnel by 2028; includes 25,000 civilian workforce
Equipment			
Previous announcements	15[a]	3	Previously announced equipment purchases, including: C-17 Globemasters C-130J Hercules Arctic/offshore patrol ships CH-47F Chinook helicopters Trucks
New major fleet announcements	20[b]	4	Fixed-wing search and rescue aircraft Destroyers and frigates Maritime patrol aircraft Fighter aircraft Land combat vehicles and systems
Other capital	25	5	Includes individual weapons, communications equipment, etc.
Infrastructure	40	8	Increased investment in rebuilding and maintenance of infrastructure of approximately $100M/year
Readiness	140	29	Approximately $140M/year in new spending on spare parts, maintenance, and training
Total spending over 20 years	**490**	100	

[a] This figure reflects only the capital component of this equipment over the 20 years. The previously announced total of $30B includes the capital and in-service support costs over the full life of the equipment.
[b] This figure represents the capital costs of the new major fleet replacements during the 20 years period reflected in the table. The total capital costs of these platforms amortized over their useful life, which extend beyond this 20 years, amount to $45–50B.
Source: Canada, Department of National Defence, *Canada First Defence Strategy* (Ottawa: 2008), 12.

policy and whether or not it should acquire the Joint Strike Fighter rather than look at other options.[42] More importantly, this amount of spending demands that the government have a coherent and broad IRB policy that moves beyond individual projects. Canada and its taxpayers can no longer afford a government that looks at each individual project on its own when assessing company bids against the IRB policy. A twenty-year plan requires a Twenty Industrial Regional Benefits plan. Only by connecting the procurement and funding in a more holistic manner can industry be confident in making long-term investment decisions, and those decisions are critical to the long economic development of new capabilities and skill sets for Canadians. Ensuring that Canadian industry has the opportunity to become a world leader in a particular area is good for Canada, good for industry, and good for the military.

Conclusion

This chapter set out to look at the connections among procurement, industry, and Canadian national interests. Accepting that economic prosperity and being competitive in the global economy is in our national interest, the chapter reviewed Canada's procurement challenges and the state of Canadian defence industry, especially the challenges associated with IRBs, and finally the planned spending articulated in the CFDS. At the end of the day, it is only by connecting procurement and funding in a more holistic manner that industry can be confident in making long-term investment decisions. Those decisions are critical to long-term economic prosperity and for the development of new capabilities and worker skill sets that enhance Canadian competitiveness in the global economy. If the government does not make the connections among defence procurement and defence industry, much of the $490 billion will be spent without lasting effect. It is in our national interest to ensure that each is connected to the other.

NOTES

1 Canada, Treasury Board, *Procurement Review Policy,* http://www.tbs-sct. gc.ca/pol/doc-eng.aspx?id=12074&section=HTML.
2 The 2004 *National Security Policy* indicates that personal security, national security, and international security are interconnected and cannot be looked at in isolation. See Canada, Privy Council Office, *Securing an Open Society: Canada's National Security Policy* (Ottawa: Privy Council Office, April 2004), 4.
3 Canada, Industry Canada, *IRB Policy Guidelines,* accessed 13 July 2009, http://www.ic.gc.ca/eic/site/ad-ad.nsf/eng/ad03657.html.
4 Todd Sandler and Keith Hartley, *The Economics of Defense* (Cambridge: Cambridge University Press, 1995), 114.
5 Some of the material in this section is based on previous work by the author as part of his PhD dissertation and from work published in *The*

Public Management of Defence in Canada, ed. Craig Stone (Toronto: Breakout Educational Network, 2009).

6 John Read, 'One PWGSC Perspective,' *FrontLine Defence* 3, no. 1 (Jan. 2006), http://www.frontline-canada.com/Defence/articles/06_01Read.html.

7 Dan Middlemiss, 'Defence Procurement in Canada,' in *Canada's International Security Policy*, ed. David B. Dewitt and David Leyton-Brown (Scarborough, ON: Prentice Hall Canada, 1995), 391.

8 John Treddenick, 'The Economic Significance of the Canadian Defence Industrial Base,' in *Canada's Defence Industrial Base: The Political Economy of Preparedness and Procurement*, ed. David G. Haglund (Kingston: Ronald P. Frye, 1988), 42. More recent figures indicate that defence spending in the domestic industrial base accounts for only 0.4 per cent of the Canadian GDP at factor cost. Brent K. Lemon, 'The Economic Impact of Defence Spending on the Canadian Industrial Base' (MA thesis, Royal Military College, 2001), i.

9 Canada, Department of National Defence, *Canada First Defence Strategy* (Ottawa: DND, 2009), 5.

10 In general, defence procurement that involves recurring purchases or items readily available in the market are tendered using a fixed price contract, under which there is little risk to the contractor or the government with respect to cost changes and quality. Most defence procurement is done on a fixed contract basis. Unfortunately, new weapons systems are generally contracted using a cost-plus or incentive type contract.

11 Alan S. Williams, *Reinventing Canadian Defence Procurement: A View from Inside* (Montreal and Kingston: Breakout Education Network, 2006), 45–7. The Assistant Deputy Minister (Materiel) is the organization within defence that is responsible for procurement.

12 Treasury Board Secretariat, 'Appendix A: Definitions,' in *Contracting Policy* (Ottawa: TB, 9 June 2003), accessed 28 Feb. 2008, http://www.tbs-sct.gc.ca/pubs_pol/dcgpubs/Contracting/contractingpol_a_e.asp.

13 'Chapter 9 Best Value,' in ibid. Of particular note to the newcomer in the study of defence procurement, cost estimation is perhaps the most complex area of defence procurement. In addition to providing data for forecasting costs, it is closely linked to the decision-making process for choosing between competing options. It is an area that involves both systems analysis and cost-benefit analysis.

14 Canada, Office of the Auditor General, 'Chapter 11 National Defence,' in *1982 Report of the Auditor General of Canada*. The report went to observe, 'More importantly, the Government takes considerable interest in these large projects because of the opportunities to achieve

objectives beyond those of DND, such as industrial and regional development. . . . Departmental management systems cannot be designed to hasten
this process; they can only be designed to provide required information
and to react to decisions when they are made.'

15 Canada, Minister's Advisory Committee on Administrative Efficiency,
Achieving Administrative Efficiency, report to the minister of national
defence by the Advisory Committee on Administrative Efficiency (Ottawa:
Minister's Advisory Committee, 21 Aug. 2003), vii.

16 In figure 4.1 SOR is Statement of Requirement and RFP is Request for
Proposal.

17 For example, Alan Williams argues that a new defence procurement
agency should be created, combining PWGSC and DND resources,
under the control of the minister of national defence. See Alan Williams,
'Procurement Reform: Fact Fantasy or . . . Trap?' *Frontline Defence* 1
(2008): 17.

18 Canada, House of Commons, Minutes of Proceedings of Evidence,
Standing Committee on National Defence, 39th Parliament, 1st Session,
20 Feb. 2007, Rick Casson, chair (Ottawa: House of Commons, 2007), 2,
http://www.parl.gc.ca/content/hoc/Committee/391/NDDN/Evidence/
EV2722736/NDDNEV37-E.PDF. PWGSC is the purchasing agent for all
departments in the federal government and acts as a separate centre of
authority on contracting.

19 Dan Ross, Minutes of Proceedings of Evidence, Standing Senate
Committee on National Security and Defence, 25 May 2009, Colin Kenny,
chair (Ottawa, Senate: May 2009), 6:34, http://www.parl.gc.ca/40/2/parlbus/
commbus/senate/Com-e/defe-e/pdf/06issue.pdf.

20 See Canada, House of Commons, *Procurement and Associated Processes*,
report of the Standing Committee on National Defence, Rick Casson, chair,
39th Parliament, 2nd Session (Ottawa: House of Commons, Feb. 2008), 4.

21 The primary DND documents – which now provide annual guidance to
the senior management on planning for the acquisition, organization, and
maintenance of the military capabilities required to meet defence policy
direction – are the annual *Report on Plans and Priorities* and the *Defence
Plan On-Line*. Those familiar with the defence portfolio will recall that this
information used to be provided in the annual Defence Planning Guidance
document. In 2000–3, this document evolved to the *Departmental Report on
Plans and Priorities* and an annual Defence Plan, which is now provided
electronically within DND via the VCDS website. These documents provide DND's translation of broad government policy objectives into strategic plans on how those objectives will be achieved. The reader should be

aware, however, that at the time of writing, there was no approved govern-ment defence policy document. The CFDS issued by the Conservative government is an articulation of how it intends to fund the military in the future and an indication of what equipment it intends to purchase. This document combined with a Departmental Investment Plan provides long-term guidance to the military, but it is neither a strategy nor a policy.

22 Alistair D. Edgar and David G. Haglund, *The Canadian Defence Industry in the New Global Environment* (Montreal and Kingston: McGill-Queen's University Press, 1995), 62. Edgar and Haglund note that the DPSA came about after Canada cancelled the Arrow program and had effectively aban-doned future domestic development prospects for major weapon systems. See also Michael Slack and John Skynner, 'Defence Production and the Defence Industrial Base,' in *Canada's International Security Policy*, ed. David B. Dewitt and David Leyton-Brown (Scarborough, ON: Prentice Hall Canada, 1995), 369–70.

23 Slack and Skynner, 'Defence Production and the Defence Industrial Base,' 370. For example, the three most prominent committees were the Material Coordination Committee for supply and raw material, the Joint Economic Committee for joint defence production and war planning, and the Joint Defence Production Committee. All three of these committees were formed in 1941 and have been used as models for more recent agreements and committees, the most important of which is the Defence Production Sharing Arrangement established in October 1956.

24 James Fergusson, 'In Search of a Strategy: The Evolution of Canadian Defence Industrial and Regional Benefits Policy,' in *The Economics of Offsets Defence Procurement and Countertrade*, ed. Stephen Martin (York, UK: The Centre for Defence Economics, University of York / Harwood Academic Publishers, 1996), 110.

25 For a detailed discussion on the state of the Canadian defence industrial base, see R.B. Byers, Michael Slack, Martin Shadwick, John Willis, and David Leyton-Brown, *Canada and Defence Industrial Preparedness: Options and Prospects* (Toronto: Centre for International and Strategic Studies, York University, April 1987); and Canada, Department of National Defence, *Defence Industrial Preparedness: A Foundation for Defence – Executive Version of the Final Report of the Defence Industrial Preparedness Task Force* (Ottawa: Supply and Services Canada, November 1987). Although dated, these are the only substantial studies of the Canadian defence industry's strengths and weaknesses. Other assessments can be found in Bernie Grover, *Canadian Defence Industry: A Statistical Overview of the Canadian Defence Industry* (Ottawa: Canadian Defence Industries Association, 1997 and

1999); and Binyam Solomon, 'The Defence Industrial Base in Canada,' in *The Public Management of Defence in Canada*, ed. Craig Stone (Toronto: Breakout Educational Network, 2009), 111–40.

26 Grover, *Canadian Defence Industry* (1997). It is important to remember that access to the U.S. defence market is not based on any treaty status agreement; therefore, despite measures like the defence production sharing agreement, Canadian access is open to change from things like the International Traffic in Arms Regulation issue.

27 Solomon, 'Defence Industrial Base in Canada.'

28 Grover, *Canadian Defence Industry* (1999), 5–7.

29 Edgar and Haglund, *Canadian Defence Industry;* and Grover, *Canadian Defence Industry* (1999), 10–14.

30 Solomon, 'Defence Industrial Base in Canada,' 112.

31 Timothy Page, 'CADSI Calls for Strategic Decision-Making,' *Frontline Defence* 3 (2006): 13.

32 Industry Canada, *IRB Policy Guidelines.*

33 Fergusson, 'In Search of a Strategy,' 110.

34 For a review of the state of Canadian defence industry, see Grover, *Canadian Defence Industry* (1997 and 1999); and Solomon, 'Defence Industrial Base in Canada.'

35 Page, 'CADSI Calls for Strategic Decision-Making,' 13.

36 Ibid., 13–14.

37 Ibid., 14–16.

38 DND, *Canada First Defence Strategy*, 2.

39 Ibid., 4.

40 Ibid., 20.

41 The government states, 'This commitment to long-term funding and to the detailed procurement strategy it supports will also provide major new opportunities for Canadian industry and produce significant economic benefits for Canadians. It will provide good jobs and new opportunities for tens of thousands of Canadians who work in defence industries and communities with military bases. It will also allow Canadian companies to align their long-term manufacturing, support, and research and development programs to better meet procurement requirements' (ibid., 12–13).

42 The government has a shipbuilding policy that indicates ships should be built in Canada. However, the lack of sustained shipbuilding activity for over a decade means the skills and capabilities are no longer resident in Canada to build warships. With respect to the Joint Strike Fighter, in February 2002 Canada joined the project as a Level Three international partner. Canada is committed to funding and services of more than US$150

million, which allows Canadian industry to compete for US$500–600 million in development phase work. This is significant, since the Joint Strike Fighter is considered to be the largest acquisition program in the United States, and access to production level contracts will provide significant economic benefits to industry.

5   Homeland Security and Defence in the Post-9/11 Era

ELINOR SLOAN

Any national security strategy for Canada must necessarily encompass the direct security and defence of Canada. Although this may seem self-evident, it has not always been the case. Surrounded by oceans, and bordering what has been a friendly neighbour for the past two centuries, Canada – like the United States – has historically felt little direct threat to its territory. The experience fostered an expeditionary 'strategic culture' under which threats to Canada are met 'over there' before they can reach our borders. It prevailed even during the Cold War, when nuclear-armed intercontinental ballistic missiles posed a direct threat to North America; because there was no effective defence against such missiles, Canada defended its security abroad, on the inter-German border. On 11 September 2001, that 'away game' emphasis was challenged, demonstrating that no matter how good a country's offence, there is always a requirement for defence. Canada's expeditionary culture remains, and the vast majority of military spending in the first post-9/11 decade was allocated to the mission in Afghanistan. But driven by the threat of terrorism and more recently by the melting polar ice cap, there has also been increased focus on the 'home game' of national security – 'homeland security' and 'homeland defence.'

Introduced in the United States, homeland security was originally associated almost exclusively with terrorism. The Bush administration defined homeland security as 'a concerted national effort to prevent terrorist attacks within the United States, reduce America's vulnerabilities to terrorism, and minimize the damage and recover from attacks that do occur.'[1] Yet natural disasters like Hurricane Katrina have demonstrated that terrorism is not the only circumstance that can put at risk the security of the homeland. Accounting for the array of issues that can affect a nation's security, homeland security can be more generally understood as civilian-led measures to protect the people, property, and systems of a country. In homeland security missions, the military could play a supporting role to a civilian agency, or it could play no role at all.

Homeland defence is a subset of the overarching homeland security concept and refers to military-led activities to protect a nation's people or territory. Traditionally, these activities have been directed against external threats, although in some circumstances the military can play a lead role in, around, or over the homeland. The last refers to airborne threats internal to the North American continent, such as the hijacked aircraft of 9/11. Responding to this threat is the responsibility of the North American Aerospace Defence Command (NORAD), as is reacting to Russian bombers approaching North America, while addressing the ballistic missile threat is the concern of both NORAD and U.S. Northern Command (USNORTHCOM). All of these aerospace-oriented homeland defence issues figure in continental defence, the subject of the next chapter, and so will not be discussed here. What follows below is a brief discussion and examination of Canada's approach to homeland security and homeland defence in and around Canadian territory, with some concluding thoughts on the Arctic region.[2]

Homeland Security

In the weeks and months after 9/11, the government of Prime Minister Jean Chrétien adopted an intelligence and legislation-based approach to addressing threats to the homeland. In December 2001, Parliament passed Bill C-36, the Anti-Terrorism Act, granting Canadian law enforcement agencies expanded wiretap powers and the authority to detain anyone for up to seventy-two hours without a warrant on suspicion of terrorism. In its 'security budget' of the same month, the government also allocated several billion dollars to increasing intelligence-gathering capabilities, improving critical infrastructure protection, enhancing border security, and improving immigrant and refugee claimant screening. In 2002 the government enacted the Immigration and Refugee Protection Act, making it easier for the government to deport individuals deemed a security threat, and it also initiated a Public Safety Act, allowing for things like the collection of information on air travellers.

But it was left to a new government to implement whole-scale *institutional* change in response to the post-9/11 homeland security emphasis.

When Prime Minister Paul Martin came to power in December 2003, one of his first acts was to create a new super-ministry called Public Safety and Emergency Preparedness Canada. Renamed by the subsequent Stephen Harper government as Public Safety Canada (PSC), the department's central mandate is critical infrastructure protection and emergency management. 'Critical infrastructure' refers to facilities and services that, if disrupted or destroyed, would have a serious impact on the safety, security, or economic well-being of Canadians – things like energy and utilities, communications and information technology, finance, health care, food, water, transportation, government services, and manufacturing. 'Emergency management' encompasses disaster prevention and mitigation, emergency preparedness, and the response to and recovery from an emergency.

All functions of the former Department of the Solicitor General are also part of PSC, including the Royal Canadian Mounted Police (RCMP) and the Canadian Security Intelligence Service (CSIS). Created in 1984, CSIS gathers security intelligence on direct threats to Canada. Whereas previously this information was gathered primarily inside Canadian borders, today CSIS increasingly collects information on threats to Canada that originate in a foreign country. Meanwhile, the RCMP heads up all law enforcement aspects of threats to Canada, both on Canadian territory and in our surrounding waters. Finally, PSC also includes the Canada Border Services Agency (CBSA). Created by the Martin government, CBSA is charged with facilitating and managing the movement of goods and people into Canada. This primarily involves administering and enforcing domestic laws and international agreements related to the movement of goods and people, notably the Canada-U.S. Smart Border Declaration and the Security and Prosperity Partnership.

Homeland Security Initiatives

In the years after 9/11, Canada instituted a whole range of initiatives to increase land, air, and maritime security. In the land dimension, the driving factor has been ensuring continued access to the U.S. market. With more than 80 per cent of Canadian exports – representing about 40 per cent of its gross domestic product – going to the United States, access to the American market is considered a national security issue from a Canadian government perspective. In December 2001 the two countries signed the Smart Border Declaration, which, with its thirty-two-point action plan, had as its objective increasing border security while facilitating the flow of legitimate traffic. Its range of activities, including fast-tracked clearance systems and advanced technologies to screen trucks and passenger vehicles for explosives and radiation, were implemented by 2005. At that time, the two countries signed the follow-on Security and Prosperity Partnership agreement, which contains still more agenda items for increased cooperation. The two countries have, for example, established Integrated Border Enforcement Teams made up of members of Canadian and American agencies involved in law enforcement, and instituted a program on the Great Lakes under which RCMP officers travel on U.S. Coast Guard boats to interdict transnational threats.

In the air dimension of homeland security, Canada created the Canadian Air Transport Security Authority to improve airport screening and to place armed undercover police officers on Canadian aircraft and in airports. In addition, the fast track clearance systems established under the Smart Border Action Plan have been extended to airports and marine ports, while the government has piloted 'dirty bomb' detectors to warn of radioactive materials in passenger, baggage, or cargo systems. Abroad, Canada has established a network of immigration control officers at selected airports to identify and stop terrorists before they can board a plane to Canada. Both Canada and the United States have also co-located customs and immigration officers in joint passenger analysis units at major international airports to identify high-risk travellers. Despite all this activity, the auditor general has persistently uncovered shortcomings in Canadian airport security. Critics have argued that its airports (and seaports) are 'riddled' with organized crime because responsibility for airport security is fragmented among numerous agencies.[3]

In the maritime dimension, one of the Canadian government's greatest concerns is that a terrorist will smuggle a weapon of mass destruction (WMD) onto the continent in one of the thousands of sea containers that enter Canadian ports every year. To address this concern Canada joined America's Container Security Initiative, under which CBSA receives cargo information on ships destined for Canada ninety-six hours prior to their arrival. It then uses an automated risk-scoring tool to identify high-risk containers, and those with a high score are not permitted to be loaded on a Canada-bound ship. In North America, Canadian and American customs agencies have established joint teams of officials at five ports to examine cargo containers that have been identified electronically in transit as potentially posing a risk. Gamma ray scanners are used to inspect the containers for dirty bombs, and almost all containers arriving in Canada are scanned for radiation. Yet, as is the case in Canada's airports, there remain security shortfalls. Most notably, there is evidence of organized crime and a general lack of policing at Canadian seaports.

Canada's National Security Policy

Under Prime Minister Paul Martin, the federal government sought to put Canada's approach to national security on a formal footing by writing Canada's first-ever national security policy. Hastily produced in the weeks before Martin was to meet with U.S. President Bush, *Securing an Open Society: Canada's National Security Policy* was released in April 2004.[4] Although the Harper government has indicated on various occasions that it would release a new statement on national security, this has not happened. As a result, the 2004 policy remains Canada's overall guidance for homeland security.

Canada's 2004 National Security Policy highlights three core national security interests: protecting Canada and Canadians at home and abroad, ensuring that Canada is not a base for threats to our allies, and contributing to international security. To this end, it put forward a number of important policy initiatives, most if not all of which are still in place. It announced, for example, the creation of an Integrated Threat Assessment Centre, a central organization housed in CSIS and charged with fusing intelligence from all members of Canada's security and intelligence community; a Government Operations Centre to provide around-the-clock coordination of key players at the federal, provincial, and municipal levels in the event of a national emergency; and two (now three) Maritime Security Operations Centres) (see below).

Border Perceptions

More than anything, the 2004 *National Security Policy* set out to assure America that Canada's 1938 security pledge still holds: Canada will not allow threats to reach the United States via Canadian territory, including its land, sea, or air space. Indeed, a key homeland security issue Canada must contend with continually is the U.S. perception that Canada has leaky borders and therefore poses a security threat to the United States. None of the nineteen hijackers involved in the 9/11 attacks entered the United States through Canada; nonetheless, Canada is seen by some in the United States as being a terrorist haven. The perspective is largely a result of the case of Ahmed Ressam, an Algerian who was arrested in December 1999 by an alert U.S. customs agent as he tried to enter the United States, apparently on his way to blow up the Los Angeles airport during New Year's celebrations. Ressam had twice been refused refugee status in Canada, yet he continued to live in Montreal and carried a phoney Canadian passport.

The Ressam incident clearly highlighted the necessity for Canada to tighten its immigration, customs, and security laws. Yet it is difficult to know how much of the perception surrounding Canada's lax borders is just perception and how much is based on concrete evidence. The only reported instance in the open literature of a terrorist going across the Canadian border into the United States is the Ressam case. U.S. Homeland Security Secretary Janet Napolitano has strongly hinted there have been others, but these names and cases have not been released 'due to security reasons.'[5]

Homeland Defence

As with homeland security, a central Canadian government response to the homeland defence imperative has been *institutional*. In 2006 Canada established four new commands, one of which – Canada Command (Canada COM) – is dedicated to the homeland defence of Canada.[6] With a mission to deter, prevent, pre-empt, and defeat threats and aggression aimed at Canada, the command is concerned with the geographic areas of the continental United States, Mexico, the Caribbean (because of hurricanes), and the Arctic approaches to Canada, in addition to Canadian territory. Canada COM works closely with PSC to provide military assistance to civil authorities, much as USNORTHCOM supports the U.S. Department of Homeland Security. Six regional joint task forces, comprising sea, land, and air elements, are located in major cities across Canada and report to the commander of Canada COM in Ottawa.

Having a joint military command dedicated to the defence of Canada represents an entirely new element in Canadian defence planning. 'In the past, Canada has structured its military primarily for international operations,' noted the Martin government in its 2005 *International Policy Statement*, 'while the domestic role has been treated as a secondary consideration.'[7] Post-9/11, it was felt that this approach was no longer sufficient. Canada COM was created as a single locus of authority for responding to an emergency, and to have a command that is concerned solely with the security of Canadian territory. Previously, all operations – at home and abroad – were the responsibility of one deputy chief of defence staff. Under the new structure, operations at home and abroad are divided between Canada COM and a separate Canadian Expeditionary Forces Command for overseas missions.

Canada's new command structure, the most extensive reorganization of the Canadian Forces (CF) since the 1960s, is still a work in progress. The immediate effect of creating several new command structures was to take hundreds of personnel out of operational positions and place them into staff positions, thereby straining an already overstretched military. But in the longer term, the creation of Canada COM is likely to prove a positive step. It provides the operational link with USNORTHCOM for homeland defence missions and with PSC for homeland security activities. Anecdotal evidence suggests that the creation of Canada COM as a rough counter to USNORTHCOM has simplified and clarified Canada–U.S. cooperation for homeland defence.[8] It has also provided an important focal point for civilian authorities in seeking CF assistance at home.[9]

The Role of the CF in Homeland Security and Defence

Canada's military has always played a role in the direct security and defence of Canadian territory. Section 275 of the National Defence Act states that the CF may 'be called out for service in aid of the civil power in any case in which a riot or disturbance of the peace [is] beyond the powers of the civil authorities to suppress, prevent or deal with.' Such circumstances, which describe a military lead-agency role on Canadian territory, have been relatively few and far between – best remembered is the FLQ (Front de libération du Québec) crisis of 1970. In the vast majority of cases, whether it be floods or snowstorms or ice storms, the military plays a supporting role to a civilian lead agency – the exception being search and rescue, an explicitly military function in Canada.

Much of the CF's activity at home has involved responding to natural disasters. Nonetheless, a central concern of the Canadian government is that terrorists could use a WMD against a Canadian city. The panic generated by such an attack would likely be such that the situation would rapidly evolve into one of aid of the civil power. During the Cold War, the CF was trained to deal with WMD overseas, long before it was ever expected such expertise would be needed at home. These skills have now been adapted for use in the event of a WMD terrorist attack on North American soil. A Canadian Incidence Response Unit has been established at CF Base Trenton and is designed to respond to a WMD attack, while Joint Task Force 2, Canada's special operations force, is also trained to operate in a WMD-contaminated environment. Beyond this, the CF is restructuring its land force reserves to create battalion-size units across the country that will be trained with specialist skills to respond to disasters – natural or otherwise – including those involving WMD. An entire battalion will be committed to the North.

Maritime Surveillance and Control

One of the CF's most important homeland defence responsibilities is the surveillance and control of the maritime approaches to Canadian territory. And yet its capabilities in this area are relatively limited. Its 18 CP-140 Aurora long-range patrols aircraft, mandated to patrol up and down the East and West Coasts and occasionally over the Arctic, are old and often under repair; as a result, they are periodically unable to carry out scheduled surveillance missions. Some are to be upgraded, but many will be phased out, and, by the mid-2010s, only a handful of aircraft will be available for maritime surveillance missions. A new Canadian multi-mission aircraft is to arrive sometime after 2020 – if the funding is available. Canada's twelve Kingston-class maritime coastal defence vessels are staffed by the naval reserves and conduct surveillance missions along the East and West Coasts. But because they were designed for patrolling and mine warfare, they are slow and ill-suited for interdicting threats. They are also too small to handle the rough seas that characterize much of Canada's 200 nautical-mile Economic Exclusion Zone. Canada's twelve Halifax-class frigates, which date from the 1990s but are being upgraded, provide an important Canadian military capability for maritime interdictions around North America that are some distance off shore. Yet they are not an ideal maritime surveillance and control vessel closer to shore because they are too big, and they are costly to operate. Moreover, their Sea King maritime helicopters, so important for extending a ship's range of view, are old, while the replacement aircraft, the Cyclone, is far behind schedule in delivery. Finally, Canada's four Victoria-class diesel-electric submarines will be able to conduct surveillance missions off the East and West Coasts, and in the summer travel as far north as the

Northwest Passage, but they will not be fully operational until the early 2010s.

Canada's existing naval vessels cannot provide the necessary maritime surveillance and control capability off Canada's East and West Coasts. The requirement is for a mid-sized naval vessel to carry out armed tasks in support of other government departments in Canada's territorial waters and out to the limits of Canada's Economic Exclusion Zone. To tackle this capability shortfall, the Harper government in 2007 announced Canada would acquire between six and eight Arctic off-shore patrol vessels by the middle of the 2010s. But by 2011 the status of this program continues to be uncertain. If it goes ahead, the size and speed of these ships will make them ideal for operations off Canada's East and West Coasts.

To fill some of the gaps in surveillance of its maritime approaches, Canada is turning to advanced technology. One project under consideration is a network of long-range radars, called High Frequency Surface Wave Radars, at spots along the East and West Coasts. Such radars transmit high-frequency waves that follow the curvature of the earth, allowing them to detect and track ships or low-flying aircraft over the horizon, up to 200 nautical miles away. The project was halted in 2006 in response to frequency concerns, but may be restarted. The CF has also experimented with the use of unmanned aerial vehicles for maritime surveillance. Exercises were held in the mid-2000s to see if drones could be used to detect smugglers off the East and West Coasts, and could be adapted to the extreme conditions of the North. Under its Joint Unmanned Surveillance and Target Acquisition System program, the CF is pursing plans for eighteen unmanned aerial vehicles that can be used for surveillance, sovereignty, and counterterrorism patrols off Canada's East, West, and Arctic coasts, as well as for international operations.

Canada's ability to conduct the surveillance of its maritime approaches, especially the Arctic region, also includes the space dimension. As a result of Polar Epsilon, a military-owned earth-imaging capability on board the commercial satellite Radarsat-2, the CF can monitor the waters and coastline of the Arctic for traditional threats to Canada's security, like weapons and military movements, and also watch for emergencies and environmental disasters. But this surveillance is not continuous because the satellite makes a pass every several hours. Under the Radarsat Constellation project, Canada plans to launch three radar satellites by mid-decade, with the mission of boosting both maritime *and* territorial security by providing continuous space-based monitoring.

Other Agencies

One complicating factor in Canadian maritime surveillance and control is the fact that there are a multitude of government organizations involved. In the United States, there is only one agency in charge of guarding American coasts: the U.S. Coast Guard, an armed enforcement organization. In Canada, by contrast, the lead agency in any given situation may be one of five government organizations, depending on the issue involved and how close it occurs to Canadian shores. They include the Canadian navy (with support from air force assets like the CP-140 Aurora), Transport Canada, the CBSA, the RCMP, and the Canadian Coast Guard. The last is part of the Department of Fisheries and Oceans and, unlike its American counterpart, has never been an enforcement or security agency. Transport Canada is the lead department for marine security; the RCMP conducts police/enforcement functions along the coasts, assisted, if necessary, by the navy; the CBSA is responsible for things like addressing stowaways arriving by ship and collecting Container Security Initiative information; and the Coast Guard can support enforcement by transporting RCMP officers to vessels of interest, but its primary mission lies in marine navigation and safety, traffic management, and pollution control. The general coastal protection role for Canada remains with the navy.

Thus, when it comes to operations off Canada's coasts, a whole host of players are involved on the Canadian side. To bring together the intelligence gathered by government departments about activity off its coasts, Canada has created a Maritime Security Operations Centre in Victoria and in Halifax. Led by the navy, the Marine Security Operations Centres have representation from the RCMP, CBSA, Transport Canada, and the Canadian Coast Guard and use advanced technologies to combine information gathered from all five agencies, thereby creating a comprehensive picture of what is happening along Canada's coasts. The information is sent to various national headquarters, such as Canada COM and the Government Operations Centre. A third centre, this one led by the RCMP, is also being established in the Great Lakes region to monitor activity on the Great Lakes and the St Lawrence Seaway.

Like Canada's navy, other government departments involved in Canada's maritime surveillance and control have limited resources.

The RCMP is overstretched and has only a few boats and a relatively small number of personnel to carry out enforcement missions along hundreds of kilometres of coastline. The Coast Guard's boats are aging; a plan to purchase new mid-shore patrol vessels was cancelled in 2008, only to be revitalized a year later, thereby setting back any projected delivery date. Moreover, although the Coast Guard has been and is being equipped with the appropriate vessels for interdiction missions within three to five kilometres of the coast, it has neither the security mandate nor the weaponry to intervene in criminal activity. This disjuncture has led many interested parties, most vocally the Standing Senate Committee on National Security and Defence but also others, to argue that the Coast Guard's mandate should be changed such that it more literally guards Canada's coasts.

Canadian Interests in the Arctic

The Arctic is an area of growing security concern for Canada. The region as a whole is getting warmer, and experts project the Arctic's sea ice could vanish in summer by the early 2010s, and that the fabled Northwest Passage could be open to unimpeded summer navigation later that decade.[10] These developments matter to Canada for three distinct yet overlapping reasons. First, as Arctic territory – roughly defined as anything above the sixty-sixth parallel – gets more hospitable, there will be growing resource exploitation, and with this could come criminal and terrorist elements. Already there is evidence of organized crime associated with increased diamond mining in the North. Second, less ice means the potential for increased traffic in the Northwest Passage, since shipping routes through the passage would cut off thousands of kilometres of transit distance between various spots on the globe. Although future ice conditions are not precisely known, the economic incentives will likely be such that at least some ships will want to transport goods through the Northwest Passage. This would bring environmental concerns like the possibility of an oil spill, and possible search and rescue issues like responding to a cruise ship in distress. Not surprisingly, Canada wants to control who and what travels through the Northwest Passage. Canada has historically maintained that the passage is an internal waterway to be regulated by Canadian national law. But the United States, along with other major countries, maintains that this is an international strait. So far the two countries have 'agreed to disagree,' but as the ice continues to melt this could prove a confrontational issue.

A third area of concern in the Arctic centres on the exact extent of Canadian territory as it extends beyond the Arctic Archipelago. The U.S. Geological Survey estimates the Arctic seabed holds 13 per cent of the world's undiscovered oil reserves, and over 30 per cent of the world's untapped gas reserves. Under the 1982 UN Convention on the Law of the Sea, countries have exclusive rights over an economic zone extending 200 miles offshore, but this can be extended if the seabed is shown to be part of a country's continental shelf. Canada and Denmark are working together to prove that an underwater ridge reaching as far as the North Pole is an extension of Ellesmere Island and Greenland. Russia, meanwhile, is taking measures to demonstrate the ridge is geologically linked to Siberia – including by sending a remote-controlled submarine to the North Pole's ocean floor in 2007 to collect soil samples. Canada also has a long-standing and unresolved dispute with the United States over the boundary delineation between the Yukon and Alaska in the Beaufort Sea, and with Denmark over the ownership of Hans Island between Greenland and Ellesmere Island.

Some consider the Arctic a potential international flashpoint of the future. A 2007 report by America's Center for Naval Analysis argued a warming Arctic holds great implications for military operations as a result of competition for resources.[11] A 2008 European Union report found the changing geostrategic dynamics of the Arctic region brought on by climate change could have consequences for international stability.[12] North Atlantic Treaty Organization (NATO) military leaders have met to examine the prospect of standoffs among nations laying claims to the Arctic's energy reserves, while NATO's secretary general has cautioned the alliance's Arctic nations to stay united, despite growing potential for conflict.[13] In 2009, Russia released a government security report that predicts possible military conflict over energy resources in the Arctic,[14] and Russia has already announced plans to create a dedicated military force to help protect its interests in disputed areas of the Arctic.[15]

A key component of Canada's policy response to Arctic issues must be increased diplomacy. Of the five nations laying claim to the Arctic, four are long-standing allies – the United States, Canada, Denmark, and Norway – while the fifth is Russia. But another component must necessarily be ensuring that Canada has the ability to exercise control over its Arctic regions. Canadian frigates, submarines, and coastal defence vessels have already begun to carry out exercises in the Northwest Passage in the summer months, notably Operation Nanook each August. At the same time, the melting ice cap will increase the stretch of northern waters in which Canada's ships and submarines can operate, and the annual number of weeks during which they will be able to do so. But none of Canada's current naval vessels can operate in ice-infested waters. Unlike their nuclear-propelled counterparts, diesel electric submarines are restricted in ice-covered areas because they must surface periodically to regenerate their power. And unlike countries such as Denmark, Canada does not have frigates or other vessels with ice-strengthened hulls. The Canadian Coast Guard does have ice-breakers, but the largest and most capable of these, the *Louis St Laurent*, is old and nearing the end of its operational life.

The Harper government has sought to rectify some of these shortfalls. Arctic offshore patrol vessels, with their ice-strengthened hulls, would significantly increase Canada's ability to conduct maritime patrols of the Arctic regions. But if acquired, they will still be far different from the three 'armed ice breakers' the Conservatives had originally promoted during the 2005–6 election. Rather than providing an ice-breaking capability, they will only be able to go through fresh ice of about one metre thick and therefore will not be able to operate in the North year-round. Their acquisition makes most sense if made in conjunction with the building of a new Coast Guard icebreaker, and for this reason it is significant the Harper government announced plans for the construction of a new Polar-class icebreaker by the late-2010s. Other Arctic initiatives include constructing a deep-water port and refuelling station in Nanisivik, Nunavut, as a staging area for vessels operating in the high Arctic; establishing a CF Arctic Training Centre for the army in Resolute Bay, Nunavut, from which the CF can conduct year-round patrols; and increasing the size of the Canadian Rangers – part-time reservists who are native to the Arctic region – by some nine hundred members to a total of five thousand by about 2012. Canada's army has designated four reserve units to form the backbone of a new Arctic force, with about five hundred personnel in total, to be created by the middle of the 2010s.

Conclusion

Canada has responded to the contemporary security environment with a whole range of initiatives and institutional changes. Organizational efforts like the creation of PSC, Integrated Threat Assessment Centre, and Canada COM have been designed to better protect Canada and respond to crises. The lack of a terrorist strike on Canadian soil in the first post-9/11 decade, and the interaction between PSC and Canada COM on homeland issues, suggest these changes are having a positive impact. Border-related efforts are also designed to increase security, but more fundamentally from a Canadian perspective, they are meant to ensure the continued free flow of goods between Canada and the United States. An even greater priority under the Obama administration than the Bush administration, border security in all of its land, sea, and air dimensions will pose a challenge to Canada in the coming years. Canada has already done much to assuage American security concerns in the post-9/11 period, but in all likelihood will have to take additional steps to demonstrate it remains serious about homeland security, and to keep the frontier open. Yet these challenges pale in comparison to what is presented by the forces of climate change and the melting Arctic. The Arctic is of growing interest to circumpolar nations and to the world's shipping lines. Threats and economic interests also intersect off Canada's East and West Coasts. It is in Canada's security interests to conduct the surveillance and control of its maritime approaches out to the 200 nautical-mile Economic Exclusion Zone. Nonetheless, its capability off its East and West Coasts is relatively limited, its Arctic surveillance ability still more so, and its capability to operate in the Arctic region much of the year all but non-existent. A number of important initiatives have been promised, but none have yet been concretely implemented.

Canada has historically had the luxury of defending its interests far from Canadian shores. Although it still makes sense to do so rather than waiting until a threat appears on one's border, the twenty-first-century reality is that this approach must be tempered with a greater emphasis on the direct security and defence of Canada's territory and surrounding waters. The nature of the primary threat to Canadian security – international terrorism – combined with the onward march of climate change, the melting Arctic, and the accompanying challenges of criminal activity, increased commercial and military traffic, and competition for resources, indicate that the 'home game' will be just as important as the 'away game,' if not more so, in the not too distant future. The Christmas Day bomber of 2009 clearly demonstrated the perils of focusing on threats abroad at the expense of those at home.[16]

The Harper government came to office proclaiming 'Canada First' as its defining approach to Canadian security, but most of its defence investments have been overseas. The requirement is for increased resources dedicated to the security of Canada's airports and seaports, and concrete investments in capabilities that enable Canada's navy and Coast Guard to conduct the surveillance and control of Canada's three coasts. The most viable long-term approach involves acquiring aerial drones, ice-capable vessels and at least one polar icebreaker, and also transforming the Coast Guard – the agency that best knows Canada's Arctic – from a constabulary force to an armed one that actually guards Canada's littorals. Clearly the issue is one not only of budgetary allocations but also of political will. Effecting the necessary changes in capability and culture among Canada's homeland security and defence agencies will be one of the Canadian government's most daunting challenges of the next decade.

NOTES

1 United States, White House, *National Strategy for Homeland Security* (Washington, DC: White House, Oct. 2007), 3.
2 Parts of this chapter were first published in Elinor C. Sloan, *Security and Defence in the Terrorist Era*, 2nd ed. (Montreal and Kingston: McGill-Queen's University Press, 2010), chaps 4 and 5. Reprinted with permission.
3 Canada, Standing Senate Committee on National Security and Defence, *Canadian Security Guide Book: Airports* (Ottawa: Standing Senate Committee on National Security and Defence, Mar. 2007), 9; Canada, Standing Senate Committee on National Security and Defence, *Canadian Security Guide Book: Seaports* (Ottawa: Standing Senate Committee on National Security and Defence, Mar. 2007), 18.
4 Canada, Privy Council Office, *Securing an Open Society: Canada's National Security Policy* (Ottawa: Privy Council Office, Apr. 2004).
5 Qtd in Sheldon Alberts, 'Napolitano Chided for Linking Canada to 9/11,' *Ottawa Citizen*, 22 Apr. 2009.
6 The other commands include Canadian Expeditionary Forces Command, Canadian Special Operations Command, and Canadian Operational Support Command.
7 Canada, Department of National Defence, *Canada's International Policy Statement: A Role of Pride and Influence in the World – Defence* (Ottawa: DND, 2005), 18.
8 Author's impression of presentations and comments by General Gene Renuart, commander USNORTHCOM, during the U.S. Northern Command Civic Leader Tour, 9–13 June 2008.

9 Author interview with J. Scott Broughton, assistant deputy minister, Emergency Management and National Security, Public Safety Canada, Ottawa, 5 May 2008.

10 Murray Brewster, 'Flying Flag in the Arctic Could Cost Forces $843 Million a Year: Documents,' *Winnipeg Free Press,* 22 Jan. 2009; David Ljunggren, 'Arctic Summer Ice Could Vanish by 2013, Expert Says,' Reuters, 5 Mar. 2009.

11 Center for Naval Analysis, *National Security and the Threat of Climate Change* (Washington, DC: Center for Naval Analysis), 38.

12 Randy Boswell, 'EU Report Warns of Trouble over Arctic Resources,' *Ottawa Citizen,* 11 Mar. 2008.

13 Randy Boswell, 'NATO Cautions against Division over Arctic,' *Ottawa Citizen,* 30 Jan. 2009.

14 Randy Boswell, 'Arctic Conflict Possible, Russian Report Says,' *Ottawa Citizen,* 14 May 2009.

15 'Russia Dedicates Force to Arctic,' *Globe and Mail,* 27 Mar. 2009.

16 Karen DeYoung and Michael A. Fletcher, 'US Was More Focused on Al-Qaeda's Plans Abroad Than for Homeland, Report on Airline Bomb Plot Finds,' *Washington Post,* 8 Jan. 2010.

6 Continental Defence: 'Like farmers whose lands have a common concession line'

JOSEPH T. JOCKEL AND JOEL J. SOKOLSKY

It is not customary in this country for us to think in terms of having a policy in regard to the United States. Like farmers whose lands have a common concession line, we think of ourselves as settling, from day to day, questions that arise between us, without dignifying the process by the word 'policy.' We have travelled so much of the road together in close agreement that by comparison the occasions on which our paths may have diverged seem insignificant. . . . On both sides the fact has been accepted that there shall be a free and independent federation in the northern part of this continent. None of this has been achieved, however, without reflection and forethought, nor will it be maintained without constant watchfulness. . . . The relationship between a great and powerful nation and its smaller neighbour, at best is far from simple. It calls for constant and imaginative attention on both sides.

Defined more precisely, our policy in regard to the United States has come with the passage of years to have two main characteristics. On the one hand, we have sought by negotiation, by arbitration, by compromise, to settle upon the basis of mutual satisfaction the problems that have arisen between us. . . . The other aspect of our relations with the United States which I shall emphasize is our readiness to accept our responsibility as a North American nation in enterprises which are for the welfare of this continent. In support of this assertion, there is a long and creditable record of joint activity. In making it, however, I might add that it has never been the opinion of any considerable number of people in Canada that this continent could live unto itself. We have seen our own interests in the wider context of the Western World.

– Louis St Laurent, 1947[1]

For over fifty years, the most visible symbol looming over the Canada-U.S. continental defence relationship has been a bi-national military organization that operationally controls forces of both countries that have been assigned to it on a standing basis. The North American Aerospace Defence Command (NORAD) – headquartered in Colorado Springs, Colorado – has a U.S. commander, a Canadian deputy commander, and a staff drawn from both the U.S. and Canadian militaries. It reports to the senior defence authorities in the Pentagon and at National Defence Headquarters. Since its creation in 1957 as the North American Air Defence Command, it has had the responsibility to warn of an aerospace attack on North America and to direct Canadian and U.S. air defences in response.

After the terrorist attacks of 11 September 2001, which those air defences were unable to block, many Canadians expected (and hoped or feared) that to deal with this new and unforeseen threat to the continent, the two militaries would be drawn more tightly together organizationally as they pursued what had come to be called 'homeland defence.' NORAD itself, created during some of the coldest days of the Cold War, might be told by Ottawa and Washington to assume substantially broader responsibilities during the new 'war on terror.' In apparent confirmation of these expectations, the two governments announced in 2002 that they had created a temporary Binational Planning Group (BPG) in Colorado Springs to study future continental defence arrangements. It certainly seemed that the way was being smoothed towards greater continental military integration.

Today, the U.S. and Canadian armed forces are indeed working together in new ways to deal with the terrorist threat. But further integration has not occurred. No new bi-national entity has been created, and when the BPG submitted its final report in 2006, the group was wrapped up and little came of its work. In fact, the trend has been a move away from bi-national cooperation. NORAD's future is very much in doubt, especially since each country has created its own homeland defence command. The United States and Canada are returning to earlier, less integrative forms of continental defence cooperation that both predate NORAD's creation and continued, during the Cold War and post–Cold War period, to exist in its shadow.

Both the United States and Canada have largely preferred a loose defence relationship. NORAD stands out as an exception. There has long been resistance on both sides of the border to integrative continental defence arrangements. Sometimes this resistance has been Canadian, sometimes American, and sometimes both. Canadians have worried about loss of 'sovereignty' to the Americans, while the Americans have worried that working too closely with Canadians would limit their freedom of action.

Origins of NORAD

While Washington and Ottawa began to recognize in the 1930s that they would need to work together to defend their shared continent, it was not until the Second World War was well underway that they actually began to do so. The Americans responsible for defence planning with Canada assumed that it would be necessary to vest the United States with control over all continental defences, including Canadian forces. The Canadians balked, and the final version of the plan for continental defence cooperation, which was put into effect when the United States entered the war in 1941, stipulated that 'co-ordination of the military effort of the United States and Canada shall be effected by mutual co-operation' and that 'each nation shall retain the strategic direction and command of its own armed forces.'[2]

No sooner was the war over than it was clear that Canada and the United States would have to cooperate to defend themselves against the Soviet Union: at some point Soviet bombers carrying nuclear weapons would be able to reach this continent. The defence planners got down to work. At Ottawa's insistence, a series of first principles were developed, agreed upon to guide the two continental partners, and thereafter released as a public statement by Prime Minister William Lyon Mackenzie King in February 1947. The statement emphasized that while the two countries would cooperate closely, each retained control over military activities undertaken on its territory and each remained free to determine the extent of its future cooperation with the other. No overarching Canada-U.S. treaty or executive agreement on defence cooperation would be negotiated, and, to this day, no such accord exists.[3]

This approach fitted well into the government's broader approach to the United States and to Canadian foreign policy in general, which King's Secretary of State for External Affairs Louis S. St Laurent had discussed a month before in his now-famous Gray Lecture. 'It is not customary,' he said, 'for us to think in terms of having a policy in regard to the United States. Like farmers whose lands have a common concession line, we think of ourselves as settling, from day to day, questions that arise between us, without dignifying the process by the word "policy."' St Laurent followed this folksy comment with a very realpolitik assessment of how Ottawa should approach the United States. Such an approach would require 'reflection and forethought' and could not be maintained 'without constant watchfulness,' given that 'the relationship between a great and powerful nation and its smaller neighbour at best is far from simple.'[4] In short, with the Cold War just months underway, Ottawa's approach to defence cooperation with the United States was in place: it would be open to addressing with the United States discrete and specific proposals on their merits while eschewing a comprehensive and integrative approach to North American security.

In the decade that followed, however, integration was exactly what happened with the creation of NORAD. As the Department of External Affairs observed shortly thereafter, 'The establishment of NORAD is a decision for which there is no precedent in Canadian history in that it grants in peace-time to a foreign representative operational control of an element of Canadian forces *in Canada*.'[5] There were charges that Prime Minister John G. Diefenbaker did not understand NORAD's significance when he granted its establishment very swift approval upon assuming office after winning the general election of 1957; he later vigorously denied these allegations.

The U.S. Joint Chiefs of Staff, for their part, undoubtedly understood fully what NORAD entailed, and so they had had their own doubts. Cooperation with the Canadian military was, to be sure, fine with them. But what if Canadian politicians and diplomats got involved? That was another matter altogether. As the chiefs wrote the U.S. secretary of defense in 1954, 'Our experience in military planning with the Canadians has been that the Canadian military planners are unable to arrive at negotiated positions without agreement on a governmental level. A combined US-Canadian command would in all probability be restricted on the Canadian side.' Therefore, any such command 'would not seem sufficiently effective to warrant the expense in money and personnel involved.'[6]

NORAD's military sceptics in the Pentagon and civilian sceptics on Parliament Hill had to yield in the face of one powerful fact: a joint air defence command made very good sense under the strategic circumstances of the day. Soviet bombers armed with hydrogen bombs would approach U.S. and Canadian cities and military installations from the north. They could be attacked best in a continent-wide battle largely over southern Canada, with the defenders relying on the vast Distant Early Warning, Mid-Canada and Permanent/Pinetree radars that had been deployed along with hundreds of U.S. and Canadian fighter interceptors and U.S. ground-to-air missiles. As a Canadian and U.S. air force panel pointed out as early as the beginning of the 1950s, the defenders were handicapped because 'forces deployed to defend against attack from one direction (for instance, from the North) are not now under one commander, which imposes serious practical limitation in day-to-day training and in our capability to conduct a properly co-ordinated air battle in case of attack.'[7] General Earle E. Partridge, NORAD's first commander-in-chief, stepped into that role in September 1957.

Still, no sooner had he begun to issue orders than both the U.S. chiefs and the Canadian civilians circumscribed his command's authority. Partridge had wanted to make NORAD the sole continental air defence command. The chiefs insisted that the purely American command – the Continental Air Defense Command – which had existed prior to NORAD's creation, remain in place, so that the U.S. strategic defence could act where necessary without the involvement of the Canadians or the approbation of their government. Throughout its existence, NORAD has always had such a 'twin' command that has shared its commander and its facilities, but has been solely American (i.e., staffed by U.S. officers and reporting solely to Washington). Canadian officials insisted and obtained Washington's agreement in 1958 that if nuclear attack were not imminent, NORAD could only go on alert if – and only if – Ottawa's permission first was obtained. Using the 'twin' commands, the U.S. strategic defences went independently on alert without taking the Canadians along during the Cuban missile crisis of 1962 and the 1973 Yom Kippur crisis in the Middle East. Ottawa refused at first to grant its permission in 1962 – and that refusal was respected by NORAD and by Washington – and was not asked to join the brief 1973 alert.[8]

Moreover, there was a lot more to the Canada–U.S. continental defence relationship during the Cold War than NORAD with its integrated force structure and bi-national headquarters. That relationship was in fact closer to St Laurent's two farmers working things out issue by issue. When established, NORAD dealt only with air defence and surveillance against manned bombers as part of strategic nuclear deterrence and, if deterrence failed, the management of an air war, mainly over Canada. Its principal function soon became warning and assessment of missile attack, to which was added a space surveillance role. Canada contributed several land-based space surveillance sensors. But there were aspects of space surveillance pertaining to spy satellites that the United States considered too sensitive for NORAD, and thus for Canadian eyes. So it set up separate all-U.S. information channels, relying on the 'twins.' When the United States briefly deployed an anti-satellite system in the early 1960s to defend North America from attack by nuclear armed satellites, it did not ask Canada to become involved and placed the system under the operational command of the 'twin.' The government of Prime Minister Lester B. Pearson decided in 1968 that Canada would not participate in the operation of a ballistic missile defence (BMD) system. That was in fact fine with the United States, inasmuch as Canadian territory was no more needed for the operation of missile defence than for anti-satellite defence. So when the United States briefly deployed a limited BMD in the early 1970s it, too, went to the 'twin.'

Maritime surveillance and defence were never part of NORAD's mandate and there was no bi-national naval organization. Any Canada-U.S. coordination at sea was handled separately by the navies of the two countries and even here, responsibility was divided between the Pacific and Atlantic. Nor was there a bi-national organization for land defence. Apart from some plans whose relevance did not go much beyond the sporadic or inconsequential, there was little bilateral coordination of continental ground forces in the absence of a threat to North America against which the armies would need to defend. To be sure, there was a Canada-U.S. Military Cooperation Committee that helped to keep the Pentagon and the defence staff in Ottawa in touch, and within the North Atlantic Treaty Organization (NATO) formal structures there was the Canada-U.S. Regional Planning Group. But this was an arrangement that fell far short of Canada's occasionally stated, but never forcefully asserted preference, to place Canada–U.S. defence relations in the larger allied context. More importantly, the very fact that North America had only a 'planning group,' while the rest of the NATO region was covered by highly integrated international commands, was a further indication of how unstructured and informal bilateral defence relations were.

The lack of anything approximating an overarching, powerful institutional structure for North American security represented, at a deeper level, a profound confluence of the St Laurent approach with that of the United States. While the ultimate purpose of U.S. defence policy and military strategy was the security of the American homeland, this was not to be achieved by direct defence but rather by nuclear deterrence, including extended deterrence and forward defence around the globe. Here Washington was in complete agreement with Ottawa: it was not interested in a 'regional' approach to North American security. As a result, while Canadians may have felt that they needed to pay 'constant watchfulness' to defence relations with the Americans, Washington actually had to pay little attention to Canada, once it had obtained agreement from Ottawa on specific matters related largely to air defence. For awhile in the late 1950s and early 1960s, Canadian officials hoped to turn Canadian participation in air defence and especially in NORAD into a diplomatic trump card in Washington. As General Charles Foulkes, who had been chairman of the chiefs of staff committee, put it in 1961, 'As we are full partners in the defence of North America, we have to be consulted every time the US contemplates using force anywhere in the world.'[9] That was, at best, very wishful thinking.

Thus the Cold War did not usher in a period of close, comprehensive, coordinated and continuing Canada-U.S. defence collaboration, and those arrangements that did exist became increasingly marginal, reflecting the fact that North America was in a sense a strategic backwater. St Laurent's two farmers almost never had any real problems in 'settling, from day to day, questions' pertaining to defence that arose between them simply because there were not many questions. Only one truly big kerfuffle ever arose between them in the Cold War over continental defence, namely in the early 1960s over whether to equip Canadian air defence forces in NORAD with nuclear weapons (along with Canadian forces in Europe), and it can be taken as the exception that proves the rule.

Right after this nuclear weapons flap, continental defence questions became still easier to address as both the United States and Canada dismantled their vast air defences, reducing them to shadows of themselves. The nuclear air defence weapons were withdrawn, and so were all the surface-to-air missiles. Only a handful of fighter interceptors were left on duty. The Mid-Canada and Pinetree radar lines were closed down, and Ottawa seized the opportunity to 'Canadianize' what remained to be done in Canada. Canadian fighter interceptors took over peacetime intercept responsibilities in the parts of Canada where U.S. aircraft once had had responsibility. Operational boundaries were redrawn so that all of Canadian airspace was controlled for air defence purposes out of Winnipeg and North Bay, putting an end to control over much of Canadian air space out of air defence centres in the United States. When the Reagan administration and Mulroney government announced in 1985 a modernization of what remained of continental air defences, its centrepiece was the replacement of the old U.S.-built and U.S.-operated Distant Early Warning line in the high Arctic with a Canadian-built and operated North Warning System. Yet with the Soviet Union's dissolution and the Cold War's end a few years later, much of the 1985 modernization program was left unimplemented. What was the point when the commander-in-chief NORAD himself pointed out in 1994 that 'there is essentially no military air threat against North America today'?[10]

USNORTHCOM, Canada COM, and NORAD's Future

This satisfactory state of affairs seemed to come to an end on 11 September 2001. The United States had been directly attacked, and by air, with suggestions that further terrorist assaults could come by sea and by land. When the new era of North American homeland defence began on that terrible morning, the militaries of both countries, specifically the two air forces and NORAD, were drawn into a highly visible role right from the start. After air traffic controllers realized that civilian airlines had been hijacked, fighter aircraft were scrambled out of bases in Virginia and Massachusetts – too late as it turned out, as was the emergency authorization given them, apparently by US Vice-President Richard Cheney – to destroy the hijacked planes. These were the first steps towards the reconfiguration of North American air defence from a system oriented to threats from outside North America to one dealing with threats both approaching the continent and arising inside it. 'You have to admit it, but we hadn't thought about this,' said General Richard Meyers, a former NORAD commander who just about the time of the attacks became the chairman of the US chiefs.[11]

The impromptu gave way to the more organized as NORAD put in place Operation Noble Eagle for air defence. Better links were established between civilian air traffic controllers and the military. Radar coverage was extended into the interior, briefly including NATO Airborne Warning and Control System aircraft, when the alliance declared, for the first time in its history, that a member country had come under attack. The number of alert sites for interceptor aircraft was increased. Eventually the emphasis was placed on the protection of the U.S. president while travelling (which had never been a NORAD mission), and on Washington, New York, and other localities when needed. These include special events such as U.S. political party conventions, summits such as the Group of Eight (G8) meeting held in Alberta in 2002, and sporting events, especially U.S. football Super Bowls and the Olympic

Games. Indeed, NORAD provided special air surveillance at the 2002 Olympics in Salt Lake City and did so again at the 2010 Vancouver Olympics.

Despite all these efforts (and others, to be discussed below) undertaken by the military to defend North America directly against terrorists since 9/11, it must be kept in mind that they are smaller in scope than the non-military ones. In other words, 'homeland security' by civilian entities is more extensive than 'homeland defence' by the military. This is true within both Canada and the United States and with respect to their cooperative responses to the threat. As described in the previous chapter, at the heart of Canadian and U.S. efforts have been augmented intelligence, law enforcement, immigration and customs, and preparations undertaken by civilian agencies to respond to contingencies. Thus in the case of civil aviation, learning about terrorist plots and detecting weapons at the airport, not shooting down a hijacked aircraft, are the first line of protection. The continent's air defences have been reconfigured and enhanced but not greatly expanded.

Two venerable aspects of the Canada–U.S. defence relationship quickly reappeared as the 'war on terror' got underway. First, to both countries, continental defence was of much less importance than forward operations. Just as both sought to defeat Germany across the Rhine and deter the Soviets at the Fulda Gap, Canada and the United States sought to drive the terrorists out of Afghanistan and to keep them out. With its invasion of Iraq, the United States hoped to set off the transformation of the Middle East itself. Second, while since 2001 there have been bilateral impulses similar to the kind that led to the creation of NORAD in 1957, they have been held firmly in check by the more powerful and permanent wariness in both countries about integrative efforts.

The strongest bi-national impulse in this case came out of the United States. After the 9/11 attacks, Washington moved to create a homeland defence command for its military, whereupon it sent signals to Ottawa that it would welcome discussions over transforming NORAD into a parallel institution – a 'North American Defence Command,' in other words. Since NORAD already had a U.S. commander, a Canadian deputy, a bi-national staff, and a mandate for continental aerospace defence, it readily formed the basis for a structure with greater responsibility. Once Washington made the decision that, in any event, Colorado Springs would be the locale for its new homeland defence command, talking to the Canadians made sense. The wariness in this case was largely Canadian. The ever-cautious Chrétien government let the opportunity pass and the Pentagon proceeded to create in 2002 U.S. Northern Command (USNORTHCOM) that shares a commander and headquarters with NORAD, whose responsibilities remained at the time exclusively related to aerospace defence. We will, of course, never know what kind of bi-national command could have been negotiated in 2002. Nonetheless, it certainly seems fair to conclude that, had there been negotiations between Washington and Ottawa and had a bi-national homeland defence command emerged, it would have been linked to a U.S. 'twin' to provide the American military with the leeway it has almost always insisted upon in the continental defence relationship.

Instead, the two governments agreed on the temporary Binational Planning Group to see what still could be worked out. But a much bigger shoe dropped when the Canadian military announced in 2005 that it was creating its own homeland defence entity, called Canada Command (Canada COM) that stood up in 2006. While some in Canada immediately tagged Canada COM as a wannabe 'true northern command,' it originated not so much as a reaction to what the United States had put in place in Colorado Springs but rather as part of a large-scale change in the command structure of the Canadian military, engineered as part of the 'transformation agenda' of the chief of the defence staff General Rick Hiller. Still, its creators saw it as the Canadian interlocutor in a bilateral relationship with USNORTHCOM. As a Defence Department planning document put it, the new command would eventually develop 'into the sole operational HQ responsible for the Canadian theatre of operations.' This 'will in turn lead to the development of close ties with US Northern Command.'[12] The two homeland defence commands have been concentrating on how the military in one country might best be able to lend support in the other in the event of contingencies such as natural disaster or attacks with weapons of mass destruction. The point of departure for these bilateral arrangements is that, just like the arrangements within each country, the military will serve only as the backup where necessary to civilian agencies. It should be added that, quite unlike NORAD's standing operational control over U.S. and Canadian air defence forces, the two have no standing command over operational forces. These are to be assigned to them as necessary, in the event of a real or immediately anticipated contingency. The exception is missile defence, which will be considered below. In 2008 the two commands signed a formal Civil Assistance Plan.

Those USNORTHCOM–Canada COM ties, the Canadian defence planners also foresaw, might eventually come at the expense of the bi-national NORAD, whose retention of the air defence mission now is something of an anomaly in the emerging bilateral structure. Canada COM is responsible for the execution of all military operations in Canada *except* for NORAD's air defence operations or operations that the chief of the defence staff decides to command personally. There is unease in USNORTHCOM at the fact that such local responsibilities as the protection of Washington, New York, and the president in transit are not, in the first instance, under the current arrangements, those of the national homeland defence command but rather of a bi-national Cold War era air defence command.

North American air defence in the age of terror raises issues of national sovereignty that tend to favour fewer integrative arrangements between Canada and the United States. This was evident right after 9/11, when the U.S. government gave authority to senior air defence officers to authorize destruction of a hijacked aircraft in an emergency if the president and secretary of defense could not be reached in time. While the list of commanders with such authority has not been released, it is evident that it includes no Canadians at NORAD. The Canadian government, for its part, has not delegated such authority, reserving it to itself. At the same time, air defence in the age of terror is increasingly localized. There will be no vast continent-wide air defence battle of the kind that NORAD was created to be able to fight. Being prepared to respond to the terrorist air threat obviously requires close working relationships with civil aviation authorities. It also entails working with federal – as well as state or provincial – law enforcement agencies and other civilian entities at various levels of government. This is particularly the case with special events, such as the Vancouver Olympics, where the Royal Canadian Mounted Police (RCMP) was the lead law enforcement agency and several others were involved.

To be sure, throughout its fifty-year history, NORAD has shown a good deal of flexibility at the command level in accommodating differences in authority delegated to Colorado Springs (i.e., NORAD or its 'twin' command) by the two governments. The Cuban missile and Yom Kippur crises demonstrated this most spectacularly. The reconfiguration along national lines of North American air space for air defence purposes has built in more flexibility for exercising sovereignty. A good deal of planning and operational authority for air defence rests with the three NORAD air defence regions, including the Canadian region, headquartered in Winnipeg.

NORAD and Ballistic Missile Defence

The bi-national NORAD is not only faced with two new national home-land defence commands that threaten to make it odd man out, but it also contends with the nature of air defence against terrorism that raises sovereignty issues and requires closer local relationships. NORAD is threatened, as well, with the loss of what has been its core function over the several past decades – warning of and assessing an aero-space attack on North America. While NORAD was created to actively defend North America, it lost the capability to do so when the United States decided to forgo the deployment of active BMD and the active air defences were largely dismantled. The bets were placed on deterrence, and deterrence depended on good warning. Ballistic missiles attack-ing the United States would travel after launch first beyond the atmo-sphere and then sharply down towards their American targets, crossing above the altitude of Canadian air space. Unlike the extensive air defence installations that were once located in Canada, no system to detect or track ballistic missiles has ever been located there or operated by the Canadian military. The United States placed these systems on its own soil, in the United Kingdom, Greenland, and in space. Nevertheless, Canadians remain involved in the NORAD missile warning role. In fact it is a bit of a puzzle why this is the case; the quality of Canadian per-sonnel at Colorado Springs and the historic importance linking missile warning to warning of bomber attack offer only a partial explanation. It may just be, as a senior Canadian defence official once mused before a parliamentary committee, that Americans simply have developed 'the habit' of working with Canadians in continental defence.[13]

But the Americans may eventually lose that habit as a result of the Martin government's 2005 decision, which still stands, that Canada would not participate in the operation of the rudimentary BMD that the United States has put in place. On the eve of a general election that it would lose, the government, which had given Washington all indications that it would be participating in missile defence, suddenly decided that votes were to be had, especially in Quebec, by renounc-ing President George W. Bush and all his works, particularly the mis-sile defences that he had ordered deployed. Despite this decision, for the moment Canada's place in Colorado Springs is not in doubt.

In yet another instance of the long-standing flexibility in accommodating asymmetries in command arrangements at Colorado Springs, a workaround based on two elements is in place. First, while Canada is not participating directly in the operation of the missile defences, the Martin government did agree that NORAD, including the Canadians in it, could support the system by providing warning and assessment of any missile attack. Second, the system is under the operational command of USNORTHCOM. To be sure, this has led to some oddities at the Colorado Springs combat operations centre. A Canadian in charge of the missile warning centre would be able to provide the warning, yet would stand by as an American deputy recommended release of the missile defence. Similarly, a Canadian general officer in command of NORAD would be able to confirm that North America was under attack, leaving it then to an American to release the BMD interceptor.

While workable, this arrangement is not likely to last very long. The problem is that the United States will be bringing on line more and more systems linked directly to the missile defence, with which Canadians cannot be involved. As James Fergusson has observed, 'As future components of the layered system come on line and the components are integrated together into a single system, NORAD's [missile warning] becomes increasingly problematic with Canada on the outside of missile defence. At best, it becomes a redundant [warning] system, with its primary function to inform the Canadian National command Authority of strategic attack and, in turn the success or failure of intercepts. At worst, the US might some day decide to bring NORAD's [warning] role to an end.'[14]

When NORAD loses its warning role, it loses its core function. It is even conceivable that the bi-national command itself will be brought to an end, but there are other potential fates for it. The two governments might not be willing to close it, and instead allow it to linger on as a vestige of Cold War bi-national cooperation, much as the famed Canada-U.S. Permanent Joint Board on Defence still lingers on, with very little to do, as a vestige of cooperation from the Second World War. Alternatively, the two governments could take up a notion that has been discussed at times in Colorado Springs, to the effect that NORAD be downgraded to the level of a bi-national task force in support of USNORTHCOM and Canada COM, whose bilateral interactions would become the heart of the continental defence relationship.

NORAD and the Limits of Maritime Warning

Another consideration that calls into question the future of NORAD has to do with its role in continental maritime security. After 9/11, there was a great deal of discussion about the potential of sea-based terrorist threats to the American homeland, including the vulnerability of U.S. ports and the potential that terrorists could attempt to bring in weapons of mass destruction on commercial ships. Both American and Canadian governments took measures to provide greater surveillance and monitoring of shipping and to enhance port security. In the United States, the lead agency for maritime homeland security was the U.S. Coast Guard, an armed service with law-enforcement functions. Coast Guard officers took positions in USNORTHCOM. In Canada, the navy as well as the Canadian Coast Guard became more involved in homeland defence and security issues.

The May 2006 renewal of the NORAD agreement added the task of 'maritime warning' to the command's responsibilities. This new role seemed to fit in well alongside NORAD's long-standing aerospace warning role. The BPG worked on the issue almost from its creation. Yet it is quite limited in its scope. As the text of the 2006 renewal makes explicit, NORAD was not given any responsibility for 'maritime surveillance and control' – in other words, for almost all of the work of naval forces in protecting the continent. The U.S. and Canadian navies were opposed to this stance, as was the NORAD commander at the time, Admiral Keating, and he said so in public. Surveillance and control would remain fully outside of NORAD and fully in national hands, although the two countries are also free to continue to coordinate bilaterally.

To provide maritime warning, a new cell at NORAD was given the responsibility to gather existing information on maritime threats to the continent from wherever it can in the two countries – especially from the intelligence and naval establishments – and then sift and compare it. As the 2006 agreement puts it, NORAD's task here 'consists of processing, assessing and disseminating intelligence and information related to the respective maritime areas and internal waterways of, and the maritime approaches to, or attacks against North America utilizing mutual support arrangements with other commands and agencies responsible for maritime defense and security.'[15] Although sceptics abound who contend that Colorado Springs is not the right place for this, the new mission could well enhance bilateral maritime homeland security efforts by adding an additional degree of analysis, synthesis, and information sharing. Nevertheless, NORAD's new warning mission was a far cry from some earlier speculation that the command might soon operationally control the forces that guard the sea approaches to the continent, much as it has controlled the defence of the air approaches for almost fifty years.

Yet, in another sense it was not too surprising that NORAD's new maritime role is a modest one. When senior American naval leaders spoke during the immediate post-9/11 years of a 'maritime NORAD,' they were not calling for an expanded role for NORAD in the maritime defence of North America. Rather, adopting the global, forward-projection view of the United States Navy (USN), what they had in mind was a series of regional maritime security arrangements with overseas allies, designed to provide comprehensive maritime domain awareness and warning and interception capabilities against a variety of threats, from terrorism and piracy to environmental dangers. As explained by the USN's chief of naval operations, 'Our goal is to extend the peace through an inter-connected community of maritime nations – a pro-verbial world navy of 1,000 ships – comprised of all freedom-loving nations, standing watch over the seas.'[16] This concept, later named the 'Global Maritime Partnership,' formed the basis of the USN's 2007 maritime strategy, *A Cooperative Strategy for 21st Century Seapower*,[17] which, consistent with the American approach to maritime security, including that toward terrorism, adopted a decidedly global perspective.

Within this USN-led maritime coalition involving different countries and different maritime forces, bilateral Canada-U.S. maritime cooperation would be just a component – and not even the most important element.[18] In a 2007 study on the maritime dimension of potential terrorist attack and protection priorities, the U.S. Congressional Research Service noted that while terrorist attacks in American waters 'may have the greatest potential to injure US citizens' and 'the greatest potential economic impact in the event of closure of a major US port ... future attacks on US interests in foreign ports, or on vessels at sea in transit to the United States, may be easier for terrorists to execute than attacks on US waters.'[19] A 2008 Congressional Research Service study by Ronald O'Rourke on the USN's role in the 'war on terror' notes the Navy's role in 'identifying and intercepting terrorists or weapons of mass destruction at sea, or potentially threatening ships or aircraft that are in or approaching US territorial waters.'[20] But the thrust of the report, reflecting the reality of the USN's posture and strategy, and indeed the overall American approach to the terrorist threat, makes clear that priority is the identification and mitigation of maritime threats as far from American shores as possible as well the prevention of attacks on deployed American forces.

In 2005 the president approved the *National Strategy for Maritime Security*,[21] which directed all U.S. government agencies to improve their cooperation to achieve maritime domain awareness. As defined by the USN, 'Maritime Domain Awareness is the effective understanding of anything associated with the maritime domain that could impact the security, safety, economy or environment of the United States.'[22] The National Maritime Domain Awareness Plan is intended to 'to facilitate timely, accurate decision making that enables actions to neutralize threats to US national security interests.' In May 2007, in support of the national strategy, the chief of naval operations released the *Navy Maritime Domain Awareness Concept*, which noted that the USN viewed maritime domain awareness in light of its 'worldwide presence' and thus it was more than 'just homeland security' but rather encompassed a global approach involving multiple global partners and coalitions. The goal was to 'secure the United States from direct attack by confronting early and at safe distances, those who would threaten us.'[23]

America's pursuit of a global maritime awareness as part of its national maritime security strategy is supported by the National Maritime Intelligence Center located in Suitland, Maryland. Established in the 1990s, the centre brings together intelligence operations of the USN, the Marine Corps, and the U.S. Coast Guard, with the Navy's Office of Naval Intelligence being the largest component. Recently, that office initiated a major expansion and enhancement of its activities at the centre.[24]

Canadians who fear that Washington would press for a greater institutional role for NORAD on maritime security matters may have little to worry about. As Canadian Commodore (Ret'd) Eric Lerhe has argued, the U.S. approach 'has little to do with institutions.' Rather, it 'focuses on adapting NORAD air defence tactics to maritime tasks to allow US agencies to detect, track, identify, and, when necessary, interdict shipping well before that shipping arrives in their ports. The approach to achieving this is usually unilateral, and direct Canadian participation is never mentioned. Frequently NORAD is specifically identified as the last place where this new process will be monitored.'[25] And although the U.S. Navy does stress the importance of global partnerships and coalitions in achieving maritime security, the primary objective is to provide information through a national maritime 'common operational picture' to U.S. national, state, and local agencies. When it comes to international partners, the U.S. Maritime Domain Awareness Plan 'makes it clear that information will be as much controlled as shared.' While that plan promises to 'establish a network-centric, near–real time information grid' that can be shared with international agencies, other elements of its 'share information' strategy do the opposite. These will involve measures that 'restrict access,' tighten classified data 'user controls,' and enhance the 'special protection' of certain information.[26]

Both the U.S. national and global emphasis on the maritime dimensions of the 'war on terror' explain in part the lack of American interest in providing new structures, or significantly expanding NORAD, in order to provide for a more structured, comprehensive, and integrative approach to North American maritime security efforts and why it appears that little has been done to expand the Command's maritime warning mission. Indeed, a recent article on NORAD's role in protecting North America from maritime threats begins by noting, 'Maritime domain awareness is a global challenge' involving the 'worldwide maritime community.'[27]

Canada, for its part, has also taken unilateral national steps to improve its maritime homeland security posture – measures that also contribute to, but are not predicated upon, the creation of a new fully integrated bi-national arrangement for North American maritime security. The strategic culture of the Canadian navy, like that of the USN, embodies a global perspective. Though small, it sees itself as and indeed operates as a 'high seas' fleet able to support the foreign and defence policies of the government on the world's oceans. However, there is an important difference; whereas in the United States it is the Coast Guard that is the lead maritime agency, including in USNORTHCOM, in Canada it is the navy, because there is no real equivalent to the U.S. Coast Guard on the Canadian side. The Canadian Coast Guard is not an armed service and it undertakes many of the roles that its American counterpart assumes in the area of marine safety (the 'black hull' fleet), while the Canadian navy is also called upon to undertake some missions similar to those of the U.S. Coast Guard, including search and rescue and exclusive economic zone surveillance and enforcement. With respect to maritime security capabilities, however, the Canadian navy also assumes the longer-range, armed enforcement, and interdiction activities associated with the U.S. Coast Guard's 'white hull' fleet.

As noted, Ottawa has through the establishment of Canada COM created a single operational command for military contribution to homeland security. Under it are six Regional Joint Task Forces, which on the Atlantic and Pacific Coasts, as well as the Great Lakes, have maritime security responsibilities directly and in support of other civilian law enforcement and safety agencies. In addition, Canada COM has broad responsibility for continental security and indeed is 'the single military command for domestic and continental operations' as well as 'the operational link with U.S. Northern Command.'[28] To this extent it would appear that the Canadian navy's continental security activities would, in part, be handled through the USNORTHCOM–Canada COM relationship. Yet while both the USN and the Canadian navy can provide assets to their respective national homeland commands, they also continue the long tradition of direct collaboration between them on continental maritime security, such the recent monitoring of two Akula-class Russian submarines that were discovered and tracked in international waters off the U.S. and Canadian coasts in August 2009.[29]

As in the United States (and as discussed in the chapter by Elinor Sloan), responsibility in Canada for homeland maritime security is shared with a number of agencies beyond the navy and Coast Guard. These include Transport Canada, the RCMP, Public Safety Canada, and the Canada Border Services Agency. In the 2004 *National Security Policy*, Ottawa announced the creation of Marine Security Operations Centres. These centres are headed by the Canadian Forces, with additional staff from the other agencies. By facilitating cooperation between Canada's maritime agencies, these centres aim to streamline coastal surveillance and interdiction. The *National Security Policy* further pledged to increase on-water patrols to better 'intervene, interdict and board ships that may pose a threat to Canada.'[30] Other measures that were taken include increasing the requirement for advance notice for vessels entering Canadian waters to ninety-six hours; in partnership with the United States, establishing enhanced security for ships entering the Great Lakes–St Lawrence Seaway system; increasing surveillance and tracking of marine traffic, including 'near real-time' identification and tracking of vessels in Canadian waters; screening of passengers and crew onboard vessels and installing new detection equipment in ports to screen containers for radiation; and new funding for the enhancement of the RCMP emergency response teams and the establishment of permanent investigator positions at major ports.[31]

Thus on both sides of the border, national policies and intra-governmental military and civilian measures have been put in place. In each country, there are a multitude of departments and agencies involved in maritime security, and it is the relationship between these Canadian and American organizations and agencies that defines the reality of Canada-U.S. continental maritime security cooperation. All of this is consistent with the traditional pattern of bilateral security cooperation, which, NORAD notwithstanding, has eschewed bi-national, comprehensive, and integrative organizations and structures.

To be sure, the USNORTHCOM-NORAD command centre now 'monitors the maritime domain,' but it does so by using 'inputs from a multitude of fusion centers.'[32] In the case of the Russian submarines discovered off North America, a NORAD spokesperson reported that 'NORAD and US Northern Command are aware of Russian submarine activity off the East Coast operating in international waters. We have been monitoring them during transit.'[33] Thus rather than creating new maritime surveillance and intelligence capabilities within NORAD itself, or placing Canadian and American maritime assets under joint command, 'successfully executing NORAD's maritime warning mission relies on formalizing existing processes and expanding cooperative relationships with multi-national mission partners and civilian agencies in the United States and Canada to enhance unity of effort.' This entails expanding relationships with 'many established and *ad hoc* partners,' in order to 'produce trust, enhance capabilities, mutual advocacy and a culture of collaboration.'[34]

The key point is that NORAD itself is not where the action is in terms of the concrete expansion of bilateral maritime security arrangements since 9/11. Rather, consistent with the tradition of overall Canada–U.S. relations, including those relating to defence and security, this new collaboration has been effected through numerous formal and informal discrete and novel arrangements between different organizations on both sides of the border that respond to specific functional needs. An example (one in which Canada and the United States share a 'common' waterway) would be the Shiprider program, an agreement signed by the U.S. Secretary of Homeland Security Janet Napolitano and the Canadian Minister of Public Safety Peter Van Loan in May 2009. The agreement, which covers waters along the international border only, is intended 'to provide the Parties additional means in shared waterways to prevent, detect, suppress, investigate, and prosecute criminal offences or violations of law including, but not limited to, illicit drug trade, migrant smuggling, trafficking of firearms, the smuggling of counterfeit goods and money, and terrorism.'[35] One key element of the agreements is that it allows RMCP and U.S. Coast Guard personnel 'to ride on each other's vessels for joint patrols and specific enforcement operations.' In the past, 'vessels have been required to stop at the border and call the other nation's agencies for help, but the pact allows ships carrying joint enforcement teams to operate in each country's territory.'[36] The agreement also includes authority to train each country's officers by the other and specifies conditions regarding the carrying of firearms and the use of force. Reflecting the law-enforcement focus and the different character of the agencies responsible in each country, the agreement designates the commissioner of the RMCP and the commandant of the U.S. Coast Guard as the 'central authorities' for implementation.

In addition to such specific agreements, the level and scope of maritime cooperation is further enhanced by joint exercises and by participation by representatives of a number of military and civilian agencies, such as Transport Canada and Canada COM, in U.S. maritime homeland security and defence workshops and war games, such as those held at the Naval War College in Newport, Rhode Island. This involvement allows Ottawa to shape its own inter-agency policies to mesh with those of Washington, while providing for the kind of contact and exchange of information that will foster greater collaboration on an ongoing basis and when emergencies arise.

Whatever changes may be made in the future, NORAD with its new 'maritime warning' role appears for now to be just one of a whole range of U.S. and Canadian military and civilians organizations dedicated to fostering common continental maritime homeland security requirements through a plethora of bilateral initiatives, procedures, and arrangements.

Conclusion

Louis St Laurent's deceptively understated 1947 remarks capture the essence of the Canada–U.S. defence and security relationship in the second half of the twentieth century and describe well what has taken place in the first years of the twenty-first. In the Cold War it was a relationship that – reflecting the differing national strategic priorities, preferences, and global standing of the two countries – encompassed a wide range of different and discrete arrangements and practices put in place from time to time, to meet specific common needs, 'settling, from day to day, questions that arise between us.' While the bi-national NORAD was deemed necessary to handle the aerospace threat to the continent, it was by no means the norm, and even within its seemingly tight organizational structure, Colorado Springs always contained lines of national demarcation; there were, in other words, boundaries downstairs if there did not appear to be any 'upstairs.' That the St Laurent approach has been the one to which both Ottawa and Washington ultimately turned after the terrorist attacks of September 2001 explains why and how the U.S. and Canadian armed forces, along with civilian agencies, are today working well together in traditional and novel ways to deal with threats to the continent.

And there is good reason to believe that, following upon the St Laurent approach, the Canada–U.S. defence and security relationship will continue to foster the national interests of both countries, given that international terrorism is likely to remain the key threat to the security of Canada and the United States, while other threats, particularly from ballistic missiles, will persist. It is an approach that meets Washington's requirement that Ottawa takes threats to the American homeland seriously and is prepared to engage in cooperative measures where necessary. Yet it also preserves for the United States the capacity to organize and employ its security forces without limiting or restricting the U.S. ability to act in ways consistent with its domestic policies and its global power and interests. Such an approach also permits Canada to attend to its own particular domestic priorities and international obligations and commitments, while eschewing the kind of integrative arrangements that not only raise sovereignty concerns, but that are not required to effect a deep and extensive level of cooperation with the United States in securing the continent. Indeed so solid is this seemingly fluid and largely unstructured arrangement that it could conceivably withstand changes such as the downgrading or even the dissolution of NORAD or continued informality in maritime homeland security collaboration. For as St Laurent so eloquently and wisely observed, the Canada–U.S. defence and security relationship works best when it is based upon 'constant and imaginative attention on both sides.'

NOTES

1 Louis S. St Laurent, 'The Foundations of Canadian Policy in World Affairs,' Duncan and John Gray Memorial Lecture, 13 Jan. 1947.

2 C.P. Stacey, *Arms, Men and Government: The War Policies of Canada, 1939–1945* (Toronto: Oxford University Press, 1975), 132.

3 *House of Commons Debates* (12 Feb. 1947) 345–8 (W.L. Mackenzie King).

4 St Laurent, 'Foundations of Canadian Policy.' For analysis, see Hector Mackenzie, 'Shades of Gray? "The Foundations of Canadian Policy in World Affairs" in Context,' *American Review of Canadian Studies* 37, no. 4 (Winter 2007): 459–74.

5 Meeting of Consultation September 30, 1957, DEA briefing book (copy for chairman, chiefs of staff), file 2509, 73/1233, Raymont fonds, Directorate of History and Heritage, Department of National Defence (emphasis in original). See Joseph T. Jockel, *Canada in NORAD, 1957–2007: A History* (Montreal and Kingston: McGill-Queen's University Press, 2007).

6 Joint Chiefs of Staff to secretary of defense, 'Proposed North American Continental Defence Organization,' JCS 1541/94 11 June 1954, files of the Joint Chiefs of Staff.

7 Qtd. in 'Nineteen Years of Air Defense,' NORAD Historical Reference Paper no. 11, May 1965.

8 In 1962 the Canadian military joined the U.S. alert a few days later.

9 Charles Foulkes, 'Canadian Defence Policy in a Nuclear Age,' *Behind the Headlines* 2, no. 1 (May 1961): 12.

10 'The most frequent question I'm asked about NORAD is, "What's the threat?" I have responded publicly that there is essentially no military air threat against North America today.' CINC NORAD to Canadian Forces Fighter Group, 7 Mar. 1994. Copy in NORAD/USNORTHCOM History office.

11 'Meyers and September 11: "We Hadn't Thought about This,"' American Forces Information Service, news articles, 23 Oct. 2001.

12 Chief of the defence staff, CDS Action Team 1 report, pt 3. Domestic environment (CANCOM) 2005.

13 Daniel Bon, acting assistant deputy minister (policy), in Standing Committee on National Defence and Veteran Affairs, *Minutes and Proceedings,* 24 Feb. 2000, 1025.

14 James Fergusson, 'Shall We Dance? The Missile Defence Decision, NORAD Renewal and the Future of Canada–US Defence Relations,' *Canadian Military Journal* 6, no. 2 (Summer 2005): 20.

15 Agreement between the Government of Canada and the Government of the United States of America on the North American Aerospace Defense Command, 28 April 2006, http://www.treaty-accord.gc.ca/text-texte.asp?id=105060.

16 Mike Mullen, USN, 'What I Believe: Eight Tenets That Guide My Vision for the 21st Century Navy,' http://www.navy.mil/navydata/cno/mullen/

proceedingsjan06.html. See also John G. Morgan, USN, Charles W. Martoglio, USN, 'The 1,000 Ship Navy: Global Maritime Network,' *United States Naval Institute Proceedings* 132 (Nov. 2005).

17 United States, United States Navy, *A Cooperative Strategy for 21st Century Seapower* (Washington, DC: USN, October 2007), http://www.navy.mil/maritime/MaritimeStrategy.pdf.

18 Joseph T. Jockel and Joel Sokolsky, 'Renewing NORAD: Now If Not Forever,' *SITREP* 66 (Sept.–Oct. 2006): 5.

19 Paul W. Parfomak and John Fritelli, *CRS Report for Congress, Maritime Security: Potential Terrorist Attacks and Protection Priorities* (Washington, DC: Congressional Research Service, 14 May 2007), 5.

20 Ronald O'Rourke, *CRS Report for Congress: Navy Role in Global War on Terrorism (GWOT) – Background and Issues for Congress* (Washington, DC: Congressional Research Service, 3 Mar. 2008), 1–2.

21 United States, White House, *The National Strategy for Maritime Security* (Washington, DC: White House, Sept. 2005), http://www.dhs.gov/xlibrary/assets/HSPD13_MaritimeSecurityStrategy.pdf.

22 United States, Department of the Navy, Office of the Chief of Naval Operations, *Navy Maritime Awareness Concept* (Washington, DC: DN, 2007), 4.

23 Ibid.

24 'Office of Naval Intelligence Begins Historic Transformation,' *Navy Newstand*, 27 Feb. 2009.

25 Eric Lerhe. 'Will We See a Maritme NORAD?' *Journal of Military and Strategic Studies* 9 (Winter 2006/7): 1.

26 Ibid., 9.

27 'Reducing Northern Exposure,' *Maritime & Port Security* (Aug.–Sept. 2009): 40.

28 Canada, Department of National Defence, Canada Command, http://www.canadacom.forces.gc.ca/site/mis-mis-eng.asp.

29 'Detected Russian Submarines "Failed" Their Military Mission, Report Says,' *Globe and Mail*, 14 Aug. 2009.

30 Canada, Privy Council Office, *Securing an Open Society: Canada's National Security Policy* (Ottawa: Privy Council Office, Apr. 2004), 38–9.

31 Joel J. Sokolsky, 'Securing the Continental Coasts: United States Maritime Homeland Security and Canada,' *IRPP Policy Matters* 6 (Mar. 2005): 55.

32 'Reducing Northern Exposure,' 41.

33 Chris Lawrence, 'US Eyes Russian Submarines off East Coast.' CNN.com, 6 Aug. 2009, http://edition.cnn.com/2009/US/08/05/russian.submarines/index.html.

34 'Reducing Northern Exposure,' 41 (emphasis in original).
35 Framework Agreement on the Integrated Cross-Border Maritime Law Enforcement Operations between the Government of the United States of America and the Government of Canada, May 2009.
36 Jeff Karoub, 'US, Canadian Officials Sign Law Enforcement Pact,' *Seattle Times*, 26 May 2009.

PART THREE

Regions and Players of Interest

7   NATO and the EU: Canada's Security Interests in Europe and Beyond

ALEXANDER MOENS

Canada has well-established and deep ties with many European states, most prominently with Great Britain and France. Especially since the ascent of the European Union (EU) in 1992, Canada has sought to complement its bilateral networks in Europe with direct ties to the EU as the latter has grown in membership and policy competence. While Canada was the first non-European state to sign a 'Framework Agreement' to enhance trade in 1976 with the then European Economic Community, trade between the two has remained modest – only one-eighth of Canada-U.S. trade in 2008.

Canada and the United States are the only non-European members of the North Atlantic Treaty Organization (NATO) members, reflecting a major national interest in Europe's security and providing an important place in European military affairs. The forward defence 'strategic culture' prevalent in Canadian history caused three Canadian interventions in European conflicts: the First and Second World Wars and the Balkan Wars of the 1990s. The same logic kept a deployment of Canadian Forces stationed in Europe under the NATO umbrella until the end of the Cold War in the early 1990s. Canada also led the United Nations peacekeeping mission in Cyprus to avert intra-NATO conflict and the weakening of the alliance in the Cold War. Both the Cyprus and Balkan operations are now being taken over by the EU while NATO's mission is expanding beyond Europe.

During the twentieth century, Canada had a direct stake in preventing tyranny or a hostile ideology from dominating Europe. Despite a resurgent Russia in recent years, world-dominating threats no longer come from Europe. Instead, Europe is now a key partner with Canada and other democracies in keeping these threats at bay and reducing the underlying causes that bring such threats to the surface. Both NATO and the EU are crucial interstate facilitators to allow Europe to play this role.

I argue in this chapter that in that role, NATO forms a *vital* interest to Canada, while the EU forms a *major* interest. NATO is of vital interest to Canada because it is the only effective vehicle through which to launch forward-based defence actions. It also binds North American and European commitments and, in so doing, projects to the world at large a strong consensus about what constitutes world stability and democratic principles. This binding is not always strong enough, as we saw during the 2003 Iraq War, but it is stronger and more coherent than any other bond, including the UN and the Group of Eight (G8), and is clearly evident in today's attempts to keep Afghanistan (and increasingly Pakistan) from degenerating into terrorist-breeding states. In comparison, the EU plays a major role in Canadian policy in several non-military aspects of our democratic values–projection policy. Canada can achieve much of its interests by working with the EU on key domestic (or homeland) security issues in the struggle against terrorism, and on other challenges such as drugs and organized crime, pandemic disease, and environmental threats.

In an optimal scenario, Canada would be able to coordinate its policies regarding NATO and the EU by a coherent strategy. However, the policies pursued through either end of Brussels (NATO and the EU) are often different, specialized, and at times even competitive. Europe itself does not always streamline actions of the military branch with the union branch. In practice, trade and domestic policy tend to dominate Canada's EU file, while Canadian military deployments in NATO missions focus Ottawa's attention in NATO affairs.

Canada and the European Union

In 1976 Canada concluded its historic Framework Agreement with the European Economic Community, with the hope that trade diversification from the United States could be achieved. It also sought to halt the slide in Canadian trade with Europe, which came as a result of Britain's new commitments to Europe rather than to its Commonwealth. But the Framework Agreement did not slow the slide in trade. Canadian free trade initiatives towards Asia in the 1980s and towards South America in the 1990s also produced equally modest outcomes. In contrast, the Canada–United States Free Trade Agreement of 1989 followed by the

North American Free Trade Agreement in 1994 built on the integrating chain of supplies in the cross-border manufacturing sector and led to significant increases in two-way trade. For Canada, the fundamental national interest of economic growth and prosperity is strongly tied to its relationship with the United States. Canadian business people continue to exploit opportunity for profits in the big U.S. market, where they know the culture and benefit from geographic proximity, an advanced infrastructure, and what seemed until only recently a bottomless consumer appetite.

However, Canadian trade with the United States is by no means guaranteed. Little progress in trade liberalization has been made since the 1994 accord. Manufacturing losses, the so-called post-9/11 thickening of the border, a possible U.S. switch away from Canada's heavy carbon resources, and a renewed American appetite for protectionism have put Canada's future trade with the United States in some flux. Many call for trade diversification to secure Canada's long-term economic interests. It is therefore no surprise that Canadians are again considering improving their trade with the European Union; the 2009 initiative to negotiate a Comprehensive Trade and Economic Agreement with the European Union is still in progress.

While any free trade deal is good for the Canadian economy, caution is warranted. As a percentage of total trade, Canada's trade with the EU has been relatively small, though it has shown some growth in the last decade from 7.4 per cent in 1998 to 9.8 per cent in 2007.[1] In comparison, Canada's trade with the United States in the same period averaged just over 80 per cent.[2] Low trade levels with Europe have persisted over the last decades, despite very high levels of foreign direct investment by European states in Canada. The growth in Canadian exports up till the economic malaise of 2008 has been mainly due to rising prices in minerals and natural resources.

Canadian imports from the EU have consistently outpaced our exports. A joint Canada-EU study estimates that expected income gains from a free trade agreement in goods and services between the two would bring only about 0.77 per cent of GDP growth for Canada by 2014, which is slightly lower than the relative growth expected for the EU.[3] Only in the case of the United States have Canadian exports consistently outpaced imports. Without Canadian exports to the United States, Canada would be running a large current account deficit. Between 2000 and 2008, Canadian exports to China rose from .89 per cent to 2.1 per cent of total Canadian exports, while Canadian imports from China rose from 3.1 per cent of total imports in 2000 to 9.7 per cent in 2008. Given the trends in exports and imports and the size of the overall economic growth, it is unlikely that the EU (or even China) will play a more important role in Canadian trade than it does today, given the modest gains anticipated in a free trade agreement.

Modest expectations for growth in trade suggest that Canada will not have a higher security stake in the EU in terms of our economic interests. If anything, better trade ties with China (and India) and therefore more interdependent security with this region are likely to be Canada's priority after its future in North America. In sum, trade diversification is good, but more importantly Canada should make ready to benefit from a U.S. economic and manufacturing revival, including expanding intra-firm production to sectors other than automotive and machinery and to regions beyond the Great Lakes.

What will make the EU an increasingly important variable in Canada's security strategy is its rise as a global political player, its strength in the World Trade Organization trade negotiations, its preponderant role in worldwide development assistance, and its centrality in multilateral negotiations such as on measures to counter climate change. Together, individual EU member states and common EU aid policies account for half of the world's official development assistance.[4] While the EU floundered in attempts to deter aggression in the Balkans in the 1990s, its diplomatic, civilian, and military role has grown considerably. The EU now leads the mission in Bosnia and is well on track to take over from NATO in Kosovo. The French-brokered peace between Russia and Georgia in the summer of 2008 and the so-called EU-3 negotiations with Iran to avert the development of Iranian nuclear weapons are recent examples of the EU's rise as a global diplomat.[5] As such, Canada-EU diplomatic coordination and cooperation on a variety of global issues is an important ingredient in enhancing Canadian national security interests.

Suffering a similar fate as the United Nations, the revamped Organization for Security and Cooperation in Europe never came off the ground as a post–Cold War diplomatic or political vehicle for crisis resolutions in Europe. Instead, it has taken on a minor role of monitoring a few missions that Russia can agree to. The EU has meanwhile assumed the leading role in lower-level conflict management. Since its first mission in 2003, it has taken on twenty crisis-management operations, some civilian and some military. For example, the EU now employs 1,900 law enforcement personnel in Kosovo alongside the 16,000 strong NATO force.[6] At the same time, it has deployed 3,500 soldiers (mainly French) to Chad.

Canada maintains in parallel to the United States a transatlantic dialogue with the EU presidency, which allows for a wide agenda. Canada signed a Framework Agreement with the European Union in 2005 on the basic parameters of Canadian participation in European Security and Defence Policy (ESDP) operations.[7] The accord was put in place to determine Canadian participation and command positions should Canada participate in any EU-only operations run through its Common Foreign and Security Policy or ESDP machinery.[8] The agreement allows for either civilian or military participation by Canada. As a non-EU member, such participation will always remain a bit difficult. The EU is interested in the experienced and highly qualified personnel Ottawa is willing to offer. However, unlike in NATO where Canada has a voice at the table, not being an EU member will always relegate Canada to a second-tier position. So far, Canada has worked with the EU only in civilian or post-conflict operations. Finally, Canada still has a small number of officers working in NATO to help the EU's military mission (Operation Althea) in Bosnia, which is the only 'Berlin Plus' operation thus far in which the EU can borrow NATO planning and command assets.

Canada and NATO

While the old transatlantic alliance is rarely the focus of policy or public debate inside Canada, it nevertheless represents one of its most important policy vehicles. After the short illusion that the UN would play a central role in the world following the collapse of the Soviet Union and the end of the Cold War, NATO has regained its prime status for Canadian security objectives and military activity outside continental North America. It was through NATO that the peace was secured in Bosnia-Herzegovina and Croatia in 1995 – after protection missions by the United Nations had reached an impasse – and it was again through NATO in 1999 that Serbian aggression towards the Kosovars was forcefully halted. Canada participated in ending both crises, sending many of its NATO-stationed troops from Lahr, Germany, to Croatia and Bosnia as UN peacekeepers in 1992 and 1993.[9] Canadian troops served in Bosnia in the Stabilization Force from 1995 onward and briefly in Kosovo in the Kosovo Force after Canadian CF-18s joined in the bombing campaign against Serbia.

As dramatically as the NATO scene changed from 1989 and 1999, so it has again between 1999 and 2011. NATO's critical role in the International Security Assistance Force (ISAF) in Afghanistan is quite a leap from securing the peace in southeastern Europe. How transatlantic is NATO when its largest military operation is in Asia? When Libyan strongman Muammar Gaddafi threatened to unleash mass murder on the opponents to his regime in early 2011, France, the United States, Britain, and Canada eventually agreed to create a no-fly zone over Libyan air space. After some political wrangling, France agreed to hand over this initial ad hoc coalition to NATO. Ottawa took an active role in these developments, sending six CF-18 jetfighters to help patrol the no-fly zone, while Canadian Lt-Gen. Charles Bouchard was given operational command of the new NATO mission.

Russia has also re-emerged both in economic power and in its autocratic tendencies. As a result, NATO finds itself in a new type of 'Cold War Lite.' Moscow is not necessarily trying to foment communist revolutions or invade the West, but it is trying to secure a ring of 'border states' who must say farewell to their democratic aspirations and take their foreign policy cues solely from Moscow. While the 'fighting allies' of the alliance such as the United States, the United Kingdom, Canada, and the Netherlands are occupied with gaining ground on the Taliban insurgency, some of the old allies of Western Europe such as Germany are assessing their options for how much to align with a resurgent Russia. In contrast, most of the thirteen Central and East European members of NATO who have joined since 1997 are clamouring for a modern version of the original NATO in which the common defence or Article V rather than far-away operations dominate defence policy and planning. NATO is torn in different directions, and Canada has a large stake in what it ends up being and doing.

From Operation Medusa onward in the late summer of 2006, Canada put nearly all its army assets into the UN-mandated and NATO-led operation in Kandahar province.[10] In 2006, Canada committed a battle group of some 2,500 soldiers. By 2009 more than 2,800 Canadian Forces personnel were deployed in Afghanistan.[11] Canada's large effort in Afghanistan is no accident of history, but a clear reflection of our interests. Our most important ally in NATO was attacked by a terrorist organization located in Afghanistan. NATO invoked its Article V on 12 September 2001. The UN-mandated ISAF mission sought to rebuild Afghanistan after the removal of the Taliban regime, which was certainly a just endeavour when compared to the prospect of leaving the war-devastated people to fend for themselves. Canada rightly decided that its forward-based defence was a valuable asset in the ongoing attempt to prevent Afghanistan from falling back into terrorist hands.

The large and prolonged Canadian deployment into a war-fighting operation brought with it a considerable increase in Canadian defence spending and acquisition of up-to-date materiel, including airlift and numerous types of weaponry. The slide in Canadian defence spending throughout the 1990s has been halted. Canada's defence budget in 2006 increased from $13.6 billion (2005) to $17.6 billion, with most new money allocated for capital funding on new equipment needed in Afghanistan.[12] Planned spending (both departmental and capital) amounted to $21.8 billion for the fiscal year 2010–11.[13]

By early 2011, 155 Canadian soldiers had lost their lives, while hundreds are recovering from serious injuries. As documented by James Sperling and Mark Webber, Canada has borne an asymmetrical burden within ISAF in troop commitments, combat fatalities, and development aid. Its combat fatality ratio as of 2008 is double NATO's average and among the top three, the others being the United States and Great Britain.[14] The estimated total cost of Canada's commitment to the south from 2006 to 2009, including $1.2 billion in aid and development, is $4.3 billion.[15] Parliament approved an extension of the Canadian deployment until 2011 after the Independent Panel on Canada's Future Role in Afghanistan endorsed the Conservative government's objectives in Afghanistan and urged it to commit more resources. When seen in the context of post–Cold War Canadian foreign policy, the human and financial investment is enormous and underscores the sea change Afghanistan has created in Canadian foreign policy.[16] It is difficult to imagine that this strong effort to prevent a victory by the Taliban could have transpired without NATO. Certainly, the UN cannot mount anything like this operation. Given the controversy over Iraq, a simple ad hoc coalition also might not have held. While in practice, it has been a fight led by the United States conjoined by several capable and willing allies, without NATO, no such coalition of the willing would have emerged.

Canada has not only risen to the top tier of fighting allies in NATO but has also committed itself to a large stake in how NATO will fare in Afghanistan and what it will do next and how it should reform. Canada has an investment in how NATO will develop in its core defence mission, in all its non–Article V operations, towards potential new members, and in how it interacts with other organizations including the EU and other non-European democracies such as Australia that are participating in NATO missions. All of these issues were on NATO's agenda as it redrafted its core Strategic Concept, which had not been fundamentally altered since 1991. NATO's new Strategic Concept was adopted at the NATO Lisbon Summit in November 2010.[17] Despite its ambitious name, the new strategic directive is best seen as a series of moderate reforms. The allies agreed to deepen security relations with Russia. At the same time, East European members were given assurance that Article V preparations for their defence would be boosted, and NATO agreed on common efforts towards missile defence. The alliance announced that it would enhance its civilian peace operations capacity somewhat but would not seek to compete with the European Union in this policy area. The new strategy document invites cooperation with other nations and does not delineate with any precision the types of security threats that fall inside or outside its mandate.

The new Strategic Concept should not be seen as a rigid framework. Allies tend to improvise as new threats emerge and as interests dictate. The direction NATO takes will be the second-largest impact (after U.S. foreign policy) on Canada's security strategy in years to come. How and when NATO acts will be of prime value to Canada. This key premise sets the remaining theme of this chapter.

Canada's Interests in the Future of NATO

Old NATO Is Still New

NATO's Article V function, concerning the common defence of allies and their territory, remains a highly relevant task, and it should include both defence and deterrence. Central European allies such as Poland have urged that NATO bring a major installation to Central and Eastern Europe, that the alliance adopt a higher profile in its defence planning related to Article V, and that it holds actual physical exercises on this core function.[18]

One could anticipate many in Canada asking, 'Why does Canada in 2011 have to participate in the defence of East European countries?' There are at least two key reasons. First, the stable development of newly admitted democracies is as vital today as it was in the 1990s, when the last Strategic Concept was written. In its amended version of 1999, NATO's Strategic Concept stated among its core functions the goal of 'a stable Euro-Atlantic security environment, based on the growth of democratic institutions and commitment to the peaceful resolution of disputes.'[19] Canada was a part of this guarantee then and should remain so. Moreover, the spread of democracy and free trade is the best long-term development of a stable international arena. This does not mean we have defence obligations towards emerging democracies everywhere, but we have them within Europe's frontier.

The solidarity around NATO's defence function is directly linked to the solidarity around military security consultations and decision-making. It is very important to a non-EU ally such as Canada that NATO remains the essential and principal forum for decision-making in the Euro-Atlantic area. There is constant pressure from various sources in Europe to replace NATO's decision venue with a more direct US-EU format, which would be a 'game changer' for Canada. While NATO leaders pledged themselves at the 2009 NATO summit to a Declaration on Alliance Security, which reaffirmed the alliance as the essential forum for transatlantic consultation, Canada needs to remain vigilant on this point.[20]

Of course the issue of democratic development within Europe's frontier touches upon the question of NATO (and EU) enlargement and relations with Russia. Russia's turn away from democratic development at home and towards 'sphere-of-influence politics' abroad has cast the old East–West relationship into a new 'Cold-War Lite.' The problem is not that Russia plans to invade the West, but that NATO must secure both its new members and potential members from being forced into a Russian zone of influence. It must preserve the opportunity for states such as Ukraine to have a choice, including the choice to develop into a genuine democracy that will not simply follow Moscow's authoritarian regime.[21] Russia's willingness to use armed force in Georgia in 2008, leaving aside differences of opinion on the cause of the conflict, drove home not only the need for NATO to be able to protect a new member, but also to choose its members wisely.

In June 2007, NATO affirmed its plans to proceed with ballistic missile defence (BMD) plans against short- and medium-range missiles.[22] Given the recent hesitation by both the American and Polish governments (amidst earlier critiques on such plans voiced by Germany and France) on deploying a strategic missile defence system in Poland and the Czech Republic, NATO will have to proceed with utmost caution. The fact remains that American plans for an X-band radar facility in the Czech Republic and ten interceptors in Poland, to provide a BMD capacity against Iranian nuclear-tipped missiles, did not pose a military or diplomatic threat to Russia.[23] Should the Iranian threat materialize, there is time to respond. The Obama administration has meanwhile changed BMD plans for Eastern Europe from defence against long-range missiles to a system aimed at intercepting medium-range missiles, which was well received in Moscow.

Canada and other allies should not hesitate to make clear to its European partners that a separate EU-Russia 'continental security agreement' accord, as raised by Moscow and welcomed to various degrees by Germany and France – no matter how lofty its principles – will be used by Russia to drive a wedge in Allied solidarity and especially so on Article V and BMD policies.[24] The root of the new NATO–Russia tension is not NATO expansion or missile defence, but rather that Russia has rejected democracy and the rule of law and therefore now sees all NATO and EU enlargement as a threat to its regime. President Obama's recent efforts at resetting the relationship might have ameliorated some of these tensions, but they have certainly not eliminated them altogether. Importantly, NATO and the EU must continue their engagement with Russia without compromising either their respective principles or their right of enlargement.

NATO's New Missions Should Be Limited in Scope and Purpose

Three Americans coined a phrase in the 1990s that 'NATO must go out of area, or it will go out of business.'[25] We have already seen that NATO's 'in-area' business is far from finished. It is not a case of either in- or out-of-area, but both. However, out-of-area operations must be limited, given the diversity of interests and scarcity of means. Before making the case for a more specific future role for NATO, I would like to sum up what we can learn from the experience of NATO operations in Afghanistan.

Most NATO countries joined ISAF to secure the new Afghan government and to facilitate reconstruction and nation-building. The problem was that Operation Enduring Freedom had not yet secured the nation when American attention and resources were diverted to Iraq in 2003. The security condition in Afghanistan worsened. Several allies such as Britain, Canada, and non-NATO allies such as Australia were willing to pick up some of the slack by changing to more robust operations, but it is now clear that they were overstretched and under-sourced and could not secure a stable order.

The problem NATO nations have faced in the south and east of Afghanistan is that they cannot establish much reconstruction and nation-building if the enemy keeps undermining basic security. Canadian Forces, for example, conquered and re-conquered swaths of Kandahar many

times. Various studies have pointed out that the peacekeeper-to-popu-
lation ratio in Afghanistan is dangerously low, twenty times below the
ratio in Kosovo under KFOR.[26] If NATO had the same troop-to-people
ratio as it used in Bosnia in 1995, there would be four hundred thousand
troops there.[27] Even if countries such as Germany, Italy, and Spain took
the caveats off their forces and were able to engage in combat and counterinsurgency operations effectively, there is no guarantee that the Taliban
would fold.

The Obama administration has drawn the conclusion that the most
robust part of the operation needs to be re-Americanized in order to
have greater unity of command and purpose and to apply the counterinsurgency lessons learned in Iraq.[28] At the same time, the spillover
of the conflict into Pakistan and the unwillingness by some NATO
allies to do more are forcing the American hand. This does not mean
that the United States wants ISAF to go home. In 2008, 50 per cent of
ISAF forces came from European allies while 5 per cent came from
Canada and 44 per cent from the United States.[29] Instead, the American
'surge' pointed to more specialization of tasks, where most European
allies focused reconstruction and training of Afghan National Army
and Police personnel, while the Americans concentrated on counterinsurgency.[30] Canada concluded its combat operations in 2011 in
order to allow its army to recover and its equipment to be repaired
or renewed. However, given the central role played by Canada in the
past, the need for reconstruction and peace stabilization forces, as
well as Afghan National Army training, Canada agreed to send nine
hundred military trainers to Kabul after 2011.[31] The NATO Summit
in Lisbon set 2014 as a strategic date for Afghan security forces to be
able to take over from ISAF. It is therefore quite likely that Canada
will remain involved with training and other possible operations in
Afghanistan until its task is finished.

The change launched by President Obama in American strategy is a
realistic reflection of what NATO should look like when it operates far
from Europe. There is an inevitable division of tasks, with Americans
doing more combat operations and other NATO allies taking responsibility for peace building. This need not undermine alliance solidarity.
The American strategic switch, combined with the attempt to start a
genuine diplomatic effort – which was led by Richard Holbrooke, special representative for Afghanistan and Pakistan, until his passing in
2010 – will increase the likelihood of success in Afghanistan and thus
success for NATO.

Ultimately, Afghanistan will make progress when local combatants realize that they can make gains on their interests only by working with and not against the new order that has been established in Kabul in 2002. To do so, the new order in Afghanistan as well as the civilian government in Pakistan must be too strong for radicals to have any hope in toppling.[32] To make them strong, NATO needs a full U.S. effort, with allies fulfilling a supporting role. The inability of the Taliban to prevent a good turnout in the August 2009 presidential elections was another sign of progress.

In implementing the new Strategic Concept, NATO members should keep three fundamentals about the alliance in mind.

First, in operations outside of NATO territory, the alliance's coherence in word and deed will be a function of the particular international security challenge at that time. Some allies will feel more threatened than others and will thus be more motivated to supply the right resources to deal with the challenge. In other words, in these operations, there will always be an element of 'coalitions of the willing' and an informal division of tasks. The principle of 'costs lie where they fall,' which is NATO-speak for the fact that allies pay the cost of their own contribution, saddles those who do most with most of the cost. Though a 'common operations fund'[33] is a good idea, it is unlikely to get much cash. Like the NATO Response Force, it is a good idea that will run into the harsh reality of cash-strapped defence budgets.

Second, NATO's main weakness remains the relative dearth of expeditionary forces and capability among most of its Continental European members. Of the two million men and women under arms in Europe, only one hundred thousand can be turned into a modern and effective expeditionary force.[34] The defence spending gap between the United States and Europe went up from US$144 billion in 1999 to $224 billion in 2005.[35] Apart from those of Britain and France, defence budgets are quite modest in Europe and in Germany continue to decline. It is true that both NATO and the European Union have been trying to overcome this structural weakness through modernization, such as NATO's Prague Capabilities program and the EU's Headline Goals (now called European Capability Action Plan). They have also set up new agencies, such as NATO's Allied Command Transformation and the European Armaments Agency, as well as new force structures such as the NATO Response Force and the EU battle groups. In spite of these efforts, the limited capacity of the alliance to act outside its home region will remain a reality for some time to come.

Third, the alliance must be asked to act only when the vital security of one or more of its members is directly affected. Europeans perceived the carnage in the Balkans in the 1990s as a direct threat to the stability of the growth of the European Union. Americans saw the Taliban–al Qaeda threat in Afghanistan as direct threat to the security of the American homeland.

No new political agreement or Strategic Concept can succeed if it goes beyond these limitations of NATO. The alliance is already global in reach, but it should be limited in scope and purpose. It should not define its threats too widely or loosely in terms of the common global interest, nor in terms of humanitarianism or the right to protect or fix any failed state. Potential conflicts over food, water, migration, climate change, and energy security are not by definition NATO's business, unless a member is directly attacked or its vital security threatened.[36] However, threats or attacks by radical Islamists on individual NATO members may well require coordinated NATO action in the future. It could be argued that some NATO allies such as Italy and France saw the growing civil war in Libya in early 2011 as a large threat to their security, given the expected flow of refugees to Southern Europe. However, the Western military response to an impending civilian slaughter was initially not a NATO action but a coalition of the willing. Given the Obama administration's reluctance to take a leading role and Germany's decision not to participate in any military operation, both NATO and the European Union were initially kept out. However, it soon became clear that there are no better alternatives to running and managing an international coalition for a no-fly zone mission than NATO. How well NATO will fare in this endeavour remains to be seen.

Gradual Membership Expansion but No Democratic League

NATO members have global security interests. Some have thus called for a global expansion of NATO membership.[37] First up are democracies (which NATO calls Contact Countries) such as Australia, South Korea, New Zealand, and Japan, some of whom have been sizable contributors to the ISAF mission.[38] Others go even further and call for NATO to morph into a league of democracies that would maintain international peace and security better than the UN Security Council. The latter concept of a global compact among democracies has bipartisan support in the United States.[39]

Canadian interests do not call for a radical overhaul of NATO, but a slow evolution in the direction of adding non-European democracies is helpful. The reasons against a world-governing democratic league with global diplomatic and military powers are many. It is no guarantee for less disagreement among democracies. NATO is already fractious and has been half-jokingly referred to recently as the coalition of the unwilling. The United States is not likely to limit its own independent foreign policy for such a league. The current legal international order does not give well-governed states (democracies) more rights than dictatorships. Obviously, China and Russia would interpret a global military alliance of democracies as a direct challenge to them and may well form a league of their own.

At this point, the costs for developing such a compact exceed the benefits.[40] The current international system that mixes United Nations and regional arrangements has enough flexibility and freedom of action for NATO members – also with participating outsiders – to pursue Canada's interests. For example, Western democracies were able to work with the UN system to liberate Kuwait in 1990, but they did not need a formal UN Security Council Resolution in 1999 to use military force to protect Kosovars from Serbian assault.

NATO Must Remain Europe's Foremost Military Forum and Power

Canada has a direct stake in a clearly defined relationship between NATO and the European Union.[41] The ESDP represents at least two political interests in Europe. As a new civilian-military blend of crisis and conflict management, rather than a military alliance, it provides an added tool for crisis management and reconstruction, which Canada welcomes. As such, it is complementary to NATO in providing a wider array of security for Europe, its neighbourhood, and the world. But there is also a Europeanist elite that wants to build ESDP into a supranational military at the expense of NATO.[42] It is not in Canada's interest for the EU to take over NATO's defence planning and command system. It is between these potentially opposing objectives that Canadian diplomacy should traverse.

At the Strasbourg/Kehl NATO Summit in 2009, French President Nicolas Sarkozy announced France's return to NATO's military structures.[43] The French move underscores the resilience of the alliance. On the other hand, France's return should not be interpreted as a final resolution of problems that have plagued NATO–EU relations. Like Quebec in Canada, France sees itself not as just another NATO member, but as a founding nation of NATO. France will always insist on a special status in the alliance, and that will not change with its return to NATO's integrated command structure.[44]

A Final Global Perspective

The greatest global security threat for Canada today is relative American weakness.[45] Its military still dominates the globe, but how long can it be sustained if budgetary conditions in the United States continue to worsen? America is weak relative to the commitment of its allies, the strength of its rivals and competitors, and the number and significance of global threats. Half of U.S. discretionary spending is now absorbed by the Pentagon, and that is before all the renewal costs flowing from Iraqi operations come due and while American operations in Afghanistan are still on the rise.[46] U.S. federal debt was 41 per cent of GDP in 2008 and is expected to rise to 60 per cent and remain high for the next decade.[47] Given the additional large unfunded liabilities in Medicare/Medicaid and Social Security in the near future, U.S. domestic restraints will sooner or later shrink its security policy. Between 2000 and 2005, the American unilateral moment came and went.

Allies must remember that one of the key functions of NATO is to keep the Americans in. The future challenge is on how to support and maintain American-led military operations in defence of liberal political and economic interests. Defining such interests and deciding how to defend them will always be a difficult debate inside NATO, but if the Americans are not there to lead, Western democracies will be divided and weak. For Canada, NATO is the key force multiplier for international security, and the United States is its engine.

NOTES

1 Canada, Foreign Affairs and International Trade Canada, *Trade, Investment, and Economic Statistics* (Ottawa: Foreign Affairs and International Trade Canada, 22 Sept. 2008), accessed 24 Oct. 2008, http://www.international. gc.ca/eet/merchandise-trade-en.asp.

2 Statistics Canada, 'Imports, Exports and Trade Balance of Goods on a Balance-of-Payments Basis, by Country or Country Grouping' (Ottawa: Statistics Canada, 9 Apr. 2009), http://www40.statcan.gc.ca/l01/cst01/ gblec02a-eng.htm.

3 European Commission and Government of Canada, *Assessing the Costs and Benefits of a Closer EU–Canada Economic Partnership* (Ottawa: European Commission and Government of Canada, 17 Oct. 2008), http://trade.ec.europa.eu/doclib/docs/2008/october/tradoc_141032.pdf. A subsequent study in 2011 lowered the estimated benefits of the agreement considerably. Canadian gains were lowered to 0.29 per cent GDP growth by 2014. Peter O'Neil, 'EU-Canada Deal Slides in Value,' *Financial Post*, 31 Mar. 2011.

4 Martin Holland, *The European Union and the Third World* (Basingstoke: Palgrave, 2002), 109.

5 Colin Dueck and Ray Takeyh, 'Iran's Nuclear Challenge,' *Political Science Quarterly* 122, no. 2 (2007): 201.

6 Asle Toje, 'The EU, NATO and European Defence: A Slow Train Coming,' Occasional Paper 74 (Paris: EU Institute for Security Studies, December 2008), 12. Of the fourteen European Security and Defence Policy (ESDP) operations undertaken by mid-2007, ten have been police, observer, legal, and security sector assistance missions. See also Alyson J. K. Bailes, 'The EU and a "Better World": What Role for the European Security and Defence Policy,' *International Affairs* 84, no. 1 (2008): 118.

7 'EU-Canada Agreement on Participation in Crisis Management Operations Signed,' European Union @ United Nations, http://europa-eu-un.org/articles/en/article_5365_en.htm.

8 Jean-François Morel argues that Canada was interested in positioning itself with the rising role of the EU, but soon lost interest when ISAF gave NATO a new lease on life. See 'Le Canada, L'OTAN, et la Politique Européenne de Sécurité et de Défense,' *Canadian Foreign Policy* 14, no. 1 (2008): 51–69.

9 Lewis Mackenzie, *Peacekeeper: The Road to Sarajevo* (Toronto: Douglas & McIntyre, 1993).

10 Christie Blatchford, *Fifteen Days* (Toronto: Doubleday Canada, 2007).

11 Canada, Department of National Defence, *2009–2010 Report on Plans and Priorities* (Ottawa: DND, 2009), 19.

12 Alexander Moens, 'Afghanistan and the Revolution in Canadian Foreign Policy,' *International Journal* 63, no. 3 (2008): 572.

13 Canada, Department of National Defence, *2010–2011 Report on Plans and Priorities* (Ottawa: DND, 2010), 10.

14 James Sperling and Mark Webber, 'NATO: From Kosovo to Kabul,' *International Affairs* 85, no. 3 (2009): esp. 503–7.

15 These are total figures, not corrected for spending on manpower. Canada, Department of National Defence, *2006–2007 Report on Plans and*

Priorities (Ottawa: DND, 2006), 93. Other estimates put the cost as high as $10.5 billion by the fall of 2008. See 'Canada's Afghan Mission Could Cost up to $18.1B,' CBC News, 9 Oct. 2008, http://www.cbc.ca/canada/story/2008/10/09/afghanistan-cost-report.html.

16 Moens, 'Afghanistan and the Revolution,' 569–86.

17 NATO, *Active Engagement, Modern Defence*, Strategic Concept for the Defence and Security of the Members of the North Atlantic Treaty Organization, Lisbon, Portugal, 29 Nov. 2010, http://www.nato.int/lisbon2010/strategic-concept-2010-eng.pdf.

18 Author's interviews with senior officials in Polish Foreign and Defence Ministries, Warsaw, Poland, 12 and 13 May 2009. See also Susan Cornwell, 'Poland Would Like NATO Base, Foreign Minister Says,' Reuters, 31 Jan. 2008, http://www.reuters.com/article/worldNews/idUSN3136436320080201.

19 The Alliance's Strategic Concept, pt 1, para. 10, 24 Apr. 1999, http://www.nato.int/docu/pr/1999/p99-065e.htm.

20 NATO, press release, 'Declaration on Alliance Security, Strasbourg/Kehl,' 4 Apr. 2009, http://www.nato.int/cps/en/natolive/news_52838.htm?mode=pressrelease.

21 I disagree with Roland Paris's argument that NATO should signal its lack of intention for admitting Ukraine into NATO. See Roland Paris, 'Madly Off in All Directions,' *Globe and Mail*, 23 July 2009.

22 Walter Slocombe, 'Europe, Russia and American Missile Defence,' *Survival* 50, no. 2 (2008): 23.

23 Ibid., 21.

24 Alvoro de Vasconcelos, 'Avoiding Confrontational Bipolarity,' *ISSues* 27 (Oct. 2008): 2.

25 The original call was made by Stephen Larrabee, Ron Asmus, and Richard Kugler, 'Building a New NATO,' *Foreign Affairs* 72, no. 4 (Sept.–Oct. 1993): 31.

26 Elizabeth Pond, 'The EU's Test in Kosovo,' *Washington Quarterly* 31, no. 4 (2008): 104.

27 Philip H. Gordon, 'NATO: Enlargement and Effectiveness,' testimony before the U.S. Senate Foreign Relations Committee, Washington, DC, 25 Mar. 2008, http://www.brookings.edu/testimony/2008/0311_nato_gordon.aspx.

28 John Vinocur, 'US Gives Absolution to Its Allies,' *New York Times*, 1 June 2009.

29 Sperling and Webber, 'NATO,' 505.

30 Peter O'Neil, 'NATO Allies Give Obama Only Modest Boost,' *National Post*, 6 Apr. 2009.

31 Keith Gerein, 'MacKay Visits Troops, Offers New Details of Afghan
    Training Mission,' *National Post*, 18 Mar. 2011, http://www.nationalpost.
    com/news/world/MacKay+visits+troops+offers+details+Afghan+training+
    mission/4467162/story.html.
32 Frederick W. Kagan, 'Planning Victory in Afghanistan: Nine
    Principles the Obama Administration Should Follow,' *National Review
    Online*, 9 Feb. 2009, http://www.nationalreview.com/articles/226851/
    planning-victory-afghanistan/frederick-w-kagan.
33 Julianne Smith and Michael Williams point out the dis-incentive of this
    practice in 'What Lies Beneath: The Future of NATO through the ISAF
    Prism,' Center for Strategic and International Studies, 31 Mar. 2008, 5,
    http://csis.org/files/media/csis/pubs/080331_nato.pdf.
34 Toje, 'The EU, NATO and European Defence,' 26.
35 Seth Jones, 'The Rise of European Defense,' *Political Science Quarterly* 121,
    no. 2 (2006): 266.
36 Jamie Shea calls these 'Global Article V Operations,' as quoted in *Atlantisch
    Perspectief* 8 (2008): 28.
37 Ivo Daalder and James Goldgeir, 'Global NATO,' *Foreign Affairs* 85, no. 5
    (Sept.–Oct. 2006): 105–14.
38 A good critical analysis of a global NATO can be found in Henning Riecke
    and Simon Koschut, 'NATO's Global Aspirations,' *Internationale Politik*
    (international edition) 9, no. 2 (2008): 31–7.
39 John McCain, 'America Must Be a Good Role Model,' *Financial Times*, 18
    Mar. 2008.
40 See also Robin Niblett's point that the concept lacks an 'implementa-
    tion strategy,' in his 'Europe's Call for a Leader by Example,' *Washington
    Quarterly* 31, no. 4 (2008): 130.
41 A good account of the overlap and lack of cooperation can be found in
    John R. Schmidt, 'Last Alliance Standing? NATO after 9/11,' *Washington
    Quarterly* 30, no. 1 (2006–7): 93–106. See also Toje, 'The EU, NATO and
    European Defence,' chap. 2.
42 Alvaro de Vasconcelos, 'Europe's NATO,' *ISSues* 29 (Apr. 2009): 1–2.
    Nick Whitney, former director of the European Defence Agency, makes
    this argument in 'The Death of NATO,' *Europe's World*, Autumn 2008,
    http://www.europesworld.org/EWSettings/Article/tabid/191/ArticleType/
    ArticleView/ArticleID/21272/Default.aspx. See also Ulrike Guerot,
    'Obama and the Future of Transatlantic Relations,' European Council
    on Foreign Relations, 20 Jan. 2009, http://ecfr.eu/content/entry/
    commentary_obama_eu_us_ecfr_guerot/.
43 Steven Erlanger, 'Sarkozy Embraces NATO, and Bigger Role for France,'
    New York Times, 8 Mar. 2009.

44 Justin Vaisse offers several arguments on this point in 'A Gaullist by Any Other Name,' *Survival* 50, no. 3 (2008): 5–10.

45 Jack. L. Granatstein, Gordon S. Smith, and Denis Stairs, *A Threatened Future: Canada's Future Strategic Environment and Its Security Implications* (Canadian Defence and Foreign Affairs Institute, September 2007), 6, http://www.airforce.forces.gc.ca/CFAWC/Contemporary_Studies/2007/2007-Oct/2007-10-01_A_Threatened_Future.pdf.

46 Michèle Flournoy and Shawn Brimley, 'The Defense Inheritance: Challenges and Choices for the Next Pentagon Team,' *Washington Quarterly* 31, no. 4 (2008): 62.

47 'A Squeaker, with More to Come,' *Economist*, 4 July 2008, 24.

8   Shift to the Pacific: Canada's Security Interests and Maritime Strategy in East Asia

THOMAS ADAMS[1]

Within the last few decades, the world centre of gravity has moved from the Atlantic to the Pacific. By virtually any metric, whether it is economic power, military power, political power, or global influence, the world centre of power has come to reside in the Pacific – with China at the heart of this profound transition. Numerous issues in the security realm make the region a potentially volatile one. As the result of regional rivalries, the importance of the region's economies, and ongoing military build-ups, the Asia-Pacific region has been likened aptly to the powder keg of Europe prior to the outbreak of the First World War. These issues, in turn, have the potential to affect Canada's national security interests, whether directly or indirectly. However, Canada's leaders have not grasped the enormity of the paradigm shift, that for the first time in five hundred years, Europe no longer sets the global agenda.

This chapter argues that Canada needs to engage the Asia-Pacific region more substantially in order to defend and advance its national interests. It makes that argument by reviewing the regional context – its importance in the global economy, trade and commerce, and the security environment – and in so doing, identifies the ways in which Canada's security interests could be harmed. It concludes by putting forth two sets of strategic policy prescriptions: first, to continue to engage China, while at the same time hedging against it strategically; and second, to reorient Canada's naval emphasis from the Atlantic to the Pacific in order to deal with threats and contingencies in that quintessentially maritime realm.

Context

The centre of global economic power, trade, and commerce now resides in the Asia-Pacific region. China, Japan, and South Korea are the world's second-, third-, and fifteenth-largest economies in the world.[2] Northeast Asia, that is to say China, Japan, and South Korea, constitutes one of the great regional *dynamos* that drive the global economy. In particular, the Chinese economy has performed in a way that is little short of stellar and indeed historic in its breadth and depth: double-digit growth, or roughly 10–11 per cent growth per annum for almost thirty years.[3] By most indications, China will continue to be a major economic force for decades to come and might even overtake the United States as the world's largest economy.[4] So China has become the classic *entrepôt*, the great engine replacing Japan as the animator of Asian economies, though Japan still has an economy that easily eclipses that of most other countries. We are looking at a new world altogether.

In 2008, merchandise imports and exports destined for and originating from Asia accounted for approximately one quarter of all global merchandise trade, with China as the world's second-largest exporter and third-largest importer of goods, and Japan as the fourth-largest importer and exporter of goods.[5] In the same year, over 5.5 per cent of Canada's exports were destined for Asia, while over 15 per cent of our imports originated from Asia.[6] The world's busiest ports are located in China, Singapore, Hong Kong, South Korea, and Taiwan.[7] China, by 2015, has an ambition to be the world's greatest shipbuilder with the biggest and most productive shipyards in the world,[8] though perhaps not the greatest high-end shipbuilder, as that credit would probably still reside with Japan and South Korea. It will also have the biggest mega-ports in the world, as well as the biggest production of containers. Additionally, the region is also home to the world's most important sea lines of communication for trade and commerce. Over fifty thousand ships pass through the Strait of Malacca each year, transporting over one-third of all global trade and half of the world's oil, including 80 per cent of China's and Japan's energy imports.[9] The 960-kilometre strait lies between Indonesia, Malaysia, and Singapore, the last being home to the world's busiest port, and represents the world's most critical strategic chokepoint.

China's unprecedented economic growth has provided the means by which it has been able to embark on its substantial military modernization. And despite a long tradition of continentalism, China has now become increasingly Mahanian in outlook. Certainly the appetite for international energy has contributed in part to China's becoming a maritime power. In their search for energy, the Chinese are becoming increasingly exposed and vulnerable to the vagaries of the maritime realm, as their sea lanes stretch back across the Indian Ocean to

Africa or across the Pacific to South America and elsewhere. They are acquiring blue-water appetites and a desire to have an ocean-going naval presence. As such, one of the primary characteristics of China's military modernization is the development of power-projection capabilities. Advanced submarines, surface combatants, and (eventually) aircraft carriers are all key components of China's military modernization, meant to provide it with the ability to project power abroad to advance its national interests.

Another part of the reason for the growth of Chinese military power is to enable China to protect its own borders and to shape the strategic environment in which the future of Taiwan may be decided. The status of Taiwan is still a matter of dispute between the island's leaders and the Chinese Communist Party. Taiwan is for all intents and purposes a de facto state, albeit not one recognized officially as a *de jure* one. Taiwan wishes to obtain such recognition, while China desires to incorporate the 'renegade province' into the mainland. Were the island to become reunited with the mainland, China would have the ability to project naval power more readily throughout the region and beyond by virtue of having unencumbered blue-water access through naval bases on the island. Currently, China has over a thousand ballistic missiles pointed directly at the island in order to deter it from declaring formal independence, and the number of missiles continues to grow. Meanwhile, Taiwan relies on the Taiwan Relations Act passed by the U.S. Congress in 1979, in which America undertakes to provide the island with the military equipment needed to defend itself, while pledging to come to its aid in the event of an unprovoked attack by the mainland. The China-Taiwan situation is the flashpoint most likely to bring American and Chinese military forces into direct conflict with each other, with potentially far-reaching or even catastrophic consequences.

Elsewhere in the region, the divided Korean Peninsula remains one of the most militarized places in the world. The ceasefire agreement signed in 1953 by North Korea and U.S.-allied forces has not yet been replaced with a permanent peace agreement. As a result, approximately 25,000 American troops are stationed south of the demilitarized zone to supplement South Korea's 687,000 troops.[10] The Democratic People's Republic of Korea is home to the world's fifth-largest army; over 1 million troops are stationed just north of the demilitarized zone, as are hundreds of tanks and aircraft, and thousands of artillery pieces.[11] For the last couple of decades, Pyongyang has been steadfastly developing a ballistic missile and nuclear weapons capability. Fortunately, since the end of hostilities in 1953, U.S. and Republic of Korea forces have arguably deterred a second North Korean invasion of the South. Tensions along the demilitarized zone remain high, however. Should war break out on the peninsula, U.S. and South Korean forces would undoubtedly prevail and, in all likelihood, bring about the end of the North Korean regime. But the war would be tremendously bloody: Seoul would most likely be obliterated by the thousands of artillery pieces and missiles pointed at it; Japan might be attacked with ballistic missiles, possibly armed with weapons of mass destruction (WMD); and depending on the state of North Korea's WMD and missile capabilities at that time, the American homeland might itself be attacked directly. While America, China, Japan, and South Korea all wish to see the complete dismantlement of North Korea's WMD programs and the reduction of hostilities across the demilitarized zone, they also desire to prevent the sudden collapse of the northern regime. The costs of unification would be tremendous, a humanitarian crisis might ensue, and the status of U.S. forces on the peninsula (and in Japan) would be called into question.

The China-Taiwan and Korean Peninsula flashpoints highlight a related issue: the endemic proliferation of WMD and ballistic missiles in Northeast Asia. China has over a thousand short- and medium-range ballistic missiles on its coast pointed at Taiwan and approximately thirty intercontinental ballistic missiles capable of reaching the North American continent. As evidenced by recent tests and pronouncements, North Korea appears wholly unwilling to halt its development of nuclear weapons and long-range ballistic missile capabilities and has shown itself willing to sell missiles and nuclear technology to the highest bidder, including countries such as Iran. Both America and Japan have missile defence assets deployed in the region to counter those threats, and Taiwan has shown interest in acquiring such a capability.

Since the early days of the Cold War, America's forward presence in Northeast Asia has brought relative stability to an otherwise unstable region. For better or worse, the United States is the great balancer by virtue of some 58,000 forward-deployed U.S. forces in South Korea and Japan and security partnerships with other regional states.[12] America's unofficial support for Taiwan has arguably deterred an unprovoked Chinese attempt to reunify the island with the mainland by force. Its security guarantee to Japan precludes that country's need to fully arm itself above and beyond the limits allowed by its constitution, which in turn has served to placate its neighbours' fears of a remilitarized

Japan. And America's forward deployment of troops in South Korea has deterred another North Korean invasion.

Thus, a contraction of America's presence in the region would compel those who currently rely on U.S. security guarantees to provide for their own security to a far greater extent than they do already. Such an outcome would be further exacerbated if China does not become more transparent about its military modernization and its overall intentions in the security realm. This would further add to existing suspicions in the region and might lead to miscalculation and even war. So while there is a great deal of anti-Americanism in Asia at the grassroots and elite levels, many are hedging their bets over and against China. What, they ask, is China's endgame? The message is, 'Do not let the Americans leave Asia.'

Canada's Security Interests in the Asia-Pacific Region

The previous section illustrated the importance of the region to the global economy and the delicate and intricate security dynamics present there. Though it may not be readily apparent to most Canadians, what happens in the Asia-Pacific region can affect Canada's national security interests directly and indirectly. This section examines the ways in which Canada's interests have the potential to be harmed as a result of instability in the Asia-Pacific regional security environment.

First, the disruption of trade and commerce. As a trading nation, Canada relies heavily on a secure and stable trading environment. As noted above, China, Japan, and South Korea are the world's second-, third-, and fifteenth-largest economies, and Taiwan is the twenty-fourth largest.[13] Those countries are home to some of the world's busiest ports, and the volume of trade taking place within and emanating from the region is significant. A severe disruption of global commerce in the region would pose a clear danger to Canadian interests. Unfortunately, it is possible for some or all of these states to become involved in a military conflict with one another. It is also likely that the United States would itself become militarily involved, whether over the China-Taiwan situation, the Korean Peninsula, or some other issue. The repercussions for the global economy generally and Canada specifically from a regional war could be devastating.

It is also possible that the Strait of Malacca would be severely compromised. Acts of piracy or terrorism or a regional power blockading the strait as part of a larger regional conflict would produce far-reaching consequences for international trade and commerce. We could see a substantial rise of shipping insurance rates, demonstrated by the recent increase due to the incessant pirate attacks of ships off the Somali coast. To avoid the threat of piracy, shipping companies might be forced to use alternative routes to reach their destination. However, this would lead to increased travel times, travel costs, insurance premiums, and costs for the exporter to ship products. This in turn would lead to reduced sales on the production side and increased prices for the consumer. In addition, the fragile oil market could be further threatened as a result of illegal seizures of oil tankers, thereby leading to increased prices in oil at home. Overseas threats, while far from our shores, can nonetheless wreak havoc for Canadians at home.

Second, the rise of China. As the result of the size of its economy, the nature and scope of its military modernization, and its growing regional and global influence, China will increasingly become a critical determinant of the security environment in Northeast Asia and the wider Asia-Pacific region. It is conceivable that China will wish to carve out a bigger role for itself in its own region, if not on the entire world stage, commensurate with its ever-growing economic and increasingly military power. Throughout history, such behaviour has typically resulted in conflicts of interest between the status quo power (e.g., the United States) and the rising power (e.g., China), as the former wishes to maintain, if not expand, what it already has, while the latter desires its own piece of the pie, at the expense of the former. War has often been the result and has decided the ultimate apportionment of regional and global spoils.

China is the most likely candidate to challenge America's unrivalled power, and there is already competition between Washington and Beijing for influence in the Asia-Pacific region. Should China seriously challenge or disrupt the regional and global status quo (e.g., through an unprovoked attempt to incorporate Taiwan into the mainland by force), its actions might elicit a serious response from the United States. To some extent, the United States and its security partners in the region are already preparing for such an eventuality. As the American presence in the Asia-Pacific region provides a modicum of security and stability in an otherwise volatile region, the rise of China at the expense of U.S. power and influence could have a profoundly detrimental effect on regional security and the security interests of the region's key players. As Canada is America's neighbour, largest trading partner,[14] and closest military ally, the state of Sino–U.S. relations will necessarily have implications for Canadian foreign and defence policy.

Thus, we have seen that the remarkable growth of China is as much an issue for Beijing as it is for Washington, London, New Delhi, and the other great capitals of the world. They are all caught in the crossfire of those who see China as an opportunity and those who perceive it as a challenge. And that ambiguity is playing itself out in many corners of the globe. We can see it, for example, in Washington, where some have coined the curious conflation 'congagement.'[15] Are they engaging China? Are they containing China? Of course, one can advance persuasive arguments that China constitutes a threat to the new world order. And indeed, one has only to read U.S. Department of Defense publications that highlight the relentless growth of the Chinese military. As Secretary of Defense Donald Rumsfeld asked publicly in Singapore several years ago, 'Since no nation threatens China, one must wonder: Why this growing investment? Why these continuing large and expanding arms purchases? Why these continuing robust deployments?'[16] So while there is much admiration for China, there is also a great deal of uncertainty, even ambiguity, about how to position oneself over and against China, whether one is in Singapore, Malaysia, Australia, or India.

Third, the proliferation of WMD. An interstate missile exchange as part of a larger regional war would severely disrupt the regional and thus global economy upon which Canada's prosperity is highly dependent. A direct ballistic missile attack against the American homeland as a result of a regional conflict would wreak tremendous damage, not only against the U.S. population, but also its economy, upon which Canada's own economy depends so strongly. It is also conceivable that a missile could strike a Canadian population and economic centre – either intentionally or as a result of a misfire. Moreover, should American security guarantees to its key allies be called into question, Japan, South Korea, and Taiwan might develop their own nuclear and ballistic missile capabilities that could greatly increase regional instability.

Canada's Current Asia-Pacific Policy and the Way Ahead

An appropriate question to ask is, 'What is Canada's view of the Asia-Pacific security environment and the rise of China as it relates to Canada's security interests?'[17] Unfortunately, the answer to this question continues to be, 'Not much.' Both the 2005 Defence Policy Statement and the 2008 *Canada First Defence Strategy* combined make mention of Asia seven times and China once. The 2005 Defence Policy

Statement, for instance, notes that 'long-standing tensions remain' in Asia and that even though those 'hot spots . . . are unlikely to erupt into major regional wars in the near future, the possibility cannot be discounted. North Korea's nuclear brinkmanship and ongoing tensions between Taiwan and China remain serious concerns in the region.'[18] In order to contribute to international stability in the Asia-Pacific, the Department of National Defence will engage in 'defence diplomacy' in the region.[19] The *Canada First Defence Strategy* says even less: 'The ongoing buildup of conventional forces in Asia Pacific countries is another trend that may have a significant impact on international stability in coming years.'[20]

As discussed in the previous section, several issues in the Asia-Pacific region can have both direct and indirect negative consequences for Canada's security interests. As security abroad helps ensure Canadian security and prosperity at home, Canada needs to make effective contributions to security in the region. This section puts forth two sets of prescriptions for Canada to follow in order to secure its interests in the region: engage with, but strategically hedge against, China, and shift naval assets from the Atlantic to the Pacific in order to deal with immediate and potential security threats.

China

Canada should engage China as much as possible to advance our mutual interests in the economic and security realms. Though Sino–Canadian relations have traditionally been good, political relations cooled significantly after the Conservative Party came to power in 2006. Fortunately, after three years in office, Prime Minister Stephen Harper made his first state visit to China in December 2009. This was a positive first step towards restoring the relationship. There is much to gain from such engagement with China, not the least of which is the great potential of Chinese foreign direct investment in Canada and the tremendous market opportunities in China for Canadian exports. Continued engagement could also encourage China to become more transparent about its intentions in the security realm.

At the same time, Canada should hedge strategically and if necessary be prepared to stand firm with the United States and other allies against China, should Beijing attempt to revise the regional and global status quo forcefully. Amicable, simultaneous relations with both America and China are in Canada's best interest. Ultimately, however, our economic and security interests lie primarily with the United States. As Canada's security and prosperity depends to a large extent on America's global pre-eminence, the rise of China – at the expense of a significant decrease in American power – would not be in our interest, especially if Sino–U.S. relations turned decidedly sour. Unfortunately, no one is as yet certain about China's true intentions in the regional security architecture. To wish for the best – that China might have a 'peaceful rise' – while not preparing for the worst could compromise Canada's interests. As such, Canada must be sufficiently realistic to avoid basing its security on purely wishful thinking.

Maritime Security

For all of Canada's naval history, the emphasis has been on Atlantic operations. There has been a natural tendency toward that approach, given the transatlantic nature of historical links between North America and Europe. These links have been solidified militarily through the North Atlantic Treaty Organization, in which Canada's primary naval role has been anti-submarine warfare in the Atlantic. Correspondingly, the bulk of the Canadian navy has always been stationed in Halifax, Nova Scotia, with a smaller force stationed in Esquimalt, British Columbia.[21] Despite the collapse of the Soviet Union and the Warsaw Pact, and despite the fact that the global centre of political, economic, and military power and influence has since shifted towards the Pacific, the Canadian navy remains primarily Atlantic-centric. It is no surprise that the Americans have moved the bulk of their naval forces into the Pacific in recognition of new geostrategic realities, and Canada's security interests would be well served by a similar shift in focus for the Canadian navy.

The most direct and meaningful way in which Canada can contribute directly to a secure and stable Asia-Pacific region in concert with its partners and allies is through forward deployment of its naval forces. As such, the second prescription made in this chapter is a reprioritization of Canada's naval assets from the Atlantic to the Pacific. Such a reorientation would enable Canada to contribute to:

- *Maritime security operations.* A secure and stable maritime environment in which trade and commerce can thrive is essential for the regional and global economies, and by extension Canada's national interests. Canada's Department of National Defence states, 'The purpose of maritime security operations is to help set the conditions for

security and stability at sea, while complementing the counterterrorism and security efforts of regional nations.'[22] As discussed above,
there are numerous scenarios in which the maritime domain upon
which trade and commerce is so heavily dependent could be compromised, whether as a result of a China-Taiwan military exchange,
a military conflict on the Korean Peninsula, or the blockading of the
Strait of Malacca. A forward-deployed naval task force comprising
like-minded states could deter threats to seaborne trade and counter
such threats rapidly and decisively, should deterrence fail. Since
2004, Indonesia, Singapore, and Malaysia have undertaken coordinated naval and aerial patrols to help counter potential threats of
piracy and terrorism to the Strait of Malacca. This is an important
first step towards ensuring the safe, unrestricted movement of international trade through this strategic chokepoint. For countries such
as China and Japan, whose economies are highly dependent upon
the free flow of goods through the strait, there is a strong interest
for them to participate in such coalition operations. Greater involvement by concerned players there and similar efforts elsewhere in the
region can help ensure a safe, secure, and stable global commons.

- *Counter-proliferation.* Canada should begin to consider more substantive ways to counter the spread of WMD beyond mere pronouncements that the nation supports non-proliferation and disarmament.
  The maritime security operations described above could also include
  engaging in Proliferation Security Initiative activities. Launched in
  2003 as a further means of countering the growing WMD threat,
  the PSI aims to deter shipments of WMD and their delivery systems, and to stop such shipments through interdiction. We know,
  for instance, that North Korea has sent ballistic missile components
  by sea through this area. A multinational naval task force here
  could provide an added layer of interception to prevent the spread
  of WMD. As a long-standing vocal and diplomatic supporter of
  counter-proliferation and a participant in the Proliferation Security
  Initiative, Canada should continue to contribute to such activities.
  The dispatch of at least one of our frigates to the region would be
  a welcome contribution as the international community comes
  together to help prevent the spread of WMD from North Korea.
- *Strategic hedging vis-à-vis China.* With changes in the Asia-Pacific
  region, which includes the rise of China, Canada must be prepared
  to defend its strategic interests through military force. Though
  it is unlikely that Canadian destroyers or frigates would engage

Chinese forces in a conflict, they might be employed to blockade, for instance, the Strait of Malacca, through which 80 per cent of China's critical energy imports move each day. Or if Canada, its security partners, and the larger international community deem a Chinese blockade of Taiwan to be an act of aggression, Canadian naval forces could be employed for counter-blockade operations.

- *Defence diplomacy, or 'showing the flag.'* There is also a diplomatic benefit to an increased role of the Canadian navy in the Asia-Pacific theatre. Besides showing the flag, participation in such a coalition task force would provide Canada and its allies an opportunity to work with non-traditional coalition partners such as China, Japan, South Korea, Indonesia, and others. Given the increasing importance of the Asia-Pacific region as a whole, this could provide Canada and its allies with a unique opportunity to engage with these important economic and military powers. It could also encourage China to become more transparent militarily, thereby reducing suspicion and fear of its intentions.

- *Humanitarian assistance and disaster relief.* There is a high likelihood of refugee and humanitarian crises occurring in the chaos associated with the collapse of the North Korean regime. Millions of North Koreans could flee into China and South Korea in such an event. Tens of thousands of North Koreans have already fled brutal conditions in their own country to seek a new life in Northeast China, further aggravating the already high unemployment there. Similarly, Seoul has often cited the enormous human costs for South Korea of a humanitarian crisis if it was obliged to embrace refugees fleeing from the north. Canada has traditionally been a strong supporter of disaster relief, as evidenced by recent operations in Haiti, Turkey, Honduras, Sri Lanka, Pakistan, and China (where Canada provided financial assistance for the rehabilitation of areas devastated by earthquakes in Sichuan province). A forward-deployed naval presence in the Asia-Pacific region would enable Canada to quickly provide humanitarian assistance and disaster relief to countries subject to political turmoil or natural calamities.

Conclusion

Historical ties, institutional links, and outbreaks of war in Southeast Europe, Southwest Asia, and Africa prolonged Canada's post–Cold War inclination to view security concerns through a Euro-centric lens. The events associated with 9/11 further reinforced this inclination,

strengthening the security dialogue with Washington and reanimat-
ing the nation's involvement in the Atlantic alliance. At the same time,
however, profound and historic forces have shifted the global centre
of economic, military, and political gravity into the Asia-Pacific region.

China is at the centre of this phenomenon. Its staggering economic
growth over three decades has accelerated the forces of globalization,
transformed the U.S. economy, and amended the geostrategic architecture of Asia. The speed and comprehensiveness of these changes caught
many off guard. Does the 'peaceful rise' of China constitute a threat or
an opportunity? China's decision to modernize its armed forces and its
navy in particular gives ammunition to proponents of the threat school.
The avalanche of inexpensive goods pouring out of China lends credence to the opportunity school. The upshot is a sense of worldwide
ambiguity. Nations are eager to trade with China but seek to keep their
powder dry, because there seems no way of knowing what China's endgame is. Canada is party to this uncertainty, and critics of Canadian
foreign policy have argued that Ottawa, captured by concerns over
China's egregious human rights record, has failed to develop a constructive dialogue with Beijing. Others have noted that the lack of an
engagement strategy with China is symptomatic of a larger Canadian
failing to recognize the new realities and opportunities represented
in Asia. Not surprisingly, in an era in which the Canadian Forces have
distinguished themselves in Afghanistan, little thought is given to the
security concerns in the rest of Asia, a number of which have the potential to be extraordinarily serious.

The Asia-Pacific region is quintessentially maritime, and this fact
has been further underscored by the dramatic growth of regional
navies and the critical importance of regional sea lines of communication for the movement of prodigious amounts of exports. Thus, the
Canadian navy is an obvious vehicle for telegraphing Canada's national
resolve. Clearly, Canada will always be a modest player in the region,
but current trends point invariably towards the emergence of maritime coalitions designed to secure the ocean commons, facilitate the
untrammelled movement of global commerce, and provide relief from
disasters – natural and otherwise. Thus, the Canadian navy can contribute materially to the maintenance of peace and good order at sea.
Hopefully, coalition operations of the sort witnessed in the anti-piracy
campaign off the Horn of Africa will foster interoperability among
navies and co-opt those navies that are a source of concern in a number
of quarters throughout the Indian and Pacific Oceans. Greater Canadian
naval involvement in those seas raises questions about rebalancing the

navy – a subject of discussion over many years. This will no doubt happen in the fullness of time as the navy of the future emerges and the incontrovertible nature of Asia's military and political power turns Ottawa's gaze towards the Pacific.

NOTES

1 The author would like to thank James A. Boutilier, special advisor (policy) at Maritime Forces Pacific Headquarters, for his comments on this chapter. The views expressed in this chapter are the author's own.
2 Central Intelligence Agency, *The World Factbook*, 'GDP (Official Exchange Rate),' https://www.cia.gov/library/publications/the-world-factbook/fields/2195.html.
3 International Monetary Fund, *World Economic Outlook: Sustaining the Momentum* (New York: IMF, 2009), http://www.imf.org/external/pubs/ft/weo/2009/02/weodata/WEOOct2009all.xls.
4 John Hawskworth, *The World in 2050*, Mar. 2006, PricewaterhouseCoopers, http://www.pwc.com/en_GX/gx/world-2050/pdf/world2050emergingeconomies.pdf; Dominic Wilson and Roopa Purushothaman, *Dreaming with BRICs: The Path to 2050*, Global Economics Paper no. 91, Oct. 2003), Goldman Sachs, http://www2.goldmansachs.com/ideas/brics/book/99-dreaming.pdf.
5 Canada, Department of Foreign Affairs and International Trade, *Canada's State of Trade: Trade and Investment Update – 2009* (Ottawa: Minister of Public Works and Government Services Canada, 2009), 18–20.
6 Canada, Statistics Canada, 'Canadian International Merchandise Trade Database,' http://cansim2.statcan.gc.ca/cgi-win/CNSMCGI.PGM?Lang=E&CIMT_Action=Sections&ResultTemplate=CII_CIMT5. Our exports to Japan, China, and South Korea (the third-, fourth-, and seventh-largest destinations for Canadian exports, respectively) alone counted for 5.3 per cent of our total global merchandise exports (customs basis), while imports from China, Japan, and South Korea (second-, fourth-, and ninth-largest sources for Canadian imports, respectively) accounted for 14.7 per cent of our total global merchandise imports. See also DFAIT, *Canada's State of Trade*, 52–7.
7 American Association of Port Authorities, 'World Port Ranking: 2008,' http://aapa.files.cms-plus.com/Statistics/WORLD%20PORT%20RANKINGS%2020081.pdf.
8 'China Expected to Become Biggest Shipbuilding Nation in 2015,' *Asia InfoServices*, 14 Aug. 2003.
9 'Balancing Powers in the Malacca Strait,' *Global News Journal*, 7 Mar. 2010, http://blogs.reuters.com/global/2010/03/07/balancing-powers-in-the-malacca-strait/;

U.S. Energy Information Administration, 'World Oil Transit Chokepoints: Malacca,' http://www.eia.gov/countries/regions-topics.cfm?fips=WOTC; Ji You, 'Dealing with the Malacca Dilemma: China's Efforts to Protect Its Energy Supply,' *Strategic Analysis* 31, no. 3 (May 2007): 473.

10 International Institute of Strategic Studies, *The Military Balance 2009* (London: Routledge, 2009), 396–8.

11 Ibid., 394–6.

12 Ibid., 43.

13 Central Intelligence Agency, *2010 World Factbook,* GDP (Official Exchange Rate).

14 China surpassed Canada in 2009 as the largest source of exports to the United States. See United States, U.S. Census Bureau, Foreign Trade Statistics for Canada, http://www.census.gov/foreign-trade/balance/c1220.html; and for China at http://www.census.gov/foreign-trade/balance/c5700.html. Canada still remains the largest destination for U.S. exports.

15 See, for instance, Zalmay Khalilzad, *Congage China,* RAND Issue Paper (Project Air Force, 1999), http://www.rand.org/pubs/issue_papers/2006/IP187.pdf.

16 Secretary of Defense Donald Rumsfeld, 'The US and Asia-Pacific Security beyond the War on Terrorism,' First Plenary Session, 2005 Shangri-La Dialogue (International Institute of Strategic Studies), 4 June 2005.

17 This paragraph reprinted with permission from Thomas Adams, 'Security in the Asia-Pacific Century: Australia's Defence White Paper 2009 and What It Means for Canada,' *Strategic Datalink* no. 10 (May 2009): 3.

18 Canada, Department of National Defence, *Canada's International Policy Statement: A Role of Pride and Influence in the World – Defence* (Ottawa: DND, 2005), 5–6.

19 Ibid., 28.

20 Canada, Department of National Defence, *Canada First Defence Strategy* (Ottawa: 2008), 6.

21 There are currently two destroyers, seven frigates, one supply ship, three submarines, and six coastal defence vessels on the East Coast and five frigates, one destroyer, one supply ship, one submarine, and six coastal defence vessels on the West Coast.

22 Canada, Department of National Defence, 'Canadian Participation in Combined Task Force 150,' http://comfec-cefcom.forces.gc.ca/pa-ap/ops/fs-fr/CTF150-eng.asp.

9 South Asia: Growing Risks, Growing Importance, and Canada's Evolving Role

DOUGLAS GOOLD

Even though Canada is a Pacific nation – as well as an Atlantic and Arctic one – it has been slow to embrace the rise of Asia, let alone South Asia. Undoubtedly, this is because Canada is the product of two European cultures and shares its only border with the United States. Historically, Canada's focus has been on the North Atlantic and on the immense power to its south, rather than on the Pacific. This is clear from our security agreements, of which the two most prominent are the North Atlantic Treaty Organization (NATO), which bridges North America and Europe, and the North American Aerospace Defence Command, which is responsible for the defence of Canada and the United States. The non-Asian tenor of much of Canada's history is also evident in the country of origin of most of its immigrants up to the 1970s, with British and American immigrants taking the top two spots forty years ago – tellingly, they are now occupied by China and India.

This Eurocentric and North Atlantic bias is reflected in previous books and government policy documents on security and defence. David B. Dewitt and David Leyton-Brown's 1995 standard, *Canada's International Security Policy*, makes few references to Asia.[1] The same is true of the long-running, widely used annual Canada among Nations series, which over the past dozen years has yielded relatively few chapters on Asia, particularly beyond China.[2] The list includes a 1999 chapter on Canada and the Asian financial crisis; 2005 pieces on emerging powers, on global China, and on re-engaging India; a 2006 chapter on developing a China strategy; and several pieces in the 2008 anniversary volume on a century of Canadian foreign policy.[3] A chapter on multilateralism and conflict in the Pacific concludes, 'For a nation aspiring to Pacific status, Canada's approach to the region has remained strongly North Atlantic.'[4]

Government policy reviews reveal a similar lack of interest in Asia generally and South Asia specifically, and what interest there is remains largely economic. While the *Commerce* volume of Prime Minister Paul Martin's 2005 five-volume *International Policy Statement* contains a substantial discussion of Canada's poor economic performance in Asia, the *Defence* volume has sections on the Canada–U.S. defence relationship, the United Nations, NATO, and the European Union, but only passing references to Asia.[5]

One of the goals of this chapter will be to redress this imbalance by highlighting the importance of South Asia to Canada and the world. South Asia can be variously defined, but includes three large countries (India, Pakistan, and Bangladesh) and four smaller ones (Sri Lanka, Nepal, Bhutan, and the Maldives). South Asia can also be defined to include Iran and Afghanistan, which we will do here – though this expands the region to include parts of Southwest Asia. Inevitably, China, which is covered in the preceding chapter, will be mentioned from time to time.

The area's rapidly growing importance was shown by the fact that when she first came to office, U.S. Secretary of State Hillary Clinton appointed three 'super sub-secretaries of state,' and two of them were assigned to the region: the formidable Richard Holbrooke for Pakistan and Afghanistan, and Dennis Ross for Iran (a third was responsible for Arab–Israeli negotiations).

The region has arguably become the most dangerous part of the globe, combining nuclear powers, aspiring nuclear powers, failed states, terrorism, and ancient rivalries – a potentially deadly combination. Canada is not exempt from these dangers, particularly terrorism. As Tarun Das, president of the Aspen Institute India, warned in an interview in New Delhi, 'You won't be saved in Canada, as the U.S. found out. You may be far away from the scene of the trouble, but it gets to you. I think the world is globalized not only from a business point of view, but also from a terror point of you. We are all in it together.'[6]

The Evolution of Canada's Role in South Asia

Certainly Canada established a bold and far-sighted precedent when Prime Minister Pierre Trudeau recognized the People's Republic of China in 1970, the first Western country to do so. But Canada never fully capitalized on its head start, and by the early twenty-first century the Conservative party under Prime Minister Stephen Harper had managed to sour thirty-five years of generally good relations by tak-ing a publicly scolding, ideological approach to disagreements over Taiwan, Tibet, and human rights. When Harper finally visited China in December 2009, he was publicly chastised by Premier Wen Jiabao for being the first Canadian prime minister to visit in almost five years. However, some progress was made, most notably China's grant to Canada of the coveted 'approved destination status,' which promises to greatly increase the number of Chinese tourists to Canada.

Canada's relations with India, by far the largest South Asian power and, alongside China the most promising of the BRIC (Brazil, Russia, India, China) countries, went in quite a different direction, from bad to not so bad. An outsider might assume that India and Canada would be natural partners, as fellow English-speaking democracies with links through the Commonwealth and a large Indian diaspora in Canada. But that assumption would be wrong. Relations started to go off the rails as early as the 1950s, when the two countries fought one another as members of the International Control Commission for Indochina.[7] They became much worse after India's surprise nuclear test in May 1974, which was particularly galling to Canada, because it was made pos-sible through Canadian technology. Nor did it help that Indian Prime Minister Indira Gandhi told the Empire and Canadian Clubs in Toronto the previous June, 'We are not interested in becoming a power, major or minor, and certainly not a nuclear power.'[8] When India exploded another nuclear device in 1998, Foreign Minister Lloyd Axworthy reacted angrily, initiating punitive measures and stating his 'firm belief that India's recent nuclear tests constitute a clear and fundamen-tal threat to the international security regime and, thus, to Canada's security.'[9] As former high commissioner to India David Malone told the author in an interview, Canada and India went into a 'thirty-year mutual sulk' over the nuclear question.[10]

Fortunately, that sulk seemed to have came to an end in September 2008, in the wake of U.S. President George W. Bush's controversial '123' nuclear agreement with India. Canada, as a key member of the Nuclear Suppliers Group, approved an exemption for India to the group's export guidelines. This pleased both the United States and India, and signalled that Canada – thirty-five years after the fact – had come to terms with the reality that India was a nuclear power, and there was nothing that Canada (or anyone else, for that matter) could do about it. Canada and India followed this up with the signing of their own Nuclear Cooperation Agreement in June 2010; alongside the United

States, India had already negotiated agreements with France, Russia, and Kazakhstan. A second indication that the tide was finally turning was that after many fallow years, there has been a marked increase in visits by senior ministers to and from India. Harper finally visited India in November 2009. Prime Minister Singh came in Canada for the Group of 20 (G20) in June 2010, the first Indian prime minister to visit Canada since Indira Gandhi in 1973, and was the only G20 leader to be given a dinner in his honour by the Canadian prime minister.

Canada's role in South Asia has evolved dramatically. In her 1973 speech, Gandhi thanked Canada for providing India with more than a billion dollars in aid. By 2006, however, India was no longer accepting bilateral aid from Canada. But Canadian development assistance to South Asia continued to loom large. For 2007–8, the Canadian International Development Agency's bilateral funding to Afghanistan totalled a whopping $280 million, by far the most to any country, and part of a planned $1.2 billion to 2011. For 2006–7, the latest year for which data are available, Bangladesh, a long-time recipient, received $65 million, and Pakistan, a recipient for more than forty years, $25 million. In 2008–9, Pakistan was promised an additional $33 million in humanitarian aid.

Canada and Afghanistan

Canada's most dramatic and costly involvement in the region has been in Afghanistan, its greatest combat role in the half century since the Korean War. Taken at the invitation of the Afghan government, and as part of its NATO obligations and under a United Nations mandate, it was a response to the terrorist attacks of 11 September 2001. While this chapter will not consider Afghanistan in detail, it is worth briefly placing Canada's role in the context of Southwest Asia.

Though the debate about motives will continue, there is no doubt that Prime Minister Jean Chrétien became involved to a large extent to placate the United States in the wake of the Liberal government's (prudent) decision not to join the American-led 'coalition of the willing' in Iraq. Afghanistan was not an obvious mission, even though it has been supported by two Liberal governments, and a Conservative one. Going to Kandahar in the dangerous south was even less obvious; in the words of Janice Stein and Eugene Lang, it was the 'unexpected war' – originally, not even referred to as a war – in which Canada thought it would be 'early in, early out.'[11] Canada didn't even have a resident ambassador in Afghanistan until the high-profile and youthful Christopher Alexander took up his post in the capital of Kabul in 2003. And before the Taliban government fell at the end of 2001, the Canadian International Development Agency contributed a modest $10 or $20 million a year to the poverty-stricken, war-ravished country.

While the military outcome is not yet known, the expectation of military victory against the Taliban and al Qaeda has faded, in a land known as the 'graveyard of empires.' Few politicians or generals in Canada or elsewhere imagined the large number of lives that would be lost – 155 by the middle of 2011 – the billions of dollars spent, and the time and energy required to make visible progress in security, governance, or development. The strategic lessons and implications are considerable for Canada and others. In March 2005, the colourful and forceful Chief of the Defence Staff General Rick Hillier persuaded Prime Minister Paul Martin that Canada could send troops to Kandahar and still have the capacity to act in areas such as Darfur, Haiti, or the Middle East. Though the Canadian Forces were able to contribute to Haiti's reconstruction after the earthquake of January 2010, Hillier overestimated Canadian capacity. Afghanistan has stretched forces, and the efforts of Foreign Affairs and National Defence, to the limit. Thousands of Canadian troops have fought in the country and many have had multiple tours of duty, and millions of dollars of equipment have been destroyed either by combat or by the terrain. Despite the efforts of nearly 3,000 troops from Canada and more than 130,000 from NATO and the International Security Assistance Force, the threat level for the region has only increased, as Islamic fundamentalism spreads throughout Southwest and Central Asia.

On a more positive note, and largely as a result of Canada's involvement in Afghanistan, the Department of National Defence has finally been able to get the resources it had been denied for so many years and the status of the military, long scorned or simply ignored, has soared. A small but telling example has been shown by the naming of the 'Highway of Heroes,' a stretch of Highway 401 in southern Ontario along which the bodies of Canadian soldiers who have been killed in Afghanistan travel after they are flown into the air force base in Trenton, Ontario.

Canada's combat role lasted until 2011, as a result of a March 2008 agreement between the Liberals and Conservatives that effectively took Afghanistan off the table as a political issue. Yet the country's problems will continue for generations, and Canada will remain involved in a training capacity until 2014. Canada's relatively high military and aid contribution, its willingness to fight and to sustain very high casualty rates (unlike some European countries, whose 'caveats' restrict their combat role), and its continued involvement in military training should guarantee the country a seat at the table in discussions about the future of the region.

Though there has been a regrettable lack of public debate about Canada's role in Afghanistan, Canada's experience there should help educate the public about the new realities of the world beyond the borders of this country. Canada is not, if it ever has been, a nation of peacekeepers quietly going about their good work for the betterment of humankind. The peacekeeping of popular imagination has been replaced by the far more dangerous peace-making, in the era of the treacherous 'three-block war,' where danger can lurk as much in a civilian setting as on a battlefield. Canadians have also begun to learn that there is a price to be paid – if not in Iraq, then in Afghanistan – for benefiting from the security umbrella provided by our powerful neighbour to the south. Canadians were never entirely comfortable with their country's role in a distant country and a war that was never fully explained to them. Hence, while the Afghan mission is central to Canadian foreign and defence policy in the early years of the twenty-first century, it is a historical anomaly and likely to be the last expeditionary mission to that part of the world for many years to come.

The Changing Geopolitical Environment

South Asia, and Asia as a whole, has undergone a radical transformation since the end of the Cold War.

China has emerged as the dominant BRIC power, both in economic and geopolitical terms, and its status is so great there is talk – if not yet acceptance – of a Group of Two; that is, a world dominated by the United States and China. China is seen by itself and others as a global power, with strategic interests throughout Asia, Africa, and Latin America.

By comparison, India is an important regional power with global aspirations, as shown by its long campaign to become a member of the UN Security Council. However, its global claims seem more an insistence upon recognition of its enhanced status than part of a strategy to accomplish particular goals. It is unclear what it wants to accomplish beyond the region, apart, like China, from ensuring access to resources. India's foreign policy is based upon a confident and tough-minded interpretation of self-interest; unlike Canada, the country is not interested in projecting values abroad. Nor, like the United States and China, is it willing to accept a multilateral approach to security. Whatever its goals, India is better positioned to achieve them after the re-election of Prime Minister Singh in 2009. Predictions of another government at the mercy of smaller left-wing parties and the Communists proved wrong. Instead, Singh and the Congress party did far better than expected. He is the first Indian prime minister since Nehru in 1962 to be re-elected after completing a full five-year term.

Both India and China are nuclear powers, and both are increasing their military capacities at an impressive rate, with India's defence budget up 34 per cent in 2009–10 and China's defence spending having grown significantly over the past two decades. Each has among the largest navies in the world, and both are building the ultimate symbol of naval power, aircraft carriers. The two wary neighbours and huge trade partners are increasingly competing for dominance in the Indian Ocean, the world's third-largest body of water and one of the most critical for trade, responsible for half the world's container and 70 per cent of its oil traffic. According to Robert D. Kaplan, 'precisely because India and China are emphasizing their sea power, the job of managing their peaceful rise will fall on the US Navy to a significant extent.'[12] With the demise of the former Soviet Union, India's long-time ally, the United States is the only outside major power in the region, and that is likely to remain the case for the foreseeable future.

Arguably the single most important geopolitical development in South Asia in this century has been the signing of the '123' agreement between the United States and India. The nuclear pact 'is of unprecedented historical significance,' notes Pratap Bhanu Mehta, president of the New Delhi-based Center for Policy Research. 'It is in some ways an emphatic acknowledgment of India's transformation from a regional to a global power.'[13] Initiated by President George W. Bush, the civilian nuclear cooperation agreement calls upon India to allow International Atomic Energy Agency inspectors into its civilian facilities and to provide safeguards, while ending the decades-old U.S. moratorium on nuclear trade and assistance to India. These terms apply only to the fourteen reactors that India has designated as civilian; the remaining eight – the military reactors – remain off limits. What this means is that the United States completely reversed its policy and accepted India as a nuclear power.

The United States was motivated both by commercial concerns and implicitly by the belief that it needed to ally itself with a counterweight to China to the west (the United States already has its allies Japan and

South Korea to China's east). Prime Minister Singh lobbied hard and successfully for the agreement, aided by the powerful Indo-American diaspora. The deal is widely seen as a triumph of Indian statecraft. While the strategic partnership has led to defence cooperation between the United States and India and sales of sophisticated weapons to India, it would be a mistake to assume that New Delhi will reciprocate by supporting American interests in the region.

Threats to Canada and Its Allies

It does not take much to discern how South and Southwest Asia pose fundamental if mostly indirect threats to the interests of Canada and its allies. The region bristles with nuclear powers, including India, Pakistan, China, Russia, and Israel. Pakistan is unstable and was a notorious proliferator – 'the Wal-Mart of illicit nuclear trade,'[14] according to the Indian academic and journalist Raja Mohan – under nuclear scientist A.Q. Khan, who helped to advance the nuclear weapon programs of North Korea, Iran, and Libya. Nor is there any certainty that Pakistan's nuclear weapons are adequately safeguarded, a worry that came to the fore in April 2009, when the Taliban advanced to within striking distance of Islamabad and Pakistan's nuclear facilities. There have also been reports that militants in Pakistan have attacked several bases that contain nuclear weapons in recent years; what is not known is whether the attackers knew about the weapons or were interested in seizing them.[15]

Iran, with its erratic, opaque, and often irresponsible foreign policy, appears to be on its way to becoming a nuclear power, and the risk is that neither tougher economic sanctions nor the threat of military action will stop that from happening. If military strikes were carried out either by the United States or by Israel, acting by itself or as an American proxy, they would run the risk of failing to destroy all the targets and hence simply delay the completion of Iran's nuclear plans. Even more important, the political consequences of bombing a Muslim state, especially one that is a signatory of the Non-Proliferation Treaty (unlike India, Pakistan, or Israel), could be devastating. As Peter Jones, who has made many trips to Iran, phrases it, 'A US or Israeli attack on Iran would be the greatest gift that could be bestowed upon the hardliners – it would be the gift that keeps on giving. Nothing would more effectively unite the people behind a government [under President Mahmoud Ahmadinejad] that is in many other respects quite unpopular.'[16]

We can add to this unhappy mix the fact that there are many failed or failing states in the region. *Foreign Policy* magazine's Failed State Index for 2009 lists Afghanistan at number seven, Pakistan at ten, Burma at thirteen, and following in the top forty Bangladesh, Sri Lanka, Nepal, Uzbekistan, and Iran, which jumped eleven spots to number thirty-eight in the past year.[17] Nuclear-armed Pakistan may be the most worrisome. Pakistan and India have fought three major wars, with their dispute over Kashmir a frequent theme, and have come close to war a number of other times. Pakistan is a concern, given its long, porous frontier with Afghanistan and the baneful influence of the Inter-Services Intelligence, its notoriously political intelligence service. The country has also provided tacit support for extremists and terrorists, most notably for the devastating attacks on Mumbai on 26 November 2008.[18]

Given all these threats, it is no surprise that a recent major United Kingdom government report on policy in Afghanistan and Pakistan concluded, 'Of the six major sources of threat set out in the UK's National Security Strategy, Afghanistan and Pakistan are relevant to at least four.'[19]

Canada's Security Interests

As outlined in chapter 2, Canada's national interests, broadly stated, are security, prosperity, a stable world order, and the projection of values such as democracy and human rights. Each of these interests is threatened, directly or indirectly, by the dangers described above.

Canada's involvement in Afghanistan – prudent or otherwise – was motivated in part by concern for security and a stable world order, which were threatened by that country's terrorist training camps. It was then shaped by Canadian values, which are evident in the federal government's six priorities for Afghanistan, which include supporting a better justice system, schools and literacy training for girls as well as boys, the eradication of polio, support for elections, and political reconciliation among Afghans.

Prosperity is a national interest for Canada. Canada has relatively modest trade and foreign direct investment in the region, though both are growing. According to Goldman Sachs, India has the potential to have the fastest growth rate of the BRIC countries by 2050. South Asia and Asia as a whole look particularly important at a time when Canada's huge reliance upon the United States is increasingly questionable. The United States is in relative decline, while Asia is in the ascendant, and it is becoming more and more difficult to send goods across the 'thick-ened' Canada-U.S. border.

The security of the region is also important, because it is a major source of immigration to Canada. Seven of the top ten sending coun-tries in 2007 were Asian, with four countries from South or Southwest Asia: India, fractionally below China in top spot, Pakistan at num-ber four, Iran at seven, and Sri Lanka at ten (South Asians replaced the Chinese as Canada's largest visible minority in the 2006 census). A small number of those immigrants pose a security problem by bringing the battles, or former battles, of their homelands to Canada – a devel-opment that Ottawa apparently never foresaw. India has never been happy with Canada's handling of the 1985 Air India crash at the hands of terrorists, which killed 329 mostly Indo-Canadians, or by what it considers the government's lax approach to the support shown over the years by a portion of the Sikh community for a homeland named Khalistan. There have also been security issues with the Tamil com-munity in Canada, the largest outside Sri Lanka, given the support that some of that community has shown for the Tamil Tigers, which Canada – alongside the United States and the European Union – has designated a terrorist organization. Canada's interest in human secu-rity has been shown by its (unfortunately unsuccessful) attempts to mediate the Sri Lankan dispute and by its provision of humanitarian assistance since the government's victory over the Tamils in May 2009.

Finally, Canada has a security interest in a whole range of unconven-tional threats that have become apparent only in recent years, as popu-lations have increasingly moved, travelled, and migrated, and borders have lost much of their historical importance. The list of concerns includes pandemics; the movement of arms, drugs, and crime groups; WMD proliferation to states and, more ominously, to terrorist groups; and the effects of global warming, which could produce disaster in a low-lying country like Bangladesh, including the migration of tens of million of illegal immigrants into India.[20]

Canada's Strategy

Canada needs to face the stark reality that the country has very limited capacity, both in hard assets (troops and money) that it is able or will-ing to deploy abroad and soft power (such as culture) that the world is interested in, as we have learned from our experience in Afghanistan. While countries such as India and China needed us thirty years ago, we now need them, and we are towards the back of a very long line of suitors. Moreover, the time for lecturing is long past. As Foreign Affairs veteran Daryl Copeland said in an interview, 'There was a time when we could take on big projects,' such as former prime minister Pierre Trudeau's peace initiative, former secretary of state for external affairs Joe Clark's North Pacific Cooperative Security Dialogue, former prime minister Brian Mulroney's initiatives on apartheid and free trade, and former foreign minister Lloyd Axworthy's human security agenda. 'That time has passed. We need to recalibrate.'[21]

Of course, in a perfect world, Canada's 3-D (defence, development, and diplomacy) capacity would be increased through more substantial funding. While the situation at National Defence has improved considerably, the Department of Foreign Affairs and International Trade has been starved of funds and to a large extent power, which has increasingly shifted to the Prime Minister's Office and the Privy Council Office. A more robust and effective foreign policy would require a shift back to Foreign Affairs, but that is unlikely to happen, given its ineffectualness and the solid grip the Prime Minister's Office has over ministries and the bureaucracy. We also need, but do not have, a strategic plan for Asia, and, for that matter, for the rest of the world. Some of these realities are recognized by senior figures in Foreign Affairs. As one said in an interview in the summer of 2009, 'Canada has no strategic view of the world . . . If Canada plays its cards right [in South Asia], the best we can hope for is a stronger voice in a more crowded world . . . India is not willing to listen to what we think they should do. We need to accept that.'[22]

However, we have done – and should continue to do – some very useful, specific, security-related and diplomatic work in the region. Since 2001, Canada has contributed to the UN, Group of Eight (G8), and NATO-supported international effort through Combined Task Force 150 to counter piracy off the coast of Somalia and in the Gulf of Aden. Part of the task has been to ensure the delivery of the UN's World Food Program shipments. Canada's participation makes particular sense because it is one of the program's largest donors in Somalia and worldwide, and the role fits in nicely with the Responsibility to Protect doctrine, which was to a large extent initiated by Lloyd Axworthy.

Canada's 12 Halifax-class frigates, five of which are on the Pacific coast, are the workhorse of these efforts, as well as for much else in the region, such as fighting terrorism and the drug trade, and for disaster relief. Given the level of activity in and around the Indian Ocean and its importance for commerce, Canada should add to the fleet, which is to be replaced starting in 2015. A quick look at a map will make it clear why sea power is critical in South Asia.

Canada and India cooperate on counterterrorism, an apparent legacy of the Air India crash. In 1997, the two countries formed the Canada-India Joint Working Group on Counter-Terrorism, which has been meeting ever since. An unnamed official commented, when the group was set up, that the decision 'will certainly help India dealing with Sikh militants operating from the Canadian soil.'[23] In subsequent years, cooperation has reportedly broadened to include terrorist financing, immigration control, cyber terrorism, and narco-trafficking.[24] Given the Air India crash, concerns about some members of diaspora groups, the Mumbai terrorist attacks of 2008, and the problem of terrorism throughout the region, Canada–India cooperation on counterterrorism is to be encouraged.

Canada has made a valuable contribution by helping to bring together Pakistan and Afghanistan – with the cooperation of the two governments – to discuss their troubled border as part of the Dubai Process. Canada has facilitated discussions and helped to set up a joint working group, as well as a 'border flag' meeting of military officers. At the same time, Canada should realize that the problems in this part of the world will ultimately require a regional solution, which includes players such as India and Iran.[25] The first steps may already be underway, with Iran hosting a summit meeting in May 2009 with neighbours Pakistan and Afghanistan. Canada should also consider building serious capacity for track-two diplomacy – private as opposed to official diplomacy – despite a mixed record in Asia.[26]

There has been very little defence cooperation between Canada, on one hand, and India and Pakistan, on the other. More can only help strengthen links between the countries involved and increase understanding between their respective armed forces. Arms sales are a different matter. In May 2009, there was a flurry of contradictory reports that the Conservative government was considering Pakistan's request to end sanctions against arms exports, imposed after Pakistan's 1998 nuclear test. Indeed, it was under consideration. Dropping Canada's ban would be a mistake. Pakistan is an unstable country that has skilfully persuaded the United States to fund billions in arms shipments by continuing to cry wolf. Until it is absolutely clear that Pakistan is using its arms to fight terrorism fully and effectively, and not simply to beef up forces aimed at India, Canada's ban should remain in place.

In August 2009, the *New York Times* reported in a front page story that Pakistan had altered missiles sold to it by the United States for defensive purposes so they could hit India.[27]

There needs to be a thoughtful plan for Afghanistan after 2011. Clearly, the balance has shifted from defence to diplomacy and development, with training of the Afghan National Army continuing beyond 2011. Continuing the emphasis on Kandahar in the difficult south makes sense, both because Canada has experience there and because our commitment will be applauded by our allies. Unless another civil war intervenes, which is a real possibility, maintaining our commitment to Afghanistan is desirable and will give us eyes and ears in a critical part of the globe. Ultimately, of course, everyone's goal is to leave Afghanistan to the Afghans to protect, govern, and develop, even though there is scepticism about the chances of that happening.

Whenever possible, Canada should pursue its traditional multilateral approach or work with its allies in the region, as it has done as a member of NATO in Afghanistan. When the opportunity presents itself, Canada should also work with non-traditional partners, as has been the case with its anti-piracy efforts, where the country gained valuable experience working with Pakistan, China, and Indonesia. As Lord Robertson, co-chair of the United Kingdom's Institute for Public Policy Research Commission on National Security said, 'When it comes to security, national self-reliance is a dangerous fantasy.'[28] It is an even greater fantasy for a declining middle power like Canada.

It also makes sense to support and work with India whenever possible, taking the initiative as we attempt to improve our bilateral relations. The two countries have much in common, and Canada has no colonial baggage. We have access to one another at the highest level through the G20 and the Commonwealth. Ideally, Canada could mobilize the diaspora to help the two countries work together in areas such as education, energy, and the environment.

Canada could propose cooperation on governance and development support for Afghanistan, taking advantage of India's knowledge of the country and its substantial assistance program. India has shown itself to be a responsible nuclear power, and the two countries could cooperate in the area, now that a nuclear cooperation agreement is concluded.[29] Canada should continue to support India's long-standing application to join the Asia-Pacific Economic Cooperation forum. In fact, we should support any credible regional grouping, since there is none, in sharp contrast to Southeast Asia. Australia's Kevin Rudd, prime minister from 2007 to 2010 and now foreign minister, has attracted considerable attention with his vision of an Asia Pacific Community – a new regional architecture encompassing the whole of Asia-Pacific, including India, the United States, China, Japan, and Indonesia.

Conclusion

Over the past century, power has shifted from Europe, to the United States, to Asia, including South Asia. It is a critical part of the globe, both for the promise it holds and the threats it poses. Canada may be thousands of kilometres away, but it a globalized world it cannot afford to ignore the region, given its security interests and the role, however modest, it can play in helping to preserve those interests.

NOTES

1 David B. Dewitt and David Leyton-Brown, eds., *Canada's International Security Policy* (Scarborough, ON: Prentice Hall Canada, 1995).
2 The one exception to this bias was the 1997 volume, *Asia Pacific Face-Off*, which contained a range of articles on Asia, in recognition of Ottawa's designation of 1997 as Canada's Year of Asia Pacific, when Vancouver hosted the Asia-Pacific Economic Cooperation forum. See Fen Osler Hampson, Maureen Appel Molot, and Martin Rudner, eds., *Canada among Nations 1997: Asia Pacific Face-Off* (Ottawa: Carleton University Press, 1997).
3 These chapters appear in the following volumes: Robert Bothwell and Jean Daudelin, eds., *Canada among Nations 2008: 100 Years of Canadian Foreign Policy* (Montreal and Kingston: McGill-Queen's University Press, 2009); Andrew F. Cooper and Dane Rowlands, eds., *Canada among Nations 2005: Split Images* (Montreal and Kingston: McGill-Queen's University Press, 2005); Andrew F. Cooper and Dane Rowlands, eds., *Canada among Nations 2006: Minorities and Priorities* (Montreal and Kingston: McGill-Queen's University Press, 2006); Fen Osler Hampson, Martin Rudner, and Michael Hart, eds., *Canada among Nations 1999: A Big League Player?* (Don Mills, ON: Oxford University Press, 1999).
4 John Meehan and David Webster, 'From King to Kandahar: Canada, Multilateralism and Conflict in the Pacific, 1909–2009,' in Bothwell and Daudelin, *Canada among Nations 2008*, 271–92.
5 Canada, *Canada's International Policy Statement: A Role of Pride and Influence in the World* (Ottawa: Government of Canada, 2005), Commerce, 14–19; Defence, 21–6; and passing references.

6 Interview with Tarun Das, New Delhi, 18 Nov. 2009.
7 Ryan Touhey, 'Canada and India at 60,' *International Journal* 62, no. 4 (Autumn 2007): 739.
8 *The Empire Club of Canada Speeches 1973–1974* (Toronto: Empire Club Foundation, 1974), 12–22.
9 Statement to the Standing Committee on Foreign Affairs, 26 May 1998.
10 Interview in Ottawa, June 2009.
11 Janice Gross Stein and Eugene Lang, *The Unexpected War: Canada in Kandahar* (Toronto: Viking Canada, 2007), chap. 1.
12 Robert D. Kaplan, 'Center Stage for the Twenty-First Century: Power Plays in the Indian Ocean,' *Foreign Affairs* 88, no. 2 (Mar.–Apr. 2009): 18.
13 Pratap Bhanu Mehta, 'Five Balancing Acts: The Indo-US Nuclear Deal,' presentation at Centre for Policy Research, New Delhi, April 2006, http://www.india-seminar.com/2006/560/560%20pratap%20bhanu%20mehta.htm.
14 C. Raja Mohan, 'Welcoming Obama's Nuke Initiative,' *indianexpress.com*, 5 Apr. 2009.
15 Jane Perlez, 'Taliban Seize Vital Pakistan Area Closer to the Capital,' *New York Times,* 23 Apr. 2009; Bill Roggio, 'Taliban Advance Eastward, Threaten Islamabad,' *Long War Journal,* 23 Apr. 2009; see also Seymour M. Hersh, 'Defending the Arsenal: In an Unstable Pakistan, Can Nuclear Warheads Be Kept Safe?' *New Yorker,* 16 Nov. 2009, 28–35.
16 Peter Jones, 'Engaging Iran,' *Policy Brief* no. 5 (June 2009): 3. For a detailed discussion of options for dealing with Iran, see Kenneth M. Pollack, Daniel L. Byman, Martin Indyk, Suzanne Maloney, Michael E. O'Hanlon, and Bruce Riedel, *Which Path to Persia? Options for a New American Strategy Towards Iran* (Washington, DC: Brookings, 2009).
17 'The Failed State Index 2009,' *Foreign Policy,* 19 Feb. 2010.
18 See Douglas Goold, 'India, Land of Short Fuses,' *National Post,* 19 Dec. 2009.
19 United Kingdom, *UK Policy in Afghanistan and Pakistan: The Way Forward* (London: Government of the United Kingdom, Apr. 2009), 5. The four sources of threats are terrorism, conflict, transnational crime, and weapons of mass destruction.
20 See Senate of Canada, Standing Committee on Foreign Affairs and International Trade, issue 5, 1 Apr. 2009.
21 Interview, 21 Aug. 2009.
22 Interview, 23 Apr. 2009. The official asked not to be named.
23 'India, Canada Agree to Combat Terrorism,' *Agence France-Press,* New Delhi, 9 Jan. 1997.

24 While there are a few references to the group in the Indian press, including
    the names of some of the participants, there has been almost nothing in the
    Canadian media, and the government is tight-lipped about its activities.
    While recognizing the sensitivities of the subject, one would hope for a
    more forthcoming approach in the future.

25 See Ajay Parasram, 'Call in the Neighbor: Indian Views on Regionalizing
    Afghanistan Strategies,' *Asia Pacific Bulletin* no. 307 (2009). See also
    Barnett R. Rubin and Ahmed Rashid, 'From Great Game to Grand Bargain:
    Ending Chaos in Afghanistan and Pakistan,' *Foreign Affairs* 87, no. 6 (Nov.–
    Dec. 2008): 30–44. The authors propose a Contact Group authorized by the
    UN Security Council.

26 See Peter Jones, 'Canada and Two Track Diplomacy,' *A Changing World:
    Canadian Foreign Policy Priorities* 1 (Dec. 2008).

27 Eric Schmitt and David E. Sanger, 'U.S. Says Pakistan Made Changes to
    Missiles Sold for Defense,' *New York Times,* 30 Aug. 2009.

28 Quoted in Gavin Gordon, 'Re-think Urged on UK nuclear Deterrent,"
    Independent, 30 June 2009, http://www.independent.co.uk/news/uk/politics/
    rethink-urged-on-uk-nuclear-deterrent-1724767.html.

29 See Anita Singh, 'The Indo-American Nuclear Deal and Its Implications for
    Canada,' *Strategic Datalink* no. 6 (Nov. 2008): 1–4.

PART FOUR

**Expeditionary Missions
and the Future of the CF**

10 From Paardeberg to Panjwai: Canadian National Interests in Expeditionary Operations

DAVID J. BERCUSON AND
J.L. GRANATSTEIN

Canada first sent troops abroad to serve the national interest in the Anglo-Boer War of 1899–1902. Canadian troops were until only recently in Afghanistan's Kandahar province serving Canadian national interests. In the more than a century that passed between the Battle of Paardeberg and the Battle of Panjwai, Canadian troops went abroad to fight in two world wars, the Korean campaign, the 1991 Gulf War, the 1999 North Atlantic Treaty Organization (NATO) bombing of Serbia, and the war against the Taliban in Afghanistan. Canada also sent troops abroad in contingents large and small to undertake peacekeeping or peace enforcement operations from the Sinai to Cyprus to the Congo and to dozens of other trouble spots. Put simply, with little direct military threat to Canada since the last Fenian left Canadian soil in 1871, the Canadian military has largely been an expeditionary military since at least the 1890s. This is very unlikely to change.

Canadian governments, from those of Wilfrid Laurier to Stephen Harper, have believed that one key mission of the Canadian military is to deploy abroad – always as part of some larger coalition – to show larger nations (e.g., Britain and the United States), international organizations such as the United Nations, or allied nations such as the members of NATO that Canada is ready and able to put a shoulder to the wheel when military forces are needed to defend allies, deter aggression, or keep or enforce peace. In other words, Canada has been willing to do its share of the hard, dirty work. Doing so wins Canada diplomatic recognition, political acceptance, entrée into arrangements, treaties, and alliances that are important to Canada and Canadians, and a voice on how future international policies will be pursued. Were Canada not to take part in such missions abroad, friends and enemies alike would have concluded long ago that Canada is of no consequence, does not deserve to be heard, and ought not to be accorded any favours in bilateral or multilateral negotiations over any matter of consequence.

An Overview of Canadian Expeditionary Operations

There can be no rational argument that Canada should not have expeditionary capability. Even those Canadians who would prefer that Canada restrict its military to 'classical' UN peacekeeping missions, as it did prior to the mid-1990s, would still see Canada sending troops abroad: the missions might be different, but the ability to send troops abroad and sustain them for those types of missions would differ little from the ability needed to mount combat operations. Presumably the real differences would be in casualties, both physical and psychological.

Canadians in large measure are unaware of these basic facts. This is demonstrated by the changed public perception of the mission in Afghanistan. In the weeks following the 9/11 attacks on New York and Washington, DC, Canadians clamoured to send combat troops – including land forces – to Afghanistan to fight the Taliban.[1] But now public opinion on Canada's military mission in Afghanistan has turned to opposition. After almost a decade in Kabul and Kandahar, Canadians still do not appear to understand why we are in Afghanistan, what our long-term goals are, and why the Canadian Forces (CF) should be spending blood and treasure in a part of the world that is utterly foreign to them.[2] Canadians dislike war and especially wars where Canada fights alongside the United States, a product of our historic anti-Americanism. Canadians dislike casualties because they believe that 'blue beret' UN peacekeeping is the only proper role for the Canadian military today.[3] And Canadian governments, always with better ways to spend vote-getting money than funding wars abroad, dislike overseas missions and casualties. There is no political upside. What no one asks today, neither the people nor their political leaders, is whether the Afghan mission – or any other military mission abroad – serves Canada's national interests. The reason this question goes unasked in contemporary Canada is primarily because Canadians rarely frame such questions.

This is not only misguided, it flies in the face of Canadian history and the actions of governments of both national governing parties, Liberal and Conservative. In 2005, for example, the Liberal government of Paul Martin released its *International Policy Statement* and noted:

- Investing in a strong military is essential to achieving our foreign policy goals and advancing our place in the world;
- Security in Canada ultimately begins with stability abroad . . . [though] we need to be selective and strategic when deploying military personnel overseas, focusing on where our interests are at stake.[4]

The *1994 White Paper on Defence*, issued by the previous Liberal government of Jean Chrétien, declared, 'The White Paper affirms the need to maintain multi-purpose, combat-capable sea, land and air forces that will protect Canadians and project their interests and values abroad.'[5] Conservative white papers have been no less supportive of the need for Canadian military forces to operate abroad so as to serve Canadian interests. The 1987 white paper, written in the last years of the Cold War by the Progressive Conservative government of Brian Mulroney, declared that Canadian troops serving in Germany with NATO were directly addressing Canadian interests: 'Deterrence is not divisible. If it fails in Europe, it fails everywhere. By contributing to deterrence in Europe, Canadian Forces are serving a Canadian interest and contributing to Canada's security.'[6] The most recent defence policy statement, issued by the Conservative government of Stephen Harper in 2008, declared that the CF 'will have the capacity to . . . Lead and/or conduct a major international operation for an extended period; and . . . Deploy forces in response to crises elsewhere in the world for shorter periods.' It called for a strengthened military in part to secure 'a stronger voice for Canada on the world stage.'[7]

Canada has not always considered its interests rationally before dispatching troops abroad. The nation's expeditionary force history began with the sending of the Royal Canadian Regiment to the South African War in 1899. That small war in many ways set the pattern for the future. English-speaking Canadians favoured joining the conflict, eager to prove their martial ardour and political adulthood to the imperial government in London. French-speaking Canadians, on the other hand, correctly saw no threat to Canada from the Boer farmers who, to them, seemed to be just another minority oppressed by aggressive, imperialistic Anglos. The French-Canadian position was arguably the right one, but the majority prevailed, and Wilfrid Laurier, Canada's first francophone prime minister, succumbed to the public pressure from English-speaking Canada and sent troops. On the suggestion of the general officer commanding the Canadian militia, General Edward Hutton, and with the active support of the governor general, Lord Minto – both British and strongly Imperialistic – the government set a condition for the Canadian expedition: the Canadian contingent was to stay together, fight together, and be commanded by a Canadian-appointed officer. Canada had virtually no capacity to mount an expeditionary operation, but partially paid for transportation in Canada and overseas, and for some logistical support.

When Britain declared war on Germany on 4 August 1914, Canada was a British colony and thus also at war. The Great War saw Canada enlist some 620,000 men and suffer more than 200,000 casualties, including 60,000 killed. The Canadian Expeditionary Force, eventually forming the Canadian Corps of four divisions plus ancillary troops, proved to be a formidable machine that played a major role in the battles on the Western Front. This time too Canada entered the war with virtually no expeditionary capability, but the government of Robert Borden was so keen to back the war – as were the great majority of English-speaking Canadians – that a transportation and logistics system was virtually thrown together in the first months of the war to send troops overseas and to support them once there. The principle established in the Boer War of 'national command,' as an integral part of a national expeditionary capability, was also followed. These political or administrative command and support systems evolved considerably through the war.

The Great War divided Canadian society sharply. Once again, francophones, this time joined by many Canadians of other ethnicities and by many farmers and labour militants, saw the war as one for British imperial interests rather than for Canadian national interests. There was some substantial truth in this view, but arguably if the Allies had lost the war, Canada's financial and trading interests might have been ruinously affected. The freedom of the seas, maintained by the Royal Navy, was very important to Canada, even if most Canadians were largely unaware of this. And Canadians, living in a democracy, had much to fear from the possible triumph of Germanic *kultur*. But whatever Canada's interests, francophones did not perceive them and showed their disagreement by refusing to enlist. Likely no more than 25,000 French Canadians joined the Canadian Expeditionary Force voluntarily, and that, as well as low enlistment rates in some English-speaking parts

of the country, led to the imposition of conscription in 1917. A very divisive general election, fought on compulsory service in December of that
year, compounded the divisions in Canada.[8]

Nonetheless, by late 1916 and early 1917 a majority of Canadians
began to see the war as a Canadian war; Canada started the war as a
colony but – through mounting costs, effort, and sacrifice – was becoming an ally. Certainly the Borden government thought so. Borden was
determined to use Canada's expanding war effort to elevate Canada
from subordinate to equal status within the British Empire. At an
Imperial War Conference in London in March 1917, Resolution IX was
adopted by the prime ministers of Britain and all the self-governing
dominions, declaring the dominions to be 'autonomous nations' with
a right to 'an adequate voice in foreign policy.'[9] As one result, Borden
signed the Treaty of Versailles in 1919, which ended the war, while
Canada was offered a seat in the League of Nations. The Statute of
Westminster in 1931 made Canada's independence in foreign policy
a reality. Thus the Canadian Expeditionary Force helped to secure
Canada's independence.

After the Great War, most politicians took the view that Canada's
most important national interest was to stay out of wars abroad lest
national unity be imperilled. There were no credible threats to Canada,
no evident need for a military or naval force, and therefore Canadian
foreign policy should be one of no commitments. Canada's expeditionary capability, developed between 1914 and 1918, was allowed to dis-
appear. The Canadian military was not even allowed to contemplate
expeditionary capability until the last years of the 1930s.

There was more than symbolism involved in Canada's separate
declaration of war on 10 September 1939. The King government was
determined that the Canadian war effort be a distinctly Canadian one
and that Canada be seen by its citizens to be fighting as an ally, for
Canadian interests, and not as a colony. Subsequent efforts to ensure
at least the symbolic distinction of the army, navy, and air force from
the armed forces of the other Allied nations, flowed from there. Once
again, Canada would send its fighting personnel abroad in such a way
as to ensure that both Canadians and Canada's allies would recognize
the country's distinct national war effort and that Canada would secure
some part in determining the peace to follow so that Canada's interests
would be considered by its larger allies.

At first Canada's policy was to fight a war of limited liability.
Reluctantly, the Mackenzie King government agreed to dispatch a

one-division expeditionary force overseas in late 1939, preferring to make its major contribution through air training and the supply of natural resources. There was sullen acquiescence to this policy from Quebec, so long as there was no conscription. But once the war turned against Britain and France in the spring of 1940, the policy of limited liability largely disappeared, more troops were raised, more were sent overseas, and compulsory service for home defence, the first bite at the cherry of conscription as one general described it, came into force. French Canada produced substantially more volunteers than in the Great War, perhaps as many as 150,000 out of a total enlistment of 1.1 million men and women, but Quebec's strong antipathy to conscription remained with a heavily negative vote in the plebiscite of April 1942 and some riots and evasion when a limited form of overseas conscription had to be imposed in November 1944.

Without doubt, the threat to Canadian national interests in the Second World War was clearer than in the Great War. The Hitler and Tojo regimes in Germany and Japan posed a real threat to the survival of democracy and had the capacity to strike at North America, if not readily to invade it. U-boats threatened the freedom of the seas once more, and Canadian trade and finances again were in peril. The hundreds of thousands of soldiers, sailors, and airmen sent abroad to fight the war, along with Canada's extraordinary industrial and agricultural productivity, won the nation a voice in some Allied decision-making arenas. Mackenzie King sought no say in grand strategy, but his government, arguing for functionalism, aspired to a role in economic and political decision-making – and secured it. As in the Great War, the large expeditionary force gave Canada the right and the leverage to advance its positions.[10]

The returning veterans hoped to lead peaceful lives. But the Cold War pitting the Soviet Union and its satellites against the Western democracies led Canada to send its first-ever peacetime military forces abroad. A brigade group went to Korea in 1950–1 serving under the United Nations flag but in reality as part of an American-led coalition to resist Soviet–Chinese–North Korean expansionism. In 1951, a second brigade group went to Germany as part of the North Atlantic Treaty Organization's forces. This too was a response to Communist expansionism, and Canada participated for two main reasons: because Communism was deemed inimical to the democracies' way of life, and to retain and expand Canada's trade and economic links to Western Europe and the United States; in other words, to continue to be viewed as a good ally. Once again, therefore, Canadian troops went abroad to secure Canadian interests. Such defence of the national interest was costly: in the early 1950s, military spending absorbed more than 7 per cent of the GDP, as opposed to a little over 1 per cent today.

Canada also did its part for the UN, participating in literally dozens of peacekeeping missions. The most important – the United Nations Emergency Force, the UN Operation in Congo, the UN Forces in Cyprus – were part and parcel of the Cold War. Canada took the lead in the UN Emergency Force in 1956, for example, because the British-French-Israeli invasion of Egypt threatened to break up NATO, so strong was the American opposition to it. Canada went to the Congo to help keep a mineral-rich new nation out of Soviet clutches, and it sent troops to Cyprus to stop a Greek-Turkish war from destroying NATO's southern flank. In other words, the Canadian national interest in peace and security, and a strong West, were directly involved.[11] The Canadian public, however, saw only idealism at work, and politicians, seeing more votes in idealism than in discussing the national interest, did not try to alter this view.

Not that idealism and national interests were not involved in peace-keeping. Canadian troops went to the former Yugoslavia as part of the United Nations Protection Force in the early 1990s to help stop geno-cidal civil wars. Ottawa did this because fighting in Eastern Europe was disruptive in the post–Cold War world, because it served NATO and American purposes, and because genocide had to be stopped. At roughly the same time, Ottawa supported the first Gulf War because Iraq's dictator Saddam Hussein had invaded Kuwait without reason and had to be brought to heel. There was idealism there but also a will-ingness to respond to U.S. global leadership. Regrettably so run-down had the Canadian army become after years of budget and personnel cuts that the Canadian contribution was derisory. Substantial efforts after 2003 have only now begun to restore CF capabilities.

Expeditionary Operations and Canadian Influence

The historical evidence is undeniable: Canada's military serves Canada's national interests by defending Canada but that defence has almost always been mounted far away from Canada. It is also clear that after wars ended, Canadian governments – up to 1949 and the beginning of NATO – quickly disavowed any ambition to maintain an effective expe-·ditionary capability, because of the threat of another nationally divisive conscription crisis.

All of this changed after the outbreak of the Korean War and with the growing perception among NATO countries that the Soviet Union might launch a sudden invasion of Western Europe. These fears solidified in late 1950 in Ottawa, Washington, London, and other Western capitals – most of them in NATO countries – when it appeared that a Chinese offensive in Korea launched in late November might push the UN off the peninsula. This fear prompted NATO to plan a massive expansion of land, sea, and air forces in Europe; Canada's contribution to the mobilization was a brigade group and an air wing of up to twelve fighter squadrons to be permanently stationed in Europe. That brigade, pulled back to Canada beginning in 1992, stayed in place for some forty years. It remains the longest forward deployment of Canadian troops in peacetime.

From shortly after the Second World War ended, Canadian governments recognized that Canada's defence policy would address three key issues; the defence of Canada; the defence of North America; and mounting expeditions, as coalition partners, to support allies.[12] Thus, whether acknowledged or not by certain politicians, members of the media, or 'experts,' the CF must maintain a capacity to send troops abroad in a timely fashion to join with allies to meet or ease international crises. In future this will be a necessary tool of Canadian foreign policy to enhance its status internationally – particularly in Washington – as Canada's relative economic influence wanes compared to other industrialized or industrializing nations. At the moment the BRIC countries (Brazil, Russia, India, and China) have all surpassed Canada's GDP, or shortly will. South Africa, South Korea, Spain, and other countries are rising rapidly and are not now far behind. Canada is clinging to its place in the Group of Eight (G8) by its fingertips. Indeed it is not difficult to see a time soon when Canada's economy might not even qualify for an invitation to a Group of Twenty (G20) meeting.

What Canada does have – nurtured from 1899 in South Africa to today in Afghanistan – is a long experience of deploying expeditionary forces. Most G20 nations and even some G8 nations have only a minimal expeditionary capability, if they have any at all. Thus it is crucial that Canada recognize that maintaining a modern and effective expeditionary capability will continue to be a key to retaining our influence in the world – especially in Washington – and in NATO, and the UN (even if not in the G8) because many larger European states refuse to allow their troops to be used in combat. Canada's 2005 *International Policy Statement* got it right when it noted, 'By participating in . . . overseas operations ... the Canadian Forces will enhance Canada's status as a responsible and contributing member of the international community, including in key institutions such as the United Nations and the North Atlantic Treaty Organization.'[13] There are other ways to enhance Canadian influence, of course, but no one should underestimate the importance of the exemplary performance of the CF in building international regard.

Canadian expeditionary operations should be based on six fundamental principles:

1   Canadian 'hard power' should never be used without a defined political objective that the government and, to the extent possible, the public agrees with and that – if achieved – will serve Canadian interests. If 'war is the continuation of policy by other means,' and we believe that it is, then that policy needs to be clearly defined by our larger coalition partners or by us. We must not, we cannot, deploy elements of the CF merely to support chimerical aims or to serve the interests of others if our interests are not also served. The Canadian deployment to Somalia in 1992, for example, was arguably not in the national interest, stemming instead from emotion and media coverage. Canada went in without the appropriate resources and with no achievable political objectives.[14] That proved a mistake.

    Thus, the basic question that needs to be asked and answered before any Canadian expeditionary deployment is always it serves Canadian national interests. Interests are not always obvious, but a vigorous debate about them is always useful to provide clarity. This is a sine qua non of Canadian overseas participation.

2   That debate should take place in – but not exclusively in – Parliament and be authorized by a vote in the House of Commons. Extraordinarily, almost all post-1945 deployments abroad have occurred without this. The federal Cabinet can and does commit Canadian Forces to action abroad without parliamentary approval or consultation. All that is constitutionally required is an order-in-council.[15] The Chrétien government in 1994 began the practice of 'take note' debates, which let members of Parliament speak but gave them no chance to reject government plans. This device was used in the Kosovo War, in Operation Apollo (after al Qaeda's attack on the United States on 11 September 2001), and to send an infantry battalion to Afghanistan in 2002. In March 2006,

however, the Harper government put the matter of an extension of the Canadian commitment in Afghanistan until 2009 to a vote in Parliament. Another vote in 2008 extended the mission to 2011. Prime Minister Harper told ABC news on 10 August 2009, 'We require that military deployments in Canada be supported by the Parliament of Canada.'[16] This is the right way to proceed, another sine qua non. No substantial Canadian military force should ever be deployed without a prior vote of Parliament or a vote taken shortly after a decision to deploy has been made (in the event of an international emergency requiring a very quick response).

3 Once a decision has been made to deploy the Canadian Forces abroad, the terms of that deployment need to be negotiated with our allies (if, as is almost always likely to be the case, Canada is a part of a coalition). Since South Africa more than a century ago, Canada has insisted that its 'hard power' must be used within the parameters developed then: a recognizable Canadian contribution with fully formed units operating under Canadian command. That does not mean that the Canadian Forces should not acknowledge higher Allied authority in the field. It does mean that a Canadian commander in the last resort must be able to appeal a command decision of his military superior to Ottawa, an essential condition of nationhood.

4 Canada should not send forces abroad into combat operations or to missions likely to require combat without some firm commitment of support for the mission by the United States. Canada should look for political and diplomatic support at the very least, but should not deploy forces if fighting is imminent unless the United States also agrees to provide logistic and technical support. The United States is still the world's only superpower and the only one with a substantial global reach and a true multi-purpose capability. International combat action will not usually be undertaken without U.S. support anyway; it will almost certainly not succeed without it. But without the United States as a political backer; without its heavy air and sea lift, without U.S. tactical air power, Canada ought to demur. NATO intervention with the United States as a component? Yes. Without it? No.

The Afghan War has conclusively demonstrated that most NATO countries are unwilling or unready to fight. Just as Bosnia proved the UN's inability to successfully mount and lead a large and complex military operation in the early 1990s, so Afghanistan has proven the inability of NATO to successfully mount and lead a large and complex military operation today.[17] There is a lesson here for Canada. Unless Canadian troops serve again in variants of 'classical' Chapter VI UN peacekeeping – interventions by peacekeeping forces following ceasefires in well-defined state-to-state conflicts – Canadian troops should always have the communications, logistics, and tactical air support afforded by the U.S. military if not also command and control.

This should not frighten Canadians. The United States is and will remain Canada's most important trade and defence partner, and both countries, but especially Canada, require a border that is as open as possible. Moreover, Canada's national interests generally run parallel to those of the United States. 'Given our shared border, infrastructure and extensive bilateral trade,' noted the Department of Foreign Affairs in 2005, 'most of the new dangers to the United States are no less risks to Canada.'[18] Obviously, it serves Canadian interests to cooperate with Washington, and sometimes that will require the commitment of the Canadian military to operations abroad. The task for Canada is to find the ways to be a good friend to the superpower next door while preserving sufficient independence to also decline to participate in operations not deemed to serve Canadian interests. The test, as always, must be an assessment of the national interest.

5 The integrity of expeditionary Canadian forces under local Canadian command and with a political/administrative chain of command to the prime minister via the commander of the Canadian Expeditionary Force Command and the chief of the Defence Staff must be guaranteed by Canada's leading coalition partners. Canada should also make every effort to field forces that are fully interoperable with the leading coalition partners – the United States and NATO. Canada should not undertake expeditionary missions unless it is capable of at least making a significant contribution to supply and communications for its own forces and, to a lesser extent, to the larger operation (i.e., to pool resources such as heavy-air-lift or medium-lift helicopters).

6 The principle of 'Canadianization,' generated in the Second World War,[19] must apply to future Canadian expeditions: Canadians should aspire to send Canadian troops trained and equipped to the highest standards by Canada, transported by sea or air by Canada, and supported in the field by Canadian arms – artillery,

drones, and tactical air, for example. At times it may prove tactically impractical for Canadians to operate together. In Kandahar,
for example, Canada had a small air wing of six CH-47 Chinook
medium-lift helicopters, escorted on their missions by armed
Griffon helicopters. They do not always lift Canadians, nor do
Canadians rely exclusively on them for lift. But this air wing is part
of a much larger NATO pool of helicopter lift capability. Because
Canada has something tangible to contribute to that pool, Canadian
troops in Afghanistan had access to helicopters whenever they are
needed.

Conclusion: An Expeditionary Force Structure for Canada

What kind of expeditionary forces should Canada be prepared to send
abroad? The 1994 white paper declared that Canada should 'maintain
a multi-purpose, combat capable force.'[20] The 2005 *International Policy
Statement* repeated the mantra as did the *Canada First Defence Strategy*
of 2008. This oft-stated intent has sometimes been equated with field-
ing a military that can do everything, from fighting modern 'nation-
to-nation' wars against advanced industrialized countries (as in the
Second World War) to Chapter VI–style peacekeeping. But that has
never been the intent of post-war Canadian governments.

From the late 1940s on, the Canadian military has focused on some
missions and ignored others. By the 1950s Canada had not only given
up a heavy bomber role but medium bombers as well. Canada never
considered a nuclear military option, though it had the capability. The
post-war navy focused on anti-submarine warfare and largely aban-
doned the small integrated fleet concept pursued by many Royal
Canadian Navy commanders in the mid-1940s. Both political and budgetary realities came into play in those instances. They still do.

Canada's optimum expeditionary force structure should aim to build
a force for a variety of important missions from Chapter VI peacekeeping to small conventional wars. Canada's interests would not be served
by trying to design a future military capability that aimed to fill 'niches'
in the military capabilities of our allies. Canada is a very large nation in
land mass, with three ocean coastlines and a decided interest in maintaining an effective naval presence in North Atlantic and North Pacific
waters for tactical purposes alone, not to mention the need to act in
coalition with allied navies in politically sensitive sea lanes that are of
vital commercial importance to Canada. This is one reason why Canada

must maintain a modern navy, large and flexible enough to address its many requirements, from defence and sovereignty patrols in Canadian waters to anti-piracy missions.[21]

Similarly Canada's large land mass and strategic placement as a Pacific, Arctic, and North Atlantic power, which also forms the back porch of the United States, dictates the need for a multi-purpose air force. As for expeditionary capability, Canada's air force must maintain tactical helicopter lift to support at least one Canadian battalion group on off-shore deployments, medium-lift helicopters, escort helicopters, aerial drones, and tactical fighter support. Such a capability has already been outlined by the air force in its 2004 doctrinal manual *Strategic Vectors: The Air Force Transformation Vision.*[22] In accordance with principle 6 above, these aircraft ought to be flown, maintained, and supplied abroad by Canadians. The same applies to medium- and heavy-lift strategic transport as provided by the recently acquired C-17s and both new C-130Js and those C-130s still in Canadian service that can be upgraded.

For expeditionary purposes, we see no need for Canada to deploy its own Joint Surveillance and Target Attack Radar System (JSTAR) or Airborne Warning and Control System (AWACS) aircraft, though their operation in a theatre to which Canada might deploy might well be a go/no go condition. But the aircraft themselves are very expensive, will require highly trained crews operating them constantly to maintain their skills, and are useable primarily in combat or pre-combat environments. Canada must ensure that the equipment it buys is as multi-purpose as possible and that its utility will fall well within the range of missions the CF will be called upon to perform. Neither JSTARS nor AWACS aircraft fit within those parameters. They are not a capability that Canada can afford to purchase because they are not a capability that Canada will use very often.

The army ought to maintain one deployable light battalion on an emergency standby basis for immediate deployment by air. A mechanized battalion group (or battle group) should be ready to follow within ninety days. The air and sea lift required to transport the battle group should be on-call Canadian Forces assets. Other, heavier forces (for example, armoured units), ought to be capable of reaching a trouble spot within three to six months via chartered transport, air or sea, if CF assets are not sufficient. Canadian special forces – Joint Task Force 2 – and ready-to-deploy companies of the Canadian Special Operations Regiment should also be ready as needed, for air transport. Again,

Canadian aircraft and helicopters should be able to deploy with them on demand. Specially trained and equipped units such as the Disaster Assistance Response Team should be made fully air transportable and capable of reaching a trouble spot within seventy-two hours.

Today, largely as a result of the refurbishment and enlargement of the Canadian Forces that began in fiscal year 2005/6, and the hard lessons learned as to what is needed and how it must be used in mounting expeditionary deployments to Afghanistan, the CF is capable of meeting many of these requirements after the Afghanistan mission ends. The three major deficiencies are lack of sufficient numbers in the CF, both regulars and reservists, the virtually complete lack of sea transport capability, and the imminent rust-out of the Canadian blue-water fleet beginning with the Auxiliary Oiler and Replenishment vessels. The first concern would be addressed if the government, as promised, expands the CF to seventy-five thousand regulars and twenty-five thousand reservists. The second – the acquisition by purchase or lease of Canadian sea lift – should be a priority of any Canadian shipbuilding strategy. Canada does not need a large standing sea lift capacity, but it needs some. Even three 25,000-tonne transports could carry a battle group. As for the deep sea fleet, new fleet tankers with some on-board repair capability to service Canadian task group ships are an absolute must. What is not needed – and could prove a very expensive gamble – is to deploy equipment forward, as has sometimes been suggested. Canada has too small a military to consider this capability. If equipment was stored, for example, in the Middle East but Canadian troops were required in Haiti, the plan would prove to be a complete waste.

The greatest challenge to maintaining Canadian expeditionary capability of any type will be political. It has been historically true that after significant overseas deployments, the Canadian military has been cut back, sometimes to the bone. The danger is thus great that the Canadian government that oversees Canada's withdrawal from Afghanistan – whichever government that is and whenever that is – will declare yet another peace dividend and, instead of maintaining a viable expeditionary capability, usher in yet another 'decade of darkness.' The years since the Second World War have proven countless times that both Liberal and Conservative government have presided over fat years and lean years for Canadian defence. Thus future Canadian expeditionary capability will be determined less by need than by the political winds of the day.

NOTES

1 Ipsos Poll, 15 Oct. 2001; Ipsos-Reid / Globe and Mail / CTV Poll, 13 Jan. 2002; Ipsos-Reid / Globe and Mail / CTV Poll, 31 Jan. 2002.
2 For example, see Adam Radwanski, 'Selling Afghanistan,' *Globe and Mail,* blogpost, http://www.theglobeandmail.com/news/politics/second-reading/radwanski/selling-afghanistan/article1243834/.
3 See Eric Morse, 'Chasing Myths: Soft Power in a Hard World,' *On Track* 14, no. 1 (Spring 2009): 47–9; Ipsos-Reid Public Affairs, 'Views of Canadian Forces,' 2008.
4 Canada, Department of National Defence, *Canada's International Policy Statement: A Role of Pride and Influence in the World – Defence* (Ottawa: DND, 2005).
5 Canada, Department of National Defence, *1994 White Paper on Defence* (Ottawa: DND, 1994), 12.
6 Canada, Department of National Defence, *Challenge and Commitment: A Defence Policy for Canada* (Ottawa: DND, 1987), 21.
7 Canada, Department of National Defence, *Canada First Defence Strategy* (Ottawa: DND, 2008), 3 and 4.
8 See J.L. Granatstein and J.M. Hitsman, *Broken Promises: A History of Conscription in Canada* (Toronto: Oxford University Press, 1977).
9 Qtd in Norman Hillmer and J.L. Granatstein, *Empire to Umpire: Canada and the World into the Twenty-First Century* (Toronto: Thomson Nelson, 2008), 57.
10 J.L. Granatstein, *Canada's War: The Politics of the Mackenzie King Government, 1939–45* (Toronto: Oxford University Press, 1975).
11 See, generally, Sean Maloney, *Canada and UN Peacekeeping: Cold War by Other Means, 1945–1970* (Toronto: Vanwell Publishing, 2002).
12 Minister of National Defence Brooke Claxton first officially defined these principles in July 1947. David Bercuson, *True Patriot: The Life of Brooke Claxton, 1898–1960* (Toronto, University of Toronto Press, 1993), 176.
13 DND, *Canada's International Policy Statement – Defence.*
14 Bernd Horn, ed., *The Canadian Way of War* (Toronto: Dundurn, 2006), 316.
15 M. Dewing and C. McDonald, 'International Deployment of Canadian Forces: Parliament's Role,' 18 May 2006, http://www.parl.gc.ca/Content/LOP/ResearchPublications/prb0006-e.htm.
16 Jake Tapper interview with Prime Minister Harper, ABC News, 10 Aug. 2009.
17 A very good in-depth study of the issues that began to beset NATO missions after the Cold War is Wesley K. Clark, *Waging Modern War: Bosnia, Kosovo and the Future of Combat* (Cambridge, MA: Perseus Books, 2001).

18 DND, *Canada's International Policy Statement – Diplomacy.*
19 For a summary of the struggle to 'Canadianize' the war effort, see C.P. Stacey, *Arms, Men and Governments: The War Policies of Canada, 1939–1945* (Ottawa: Queen's Printer, 1970), pt 5.
20 DND, *1994 White Paper on Defence*, 11.
21 David Hudock, 'The Canadian Navy and the 21st Century Global Battlespace,' *Naval Forces, International Forum for Maritime Power* 28 (2007): 16–20.
22 Canada, Department of National Defence, *Strategic Vectors: The Air Force Transformation Vision* (Ottawa: Director General Air Force Development, 2004), 41.

11 Stabilization Operations in Afghanistan and in the Future: The Need for a Strategic Canadian Approach

ANN M. FITZ-GERALD

Since its 2005 troop deployment to Afghanistan's Kandahar province, Canada has demonstrated its commitment to servicing stabilization interventions and furthering the stabilization debate, both at the bilateral level and within the multilateral and regional security organizations it supports. While this has resulted new structures and department-specific reforms, Canada could go further in developing a clearer strategic direction on its future approach to stabilization interventions. On the basis of the way in which the Harper government has appealed to its public for continued support in Afghanistan and a presence that takes it beyond its original withdrawal date of February 2009, it appears that the government has made some arguments that link its activities in Afghanistan with the country's national interests and values that the public would wish to see protected and defended. There is an opportunity to build on these policy efforts and develop a clear and coherent strategy supporting a 'whole-of-government' approach to stabilization operations in the future.

This chapter will examine the current discourse on stabilization and assess Canada's contribution to the evolving debate. It will then discuss the need for strategic clarity supporting stabilization as a 'joined-up' policy area that could harmonize a range of existing instability-related policy initiatives. Lastly, it will look at the capacity and strategy gaps across the executive and Cabinet levels of the Canadian government that require either sustained innovation and development, or serious reform.

Background

Stabilization operations has become an all-encompassing term used to describe a wide spectrum of security activities in post-conflict interventions – these activities are meant to *stabilize* the country and thereby create the necessary foundations for nation-building. A number of donor countries have developed their own approaches to stabilization, with some countries, primarily the United States and the United Kingdom, even developing cross-governmental (or 'joint') doctrine and guidelines supporting the concept.

Over the past seven years, a number of bilateral efforts have illustrated a firm structural and institutional commitment by the Canadian government to stabilization operations. In September 2005, the government developed the Stabilization and Reconstruction Task Force (START), an interdepartmental body housed in the Department of Foreign Affairs and International Trade (DFAIT) that attempts to coordinate and implement activities of the 3-D (defence, development, and diplomacy) approach of the government.[1] START serves as the first real cross-government operational response team for wider peace operations.

In 2004, in the wake of the reconstruction debacle in Iraq and based on a decision by the Bush administration to supplement the traditional approaches to peace-building and complex emergencies, the National Security Council Principal's Committee approved the creation of a Stabilization and Reconstruction Office for the U.S. government.[2] Despite much debate over the location of the office, in the end a decision was made to house the new team in the State Department as the key implementing instrument for the secretary of state's new mandate to lead the inter-agency process for post-conflict reconstruction.[3] This mandate was formalized in 2005 under the National Security Presidential Directive 44.

Also in 2005, the U.K. government pursued similar efforts to bolster its capacity to provide improved cross-government planning and operational support for stabilization. On 7 December 2007, the Post-Conflict Reconstruction Unit changed its name to the Stabilisation Unit to better reflect the core work of the unit in stabilization and also the unit's role in the management of the U.K. Ministry of Defence's £269 million Stabilisation Aid fund announced as part of the government's Comprehensive Spending Review in September 2007.[4]

In addition to the growing stabilization discourse evolving in a number of other European countries, particularly in the Netherlands and Scandinavian countries, the discussion has also enjoyed significant debate in multilateral organizations, including the North Atlantic Treaty Organization (NATO), the United Nations, and the African Union.

Across these bilateral and multilateral actors, both the U.K. and the U.S. governments have endeavoured to offer more concise definitions, doctrine, and concepts supporting stabilization operations. While the terminology and the fundamentals underpinning stabilization are complementary between the two countries, the focus of each is slightly different. Each national approach makes the link between the requirement for stabilization interventions in places where host governments are weak or have lost the capacity to govern effectively, thus stressing the threat posed by instability and fragility.[5] As a result, some analysts have observed that those conducting such operations must often assume, at least temporarily, many roles of the state while simultaneously trying to rebuild that capacity.[6]

The U.K. government's Stabilisation Unit defines stabilization as 'the process by which underlying tensions that might lead to resurgence in violence and a break-down in law and order are managed and reduced, whilst efforts are made to support preconditions for successful longer-term development.' Stabilization, as the unit's *Guidance Note* continues, 'is a summary term for the complex processes that have to be undertaken in countries experiencing, or emerging from, violent conflict to achieve peace and security and a political settlement that leads to legitimate government.'[7] A second U.K. definition is provided in the *Joint Doctrine Publication 3-40*, which defines stabilization as 'the process that supports states which are entering, enduring or emerging from conflict, in order to prevent or reduce violence; protect the population and key infrastructure; promote political processes and governance structures which lead to a political settlement that institutionalises non-violent contests for power; and prepares for sustainable social and economic development.'[8]

Embraced by the 2008 U.S. doctrinal publication *Field Manual 3-07 Stability Operations*, the American definition of *stabilization* – or 'stability' – operations is that it is 'an overarching term encompassing various military missions, tasks, and activities conducted outside the United States in coordination with other instruments of national power to maintain or re-establish a safe and secure environment, provide essential governmental services, emergency infrastructure reconstruction, and humanitarian relief.'[9]

The American think tank RAND defines stabilization as

the effort to end conflict and social, economic, and political upheaval. . . . Stabilization, thus defined, is one component of a wide range of possible operations ... stabilization can be carried out as part of an intervention. Indeed, it can be the express purpose of an intervention to end violence. It is also crucial in the aftermath of combat operations, which may have intentionally or unintentionally helped spur additional conflict. Stabilization is also an accepted component of counterinsurgency operations because efforts to gain local support, which are so central to counterinsurgency, generally require ending violence and upheaval. Counterterrorism operations may also include a stabilization component.[10]

Lastly, a more recent definition was published in 2009 by the Netherlands Institute of International Relations Clingendael, which states that

stabilisation operations are military missions that are aimed at creating stability in a certain area, stability meaning a stable, safe society with no place for insurgents, terrorists, and other safety-undermining elements. A specific feature of stabilisation operations is that they incorporate a certain level of violence due to resistance to the stabilisation forces by (irregular) combatants or insurgents. It is this violent character that amounts to the difference between stabilisation operations and the real peace operations based on peacekeeping although the difference between stabilisation operations and peace enforcing operations is less clear.[11]

While Canada has yet to develop its own definition of stabilization operations, the custodian of stabilization, START, is much 'in tune' with the evolutionary approaches being pursued by its American, British, and Dutch counterparts. At the time of writing, Canada has sent a limited number of staff to both the British and American training initiatives and plans to use this experience to inform its own training requirements and capacity needs. However, the START team has gained many plaudits for the cross-government coordination experiences it has led on, including its response to the 2010 Haiti earthquakes.[12]

Each of the above definitions emphasizes a more comprehensive approach to addressing the short-term security needs and the longer-term development requirements. Thus, one could argue that the stabilization concept goes some way to addressing the operationalization of the security-development agenda – an issue that many critics have argued represents a major challenge to whole-of-government approaches to addressing fragile states and countries emerging from conflict. Beyond tackling violence, the existing definitions also underscore the key pillars of a much wider state-building agenda that go beyond institutional support and include economic development and efforts to promote good governance across society. This common aspect of each definition also recognizes that security-sector reform, which traditionally takes place in relatively benign environments, can also occur in parallel with 'sharp end' security activities. Lastly, linkages made between stabilization and wider foreign policy objectives such as counterterrorism or humanitarianism – and the subsequent coordination of a number of instruments of power – suggests that stabilization as a whole-of-government agenda should be treated as an instrument that supports macro-level policy goals.

'Stabilization' and the Lack of Strategic Clarity

Beyond the wealth of definitions, as a result of the wide range of activities and communities involved in stabilization, a number of different interpretations develop, depending on the prism through which each community views the concept. For example, the humanitarian community and more conventional development communities tend to view stabilization as 'early recovery' activities, while the military often links stabilization with counter-insurgency operations.[13] In the current era of emerging policy debates on 'state-building' and 'peace-building,' it is also the case that diplomatic communities interested primarily in political settlements and peace agreements will approach stabilization from a state-building focus, which prioritizes institutional development. Not surprisingly, the humanitarian and development communities, which are more concerned with the 'grass roots' elements of a stabilization intervention, tend to align themselves with the peace-building agenda. The interest of these communities is often geared towards issues such as the structural causes of conflict, rural livelihoods, and participation. In a recent evaluation of Canada's development contribution in Afghanistan, the Canadian International Development Agency (CIDA) refers to one of its key programs as the 'Afghanistan Stabilization Program,' but emphasizes its focus on rural livelihoods, basic service provisions, and increased standards of living.[14] These activities contrast with the focus of capacity-building of security institutions such as new armies, police forces, and the requisite mentoring support to relevant government ministries. These differences in the interpretation of the concept have implications for improved cross-government efforts at stabilization.

The background provided above underscores the level of intellectual energy and policy efforts needed to develop the stabilization concept and evolve the debate on the future of stabilization operations. It also illustrates that, although much has been done to further efforts at the bilateral and multilateral levels, the term still lacks strategic clarity because of the different perspectives a wide range of contributing stakeholder groups bring to stabilization. Notwithstanding these different levels of interpretation and understanding, and the divided allegiance shown between the state-building and peace-building agendas, questions have also been raised about the degree to which stabilization has been developed as a strategic policy instrument for national governments.

Most donor governments contributing to stabilization interventions have called for more integrated approaches to planning and implementation. As the 2007 *Report of the Independent Panel on the Future of Canada's Role in Afghanistan* – also known as the 'Manley Report,' which takes the name of the chair of the independent panel, John Manley – emphasized from a Canadian perspective, there is also a need for stabilization deployments regarded as national priorities to be led and coordinated by executive offices in national capitals and 'serious political authorities' locally.[15] Not surprisingly, following the publication of the Manley Report and in line with its recommendations, a decision was taken by the Canadian government to appoint a senior civilian representative in Kandahar (in addition to Canada's ambassador in Kabul) and to create a Cabinet Committee on Afghanistan. These efforts reflect similar mechanisms developed by the governments of other major donor countries contributing in Afghanistan, including the British government, which has created a Senior Officials Group on Afghanistan (which meets at Cabinet level) and appointed a senior Foreign Office civilian representative as head of its operations in Helmand province.

In addition to rethinking the seniority levels of key personnel supporting stabilization priorities, both in theatres and in national capitals, a more elevated discussion on stabilization should also be reflected in executive-level strategy documents and policy papers, such as those addressing national security. Interestingly, the national security framework documents of most nations contributing to stabilization in Afghanistan make infrequent (if any) and scant references to 'stabilization operations' and are devoid of specifics about the environments to and circumstances under which stabilization operations may be initiated as a whole-of-government policy instrument. Furthermore, many of the national contributors in Afghanistan are also committed to the Fragile States agenda, which has been led by the Development Assistance Committee (DAC) and which has generated a life of its own among leading development actors, including Canada. In fact, Canada's 2004 *National Security Policy* makes no mention of stabilization but includes a few general statements about supporting failed and failing states.[16] One could also argue a similar view in terms of the ever-growing security-sector reform debate – to which (similar to the Fragile States agenda) Development Assistance Committee members, including Canada, have firmly signed up.

In addition to the different policy discourse in support of failed and failing states, a number of United Nations member states, including Canada, have made significant efforts to promote the 'Responsibility to Protect' (R2P) campaign – a policy agenda underwritten by international humanitarian law. An August 2008 Stanley Foundation international policy brief quotes Kofi Annan, former UN secretary-general, on his successful January–February 2008 efforts to mediate the post-election crisis in Kenya: 'I saw the crisis in the R2P prism with a Kenyan government unable to contain the situation or protect its people. ... The problem is when we say "intervention," people think military, when in fact that's a last resort. Kenya is a successful example of R2P at work.'[17] The report clearly highlights the R2P policy agenda as, in this case, what mobilized stakeholders to come together to contend with the high levels of instability in Kenya.

Policy agendas such as R2P help illuminate the linkage between shared national interests and universal values such as the protection of human rights, social justice, and rule of law. The example of the post-election Kenyan intervention could also describe a present-day stabilization intervention, but one that several UN member states may rationalize as their diplomatic, development, or defence contributions based on the impact on the national interests and core values, which form the pillars of the R2P policy discourse. As an active member of both the OECD's Development Assistance Committee and the United Nations, Canada remains firmly committed to many different policy agendas relating to 'instability' and could therefore employ the services of a cross-government stabilization policy instrument.

The lack of strategic clarity supporting stabilization interventions could be explained by three dynamics. Firstly, the lack of harmonization across a wide range of the policy agenda on countries at risk of instability; secondly, the fact that the discourse on stabilization is still less than a decade old and is therefore not yet sufficiently mature as a policy agenda to significantly influence macro-strategic policy documents; lastly, due to the level of resources commanded by interventions in countries such as Sudan, Iraq, and Afghanistan, there is a risk that stabilization efforts will become (and arguably already have been) 'hijacked' by the post-conflict experience. It is critical for donor states leading stabilization operations to be prepared to respond to a range of instabilities – whether a Rwanda-like genocide (1994), serious economic vulnerabilities as witnessed during Mexico's economic crisis (1994), natural disasters in Montserrat (1997), Indonesia (2006), or Haiti (2010), or supporting more professional, adequate, and appropriate security forces in Afghanistan (2006–11). Each serves as an environment to which, depending on the national interests affected, a type of stabilization response could be activated.

Widening the stabilization debate, and harmonizing the range of agenda that may fall under this area, is an exercise required to promote improved whole-of-government approaches to existing and future stabilization interventions. Of course, this harmonization exercise will differ among donor states and will depend on larger issues such as national values and interests and the way in which each country aspires to promote, protect, defend, and pursue those national interests – at home and abroad.

Although Canada has not led on the development of definitions and doctrine supporting stabilization, it has demonstrated laudable efforts to draw linkages between its support to stabilization operations in Afghanistan and its own national interests and priorities laid out in the 2004 *National Security Policy*. This effective level of strategic policy communication has provided consistency across key statements and speeches delivered by Prime Minister Harper and a range of other key Cabinet ministers. The approach has also earned the Canadian government increased support and hardened resilience across a domestic public that maintains deep concern over the limitless nature of the Afghanistan intervention, the high number of Canadian casualties (the highest per capita rate among all contributing NATO nations),[18] and the global economic recession. This level of public support has conditioned the political enabling space for Canada to not abandon its efforts and continue to build much-needed capacity within key institutions such as the Afghan National Army and the Afghan National Police.

Beyond Policy: Strategy and Institutional Commitment

However, the expression of strategic national interests and the linkages to Canada's support in Afghanistan will not, on their own, provide the strategic direction necessary to sustain accountability to the public and the cast of local actors. The clear identification of strategic priorities must continue to cascade both downwards – in order to inform 'joined-up' strategies – and laterally, in order to inform more individual departmental strategies. Whereas Canada appears to be well-served in policy statements, the same cannot be said for the clear articulation of the means and ends supporting policy. This illuminates the distinction between policy and strategy, as well as the mutually reinforcing nature of the two concepts, in order to enable policy to move beyond an academic discussion. Indeed, one could argue that clearly articulated means and ends may not have steered the Canadian government towards the initial February 2009 troop withdrawal date from Afghanistan – the questionable operational logic for which was underscored in the 2007 Manley Report.[19] One could argue that this reflects the government's adherence to policy (the 'what' and the 'why'), but without the means and ways (the who, where, how, and when) to guide progress.

As Colonel Craig Hilton highlights, Canada's policy declarations must be backed by choices and prioritization – decisions that, as he describes, 'will go far toward answering the question most frequently asked and most difficult to answer – why a particular course of action?' As Hilton goes on to note, 'In the future, such public documents must be regarded as indispensable keys to gaining Canadian domestic support, and therefore national unity of effort, in a complex and uncertain world.'[20]

Such firm and resolute direction could also go some way to achieve what Prime Minister Harper has described: '[The] objective is to make Canada [a] leader on the international stage ... in a shrinking, changing, dangerous world, our government must play a role in the world. And I believe that Canadians want a significant role – a clear, confident, and influential role. As proud citizens, they don't want a Canada that just goes along; they want a Canada that leads. They want a Canada that doesn't just criticize, but one that can contribute. They want a Canada that reflects their values and interests, and that punches above its weight.'[21]

Defining means and ends requires an executive-level strategy but also a firm commitment to strategy development supporting stabilization interventions at the ministerial level of government. Canada's Privy Council Office must reassume 'custodianship' of the 2004 *National Security Policy* and initiate a national security strategy development exercise that prioritizes across the pillars set out in the policy – particularly during the current global economic recession, which demands that all donor states make hard choices about a number of national security policy goals.

Bridging what Colonel Hilton refers to as Canada's 'strategy gap' also demands serious institutional reform in Ottawa. The 3-D and whole-of-government concept, the achievement of which Canada has long prided itself, have yet to be fully operationalized. The most capable planners must no longer only sit within the corridors of the Department of National Defence. Strategic capacity is required for each whole-of-government contributor. This is critical for supporting the harmonization of a strategic whole-of-government agenda such as stabilization – or whatever label the Canadian government may choose to refer to the stabilization agenda in the future.

Despite criticism that the two non-defence 3-D pillars 'have largely lost their way,'[22] progress towards institutional change and strategy development in support of stabilization is already underway. At the time of writing, Canada's former top civilian diplomat in Kandahar, Elissa Goldberg, has returned to Ottawa to assume leadership of the DFAIT-led START. Under Goldberg's leadership, START has taken an assiduous and measured approach to consolidating cross-government corporate knowledge on stabilization. These efforts have also included a significant commitment to improving programmatic coherency and devolving more project responsibility to theatre.[23] The 'learning by experience' approach being taken by START also places emphasis on consolidating the right people to take forward future approaches to stabilization.

The DFAIT-led efforts by START have also prioritized human resource development – arguably the most important variable that continues to undermine local 3-D approaches. These efforts include consolidating expert rosters (including the extensive CANADEM[24] database) to identify 'tiers' of essential intervention expertise. Recently returned START operatives also provide regular briefings to others based on their experience. Beyond these personal and professional development tactics, more formal and structural efforts have been taken to develop job 'packages' for key potential senior and middle-management recruits, which includes time and space for experiences to be socialized in order to enhance a short-term 'backfill' capacity for those returning for rest and recovery.[25]

The progress described above will go some way to developing the civilian deployable capacity required to achieve whole-of-government stabilization. However, the level of required staffing should not be underestimated. Indeed, the socialization initiated by START should extend to staff secondments to the Canadian Forces College in Toronto, and other similar mechanisms that bring together a wider cross-section of deployable communities and provide both formal and informal space for discussing challenges related to deployable staff. Such socialization strategies should also be aligned with education and training that supports staff development. START should consider initiating stabilization training similar to what has been recently developed by the U.K., which has involved the development of two mandatory 'modules' (1 and 2), with the first module focused on initiating stabilization planning and the second focused on in-theatre planning. The participants who attend these courses include representatives from the Stabilisation Unit's roster of experts, and cross-government representatives who, having completed the modules, will form part of the U.K. government's thousand-strong civil service cadre. It is hoped that this DFAIT-led momentum supporting stabilization will not only feed upward into a wider national security strategy formulation exercise but also develop strategically at the Cabinet level to provide more strategic clarity to the concept of stabilization and harmonize the wide range of 'instability-related' policy agendas.

Beyond the defence and diplomacy pillars of 3-D sits the development instrument of power, which many have acknowledged is an area of much-needed reform. Over the years, CIDA has served as an international development agency that was formed by an act of Parliament (the International Development Act) and committed to multilateral principles supporting overseas aid (e.g., official development assistance). As with its counterparts elsewhere, CIDA has evolved as a reasonably independent agency that prioritizes support to its multilateral partners as opposed to supporting Canadian national interests. By moving away from a less conventional development paradigm to a more security-related development focus – one that recognizes that the majority of poverty-stricken and underdeveloped countries are emerging from conflict – CIDA could build an ethos more conducive to supporting cross-government stabilization planning. Such planning could expose the environments and circumstances in which CIDA may contribute, or even lead, in future stabilization activities, and help inform ways in which development could be a core instrument of national power in the future. One could argue that a clear strategic commitment to Afghanistan over the next five to ten years may, at some stage, involve a development rather than a military lead.

But encouraging development to become a like-minded player supporting whole-of-government stabilization will also require a less 'passive' and more 'active' approach to funding overseas aid. While the author acknowledges the limited capacity for development agencies worldwide to support direct implementation, CIDA could engage in more 'direct enabling' and coordination. More direct enabling would not deem it necessary to route 80 per cent of its funding for countries like Afghanistan through multilateral organizations like the World Bank and the UN Development Program,[26] unless perhaps a reasonable argument can be made that multilateral organizations can lead Canada's development efforts (and part of Canada's diplomatic efforts) locally more effectively than anything that can be offered bilaterally. With such a high proportion of funding in Afghanistan being channelled towards multilateral institutions, one could question the potential negative impact that this large element of multilateral bureaucracy could have on Canada's overall strategic approach to stabilization in Afghanistan, not to mention the impact felt from having a development strategy bereft of Canadian ownership.

Critics have recently described CIDA as a 'poorly run organisation . . . contributing to a mission which is heavy on combat and light on reconstruction.'[27] Other analysts such as the University of Ottawa law professor Amir Attaran and NDP foreign affairs critic Alexa McDonough state that a distinct tracking of Canadian cash through CIDA is required.[28] Auditing and the tracking of funds were also exposed in a 2007 Senate report that unveiled frightening details of the proportion of the initially disbursed Canadian aid funding that ends up in the possession of local authorities.[29] Perhaps Canada should revisit what it regards as its core competencies in support of development priorities in the 2004 *National Security Policy*. On completion, if Canada still feels that the development contribution to stabilization operations requires a multilateral lead and the expertise of those institutions, then hard decisions should be made about the contribution Canada makes to improving the effectiveness of these institutions and the risks of outsourcing its development capacity to the multilaterals. This would have serious implications for the way in which CIDA may be downsized to fill a support role in areas such as monitoring and evaluation and liaison roles supporting the national and multilateral interface.

The questions surrounding CIDA's ability to act strategically and actively to reinforce the international security element of (and thereby the means and ends that help to underpin) Canada's *National Security Policy* need to be clarified. This would add lucidity to what Stephen Saideman recently described as the 'multilateralism which is in the Canadian blood as a result of its history, its relatively small population and its geographical situation.'[30] Promoting stability across regions of strategic importance to Canada will require a more harmonized approach to stabilization as well as a stabilization concept that suits Canada. While this chapter has argued that both the defence and diplomatic pillars have gone some way in developing the debate and the practice, these efforts must include a significant multinational element in order to further harmonize approaches across the wider international community. This is not to say that primacy should be given to multilateral organizations such as the World Bank and the UN, but that a multinational approach of 'like-minded' coalitions should be taken.

The government of Canada should undertake a national security-strategy formulation. This would fill a void at the macro-strategic level of government that – if addressed – could usefully inform the policies and strategies of individual departments and ensure more effective approaches to a cross-government security agenda, including stabilisation. Furthermore, this would help inform priorities across the country's wide international stakeholder group and help identify the 'means' to support stabilization as, on its own, each individual donor country can offer no more than a 'light footprint' in strategic effect. Even now at the time of writing, with many troops having already served multiple rotations in Afghanistan and the high number of casualties incurred, a multinational comprehensive approach to stabilization could bring together a group of primary allies to share the burden across both military and civilian contributions. This would not necessitate a Canadian withdrawal from Afghanistan, as Canada would remain firmly committed to meeting its obligations within a wider Afghanistan strategy – one that would not involve a linear rotation of national troop donations (and arguably ongoing national 'abandonment') but one that could bring like-minded countries into areas where they could achieve the best collective effect. Such an approach would also ensure that

Canada's multi-year effort thus far would not become overshadowed or undermined.

Conclusion

Its deployment in Afghanistan notwithstanding, Canada has been engaged in stabilization interventions of many different guises for many years. The more recent experience in Kandahar has only further enriched Canada's stabilization capacity and has encouraged the development of cross-government mechanisms such as START to become the driving force behind the evolution of Canada's future approach to stabilization. While the development of stabilization terminology, concepts, and doctrine has been led by a number of Canada's primary allies, Canada has not underestimated how its local stabilization efforts become directly linked with the national values and interests enshrined in its *National Security Policy*, and the measures it must take in countries like Afghanistan to pursue, promote, and defend these interests.

However, despite the availability of reasonably coherent strategic policy documents and effective strategic policy communication in arguing for a continued and bolstered presence in Afghanistan, this chapter has highlighted the missing elements of strategy that must enable policy to be taken forward. Not only does this necessitate decisions to be taken on preferred policy directions – and on means and ends required to achieve the prioritized goals – but also on the question of strategic plans across each 3-D player that help make Canada's whole-of-government approach a reality. Encouraging strategy to unfold more coherently at both the executive and Cabinet levels of government will require clarity on Canada's approach to stabilization – clarity that will cut across divisive cross-government cultures and harmonize the many different instability-related policy agendas to which Canada subscribes.

A Canadian concept for stabilization must be both whole-of-government and multinational. This concept would require a hard look at the way in which Canada uses the 'development' element of the 3-D concept. It would also rely on the continued DFAIT-led efforts to create an environment conducive to greater levels of civilian deployability.

NOTES

1 While the Canadian cross-government debate on wider security interventions began with the '3-D' reference, Canada also uses the Organisation for

Economic Cooperation and Development's (OECD) language of 'whole-of-government approaches.' Discussion with Canadian government representatives dating back to 2006 confirmed a preference for the term *whole-of-government* rather than 3-D. This has been justified even on the basis of Canada's ongoing experience in Haiti, which has involved prison officers, health officials, and government representation extending beyond 3-D.

2 Dane Smith Jr, *An Expanded Mandate for Peace Building: The State Department Role in Peace Diplomacy, Reconstruction, and Stabilisation* (Washington, DC: Center for Strategic and International Studies, 2009), 18.

3 Ibid.

4 See the UK Government Stabilisation Unit website at http://www.stabilisa tionunit.gov.uk.

5 Stephanie Blair and Ann Fitz-Gerald, 'Stabilisation and Stability Operations: A Literature Review,' research paper submitted to the UK Defence Academy Directed Research Program, 14 July 2009, 3.

6 Nora Bensahel, Olga Oliker, and Heather Peterson, *Improving Capacity for Stabilisation and Reconstruction Operations* (Washington, DC: RAND, 2009), 13.

7 United Kingdom, Stabilisation Unit, *Stabilisation: UK Experience and Emerging Best Practice,* Stabilisation Unit Guidance Note, Nov. 2008, 2, http://www.stabilisationunit.gov.uk/resources/Stabilisation_guide.pdf.

8 United Kingdom, Joint Doctrine Publication 3-40, *Security and Stabilisation: The Military Contribution,* AH Working Draft, 31 Jan. 2009.

9 The U.S. Army's Peacekeeping and Stability Operations Institute uses concepts from U.S. Army Field Manual 3-07 *Stability Operations,* Oct. 2008, Glossary-9.

10 Bensahel, Oliker, and Peterson, *Improving Capacity,* 3.

11 Sico van den Meer, 'Factors for the Success or Failure of Stabilisation Operations,' Clingedael Security Paper no. 11 (Netherlands Institute of International Relations Clingendael, May 2009), 2.

12 John Geddes, 'Yes, We Have a Plan: Canada's Speedy Response to the Haiti Crisis Was No Accident,' *Maclean's.ca,* 4 Feb. 2010, http://www2.macleans. ca/2010/02/08/yes-we-have-a-plan/.

13 Stephanie Blair and Ann Fitz-Gerald, 'Stabilisation and Stability Operations: Addressing the Lack of Conceptual Clarity,' *Journal of Intervention and Statebuilding,* forthcoming.

14 *Review of the Afghanistan Program,* OECD Development Assistance Committee's Evaluation Division – Performance and Knowledge Management Branch, May 2007, 39, http://www.oecd.org/dataoecd/ 49/63/39591223.pdf.

15 Canada, *Report of the Independent Panel on Canada's Future Role in Afghanistan* (Ottawa: Government of Canada, May 2007), 20.

16 Canada, Privy Council Office, *Securing an Open Society: Canada's National Security Policy* (Ottawa: Privy Council Office, 2004).

17 Roger Cohen, 'How Kofi Annan Rescued Kenya,' *New York Review of Books*, 14 Aug. 2008, 13, qtd in Edward C. Luck, 'The United Nations and the Responsibility to Protect,' Policy Analysis Brief, Stanley Foundation, Mar. 2008, http://www.stanleyfoundation.org/publications/pab/LuckPAB808.pdf.

18 Lewis MacKenzie, 'Canada Will Not Abandon Afghanistan,' *Globe and Mail*, 17 Aug. 2009, http://www.theglobeandmail.com/news/opinions/canada-will-not-abandon-afghanistan/article1249819/.

19 Canada, *Report of the Independent Panel*, 30.

20 Craig Hilton, 'Shaping Commitment: Canada's Strategy Gap in Afghanistan and Beyond,' Carlisle Paper in Security Strategy, Security Studies Institute, US Army War College, July 2007, 10.

21 Stephen Harper, 'Reviving Canadian Leadership in the World,' speech to the Woodrow Wilson International Centre for Scholars, Calgary, 5 Oct. 2006, qtd in ibid., 6.

22 Hilton, 'Shaping Commitment,' 9.

23 Based on discussions with members of the START, 28 May 2009, Ottawa.

24 CANADEM is an acronym used for the International Civilian Reserve. Established in 1997 with start-up funding from the Canadian government, CANADEM is a non-profit non-governmental organization whose purpose is to bolster peace, order, and good governance efforts worldwide. See http://www.canadem.ca.

25 Ibid.

26 Such was the case at the time of the OECD Review of the Afghanistan Program in May 2007.

27 'Prof Calls for Audit of Aid Money to Afghanistan,' Canadian Press, 10 Jan. 2007.

28 Ibid.

29 Canada, Senate Committee on Foreign Affairs and International Trade, *Overcoming 40 Years of Failure: A New Road Map for Sub-Saharan Africa*, February 2007, http://www.parl.gc.ca/Content/SEN/Committee/391/fore/rep/repafrifeb07-e.pdf.

30 Stephen Saideman, 'The Afghan Pullout Reconsidered,' *Globe and Mail*, 21 Aug. 2009, http://www.theglobeandmail.com/news/opinions/the-afghan-pullout-reconsidered/article1257498/.

PART FIVE

Issues, Risks, and Threats

12 Canada's Defence and Security Policies after 2011: Missions, Means, and Money

DOUGLAS L. BLAND AND
BRIAN MACDONALD

> There is no such thing as a threat to the national security of the United States which does not represent a direct threat to this country.
> – Prime Minister Stephen Harper, 2009[1]

> Canada's government has made it clear that re-engagement in the Americas is a critical international priority for our country.
> – Prime Minister Stephen Harper, 2007[2]

The fundamental purpose of the Canadian Forces (CF) is to employ military armed forces, including deadly forces, lawfully at home or abroad at the direction of the government. Governments decide with advice from the chief of the Defence Staff which means, which military capabilities, they will provide to meet this purpose as governments define it. The selection of specific capabilities is conditioned by many factors, among which the protection of national interests vulnerable to attack by hostile forces, anticipated missions at home and abroad, and money are most important.

This chapter, as an example of defence policymaking in Canada, will outline a national defence strategy derived from assessments of developing armed threats to national interests, evolving Canadian foreign policy choices, and anticipated military missions. It will describe in brief the essential military missions, capabilities, and monies necessary to meet the demands of a reoriented national defence strategy set in a dynamic domestic and international security environment. Finally, the chapter will conclude with an assessment of the likelihood that Canadians can expect to see after 2011 a reasonably coherent national defence strategy – a joining of policy ends and adequate annual budget allocations – to provide the CF with the necessary means to build and sustain the capabilities the government's strategy demand.

The Fast-Fading Cold War Policy Framework

Two long-standing ideas have defined Canada's national interests and served as the foundation for our national security: defence and foreign policies. But can they serve us well into the future? We should begin, therefore, by assuming that it is not beyond the wit of Canadians to amend these ideas if the circumstances that brought them into being have passed and emerging realities demand policies set in new ideas.

The continuance of Canada as a unified and secure liberal democracy is the cardinal idea, the foundation underpinning all aspects of our national interest. It is embedded in our history and constitution and expressed in our laws and in the deliberations of Canada's courts and, most importantly, in the minds of a vast majority of Canadians. National unity and the sovereignty of the people is the garnish on every politician's rhetoric. Even when some, such as Quebec separatists, challenge the idea of Canada, they have been turned away by citizens, if not defeated entirely. Yet today, other domestic and internal challenges to national security are overriding the traditional assumptions that the missions and duties of police agencies and the CF are separate and independent of each other.

The second imperishable idea holds that Canada is naturally secure by virtue of its geography and because a secure and peaceful Canada is a vital interest of the United State. Sir Wilfrid Laurier defined, seemingly for all time, the essence of Canada's national defence strategy: 'You must not take the militia [today, the CF] seriously,' he declared. 'It will not be required for the defence of the country, as the Monroe Doctrine protects us from enemy aggression.'[3] The idea that there is no threat to Canada and if there were one the United States would save us – which might be termed the 'Laurier Doctrine' – has comforted prime ministers from Laurier to Chrétien.[4]

Canada's national defence policies, except in the early years of the Cold War, have therefore been concerned not with preparing for national defence, but with avoiding wars and military commitments for fear that entanglements in imperial or allied adventures would threaten national unity. Thus, safeguarding national unity and Canada's 'natural security' often negate in the eyes of politicians any need to build 'multi-purpose combat capable armed forces,' no matter the rhetoric of defence and foreign policy white papers.[5]

Our defence and foreign policies have reflected at least since the beginning of the Cold War a struggle among three sometimes competing concepts. First, that Canada's economic and security well-being depend on a compatible but respectful relationship with the United States. Second, that Canada is a North Atlantic nation whose interests are inseparable from the bonds of history joining us to Europe and our 'like-mindedness' with Europeans generally. This 'Atlantic-ness' is demonstrated explicitly by Canada's long association with Europe within the North Atlantic alliance and in various commitments to NATO. Finally, both these orientations are challenged – vigorously between 1993 and 2003 – by a belief that our interests are best served by allegiance to the theory of collective security as managed by the United Nations.

These ideas and the assumptions and policies they have prompted are changing, illustrated most obviously in the absence of CF units deployed in UN missions and by the government's nearly total concentration on relations with the United States and its attention to Group of Eight (G8) and Group of Twenty (G20) affairs. Canada has no permanent obligation to any alliance or any international organization. As there are no permanent commitments, there can be no immutable or binding structure for the CF. There is only a permanent vital national interest to maintain Canada as a free, united, and secure liberal democracy, the protection of which invariably requires major or minor revisions to domestic policies, national institutions, international agreements, alliances, and commitments as national and international circumstances change. It is these revisions that will determine the major and minor transformations of the capabilities, structures, and resources of the Canadian Forces.

2011 will be remembered as a year in defence history unequalled by any other since 30 January 1951, when in a Speech from the Throne the Canadian government announced the deployment of a permanent military standing force to Europe. That single decision defined Canada's defence and foreign policies and subsequently the capabilities of the Canadian armed forces for almost a half century. But that Throne Speech and that commitment can now be safely and responsibly placed on display in the National War Museum, a mere curiosity for future generations. The return of all combat units from Afghanistan in 2011 marked the first time since 1951 that Canada has no permanently deployed armed forces stationed outside its territory – and thus the beginning of a new defining era of national defence policy and a significant transformation of the CF.

NATO, since 1950, has been the essence of our defence and foreign polices and the principal institutional link to Europe. It has served us well. But Berlin, Paris, and London are secure. Since at least the end of the Cold War, NATO has evolved from a defensive alliance organized to deter war with the Soviet Union into a European 'security community' where the bonds of community make wars and armed conflicts between its diverse members all but impossible. Indeed, unified Europe seems to be turning inward, no longer interested as a community in occupying practically its once commanding place on the world stage. This retreat in European defence policies is evident in the great reluctance in most European states to play an appropriate role in Afghanistan and especially in their fast-falling defence budgets.

Canada's national security ties to Europe are weakening as memories fade and Canada's pattern of immigration significantly alters citizens' perceptions of Canada's place in the world. The once 'special relationship' between Canada and Western Europe, and the United Kingdom especially, is of little account in Europe's policy world today. Indeed, it is impossible to invent any credible scenario in which Canada would again rally to send large armies to defend Europe or in which Europe would spend one soldier's life in the defence of Canada's interests. Most Canadian policies are inconsequential to European security interests and have no influence on where Europe will travel.[6] This shift in policy is most obvious in the near-complete withdrawal of the CF from NATO commands in Europe, and in the shift in Canadian military doctrine and training from NATO European 'interoperability' standards to doctrine and training and equipment necessary to provide the CF with interoperable capabilities more closely compatible with those of the U.S. armed forces.

In matters of national defence, Canada's interests after 2011 will be most efficiently served if Canada remains as it is today, nominally allied with Europe within the North Atlantic alliance, but discouraging Europeans from any assumption they may have that Canada would, except in extremis, deploy military forces in the defence European interests. These realities are providing the foundations for Canada's present and future defence relations with Europe and the Atlantic alliance generally. They are clearly evident in planned military redeployments of the CF from the NATO mission in Afghanistan and in the government's military capabilities decisions since 2005 and in its procurement plans, none of which have any explicit relationship to standing NATO commitments.

The United Nations is gradually moving under the control of states that do not share, and in some cases are openly hostile to, our core values – the defence and maintenance of liberal democracy. Though some true believers may hold to the *idea of the UN* as a parish priest is held to his religion, by faith alone ('a belief not requiring proof'), Canadians should dismiss the ideas that faith in the UN and the theory of collective security will assure Canada's unity and liberal democracy or its national defence. If Canadian defence and security-policy choices are to escape the subordination of Canada's interests to the desires of the 'global community,' then governments must begin by diminishing the power of peacekeeping myths some Canadians love to declare as evidence of the central importance of the UN to Canada's vital interests.[7]

In 1947, Brooke Claxton, the minister of national defence at the time, defined Canada's international security interests as a willingness 'to carry out any undertaking which by our own voluntary act we may assume in cooperation with friendly nations or under *any effective plan* of collective action under the United Nations.'[8] Clearly, there was no commitment here. Rather, the policy statement sent a loud announcement of Canada's unconditional sovereignty in international affairs and a stronger message that Canada's Parliament would decide what is to be done in each and every circumstance, all of which were expected to be distinct.

The Conservative government is reconceptualizing Canada's defence and foreign policies, to bring them home to the pre-1950 assumptions at the heart of the 'Claxton Doctrine.' The *Canada First Defence Strategy,* rather than being defined by Canada's borders, declares that policies, resources, and activities by all the agencies responsible for the interrelated aspects of national security will be directed primarily towards the defence of Canada's national interests. In particular, it illustrates that Canada now has no military obligations to the so-called global community and that Canada will stand ready to undertake only 'voluntary acts' in support of the UN that clearly reinforce Canada's national interests and those of our close allies. While the UN operations occasionally may have some importance to Canada – otherwise we would argue here for a complete withdrawal from the organization – their importance and relevance to Canada since 1990 has fallen dramatically. Canada's allocation of military resources to United Nations missions and operations in particular has practically ceased, and allocations to the UN such as in Afghanistan are in reality commitments to the American-led strategy in that country, and have been substantially reduced since 2011.

Safeguarding Canada in the Americas

If Canada is not an Atlantic nation as Canadians once assumed, and if the UN is incapable of guarding our national interests, then whither Canada? The answer is implicit in the Laurier Doctrine. While assuring that Canada's national unity is Canada's primary vital national interest, acting to assure the security, prosperity, and liberal democracy of the United States is invariably Canada's second most vital national interest, because it reinforces (some would argue, implicitly guarantees) Canada's primary national interest.

These unalterable interests embed in Canadian defence polices two intertwined strategic imperatives: the defence of Canada by Canadians and the defence of North America in cooperation with the United States. In the Cold War era, the defence of North America meant the defence of the Atlantic, and Arctic sea and air approaches to the continent. In the post–Cold War era, the defence of North America will mean an increasing commitment to cooperate with the United States (and perhaps in the future with Mexico) in the defence of the southern and Pacific approaches to North America.

All other commitments, such as UN peacekeeping missions and anti-pirate operations outside continental North America, for instance, will remain 'voluntary acts' (e.g., choices Parliaments might make from time to time as circumstances and national interests dictate). Changed international circumstances and Canada's strategic imperatives, as well as the predictable parsimony of Canadian governments in funding military capabilities, therefore, bring Canadians home to America, home to the idea that Canada is a natural constituent in an enormous political and cultural entity – the western hemisphere. Thus, the strategic imperative, the defence of North America in cooperation with the United States, will mature as a concept to mean the defence not only of the northern and eastern approaches to the continent from 'traditional' military threats, but also the defence of the southern and western approaches from military and other non-military security challenges.

The practical evolution of the idea that Canada is a western hemispheric nation is advancing steadily. The Conservative government acknowledged this fact in two seminal policy statements: *Canada First Defence Strategy* and *Canada and the Americas: Priorities & Progress.*[9] Several government departments and agencies, including the Department of National Defence and the CF, the Department of Foreign Affairs and International Trade, and the Canadian International Development Agency are already intensifying their activities in the region.[10]

The several recent visits to the region by the chief of Defence Staff, significant increases in military assistance and training programs in Latin American and the Caribbean,[11] the deployment in Mexico, Latin America, and the Caribbean of five senior military attaches where none existed before 1990, and most spectacularly, the deployment of CF warships and submarines on drug interdiction operations in the Caribbean Sea and the Gulf of Mexico are witness to a gradual reorientation of national defence policies and priorities in the western hemisphere.

Three major CF operational missions are developing in Latin America and the Caribbean region, and they are most likely to expand after 2011.[12] Naval operations to deter and intercept drug-runners and contraband and human smuggling activities in the region, in cooperation with the United States and other Organization of American States (OAS) nations, are a growing priority. Training Latin American and Caribbean military officers and the development of 'counterterrorism operational groups' and 'counterterrorism capabilities' – particularly in 2008–10 in Jamaica – are high-profile missions aimed at enhancing 'stability in the Caribbean.'[13] The CF is committed to training of OAS military officers in strategic analysis, defence management, and civil-military relations, among other topics, at military facilities in the Latin American and Caribbean Community region and at CF schools and colleges in Canada.

The swift Canadian humanitarian relief mission to Haiti in the winter of 2010 is an indication of the importance of the region to Canada's national interests. The rapidly made decision to lead the relief expedition in cooperation with the United States signalled to the international community that the Caribbean region in particular is in Canada's backyard. Moreover, swift action indicated that the government understood that Canadians have an implicit expectation that Canada has a special relationship and responsibility to security and the well-being of people in the near–western hemispheric region. While these activities were comparatively small in 2009, after 2011 it is anticipated that significant 'whole-of-government' deployments will take place in Haiti, where humanitarian and 'stabilization operations' will involve the Canadian Forces and many other departments of government and agencies for several years. Indeed, some type of permanent basing in Haiti, as was common in Europe in the Cold War era, is under discussion in Ottawa today.[14]

Among other major issues defence interests in the Americas, Canada is particularly interested in encouraging the growing commitment to UN peacekeeping operations by countries in the Americas – commitments that 'help to reduce the demands placed upon the Canadian Forces by high operational tempos.' Other central defence engagements in the region include building sound democratic civil–military relations, providing training and the 'tools to fight terrorism' in the region, deterring the advance of 'extra-territorial actors ... that do not share Canada's values' from establishing footholds in the Americas, and preparing regional states 'to alleviate the impact of [natural] catastrophes.'[15]

The Canadian government is also reinforcing its foreign policy statement *Canada in the Americas* not only by increasing military missions there but also by direct diplomatic and ministerial contacts in the region. In January 2010, for instance, Minister of State for Foreign Affairs (Americas) Peter Kent visited Venezuela and Bolivia 'as part of Canada's foreign policy priority of deepening engagement in the Americas.' Kent remarked that his visit was intended 'to advance [Canada's] key objectives [building] democratic governance, prosperity, and security' in the region.[16] While in Cuba in late 2009, Kent emphasized the economic benefits and advantages Canada has in the region: 'Our government has made trade across the Americas a priority, and we are seeing tremendous potential for growth in Canadian exports to Cuba and across the hemisphere.'[17]

Although Canada has not publicly acknowledged direct involvement in security operations in Mexico, the continuing criminal insurgency in that state has become a major Canadian security concern. The insurgency is particularly violent and deadly, forcing thousands of Mexicans out of contested regions and prompting thousands to travel to Canada in the hope of claiming refugee status to escape the chaos at home. American and Canadian officials and security agents are worried that if Mexico cannot at least contain the insurgency, then the spreading violence and growing power of the drug cartels especially will migrate to the United States and Canada. Indeed, some suggest that the cartels are already conducting 'punitive raids' across the U.S.-Mexican border.[18]

Under the Canada and the Americas strategy, Canada's essential foreign policy objectives are to enhance Canada's self-interests by defining itself as a western hemispheric nation, to support U.S. security and counter-crime operations in the region through the reasonable acceptance of America's views of its national interests in the region, to develop cooperative and appropriate regional security policies and capabilities with the OAS and Caribbean Community in particular, and to lead in helping to advance a new coalition of stable liberal democracies in the western hemisphere.

Canada has a strategic advantage – a competitive advantage – in the western hemisphere over most other nations from outside the Caribbean and Latin American region. For example, Canada has a long and friendly relationship with the Commonwealth Caribbean nations and many other historic and cultural, military, business, and family links into the region. Canadian business leaders are also using their considerable entrepreneurial and managerial skills and business connections to build strong economic and private trading relationships in the region to the benefit of Canada and other regional partners. Canada – understatedly, in Washington's eyes – could be to many Latin American and Caribbean states 'not the United States.' The Canadian government today seems prepared to seize these advantages through its clearly stated policy of 're-engagement in the Americas.'

In his remarks commemorating the twentieth anniversary of Canada's joining the OAS, former prime minister Brian Mulroney praised that decision and its importance to Canada in 2010 and in the future: 'Above all, 20 years after the fact, the lesson from our decision to join the OAS, and our experience as a full-fledge member, is a more confident assertion of who we are and where we are. [That decision shows] also how the values we cherish ... can be advanced throughout the hemisphere. Our decision to join was an acknowledgement of a geographic reality, a declaration of serious political intent and a commitment to serve the interests of our own hemisphere.'[19]

Canada's engagements in the Americas have not gone unnoticed in Washington. In a 2010 meeting in Washington, DC, at the Center for Hemispheric Defense Studies (a meeting at which no Canadians were present), Deputy Assistant Secretary of Defense for the Western Hemispheric Affairs Frank Mora remarked, 'I have been very pleased with the progress we've made on expanding our relations with Canada to work more closely on mutually beneficial hemispheric issues.' He continued, 'In November [2009] the [Canadian] minister of national defence and [Defence Secretary] Gates met in Halifax for a one-on-one. It was, I believe, the first time that there was a meeting in which the two met for the sole, specific purpose of talking about continental and Western hemispheric issues. So one of the relationships that we have intensified is that with Canada because we are now working together ... [and] steadily exploring cooperation in the Western Hemisphere. It is all rather unprecedented and very encouraging.'[20]

These initiatives are evidence of the 'reorientation' of Canada's post–Cold War defence and foreign policies towards safeguarding Canadian national interests in the Americas. Military acquisitions – such as the purchase of C-130J and C-17 transport aircraft and the policy to allocate $50 billion to a national ship-procurement plan over the next twenty years – are part of a wider plan to build a modest 'expeditionary capability' in the CF. The intent to use these new resources to support national objectives at home or in Canada's near-at-home in the western hemisphere do not explicitly eliminate the possibility of short-term commitments to other NATO and UN operations. Remaining 'notionally' attached to the alliance and to UN peacekeeping missions – a mostly cost-free strategy – is a reasonable position for Canada to take. But simply because NATO-Europe was the main focus for deployments in the past and the UN needed the CF in its early days of peacekeeping, why should they hold the same station indefinitely? In a military world of ever-rising capability costs and scarce budget – the defence budget ceiling in Canada being always 2 per cent of GDP – military capabilities must be assigned to meet high-priority foreign policy and security needs. The expeditionary force model suggested later in this chapter, termed the Canada First Expeditionary Force (CFEF), does just that. It is in the main a flexible, air/land/sea armed force that could be deployed almost anywhere in the world, but it is especially designed to meet evolving national security challenges in and close to Canada.

The Canadian Forces and Security at Home

The continuance of Canada as a unified and secure liberal democracy, which as noted earlier underpins all aspects of our national interest and defence and security policies, may also be on the verge of a destructive *internal* security challenge. Scholars warn that insurgencies often occur when conditions for underprivileged people are improving and then their expectations of a better future are suddenly dashed. They also warn that whenever governments, for whatever reasons, fail to assert their sovereignty in contested areas, be they cities or rural communities, other, usually subversive organizations will take their place. Mexico's criminal insurgency in particular warns Canadians that failure to act forcefully and immediately to the threats posed by internal security weaknesses and 'transnational criminal organizations' can rapidly undermine not only law and order, but also the very basis for national unity and sovereignty, even in advanced states. Canada's vulnerability to both threats is real and increasing.

The Seeds of an Aboriginal Insurgency

Canada's aboriginal communities face a rapidly growing and increasingly frustrated young population on reserves and in our cities, open operations by criminal gangs in reserves and in other segments of the aboriginal community, and rampant drug and alcohol abuse throughout the communities. Aboriginal leaders continue to warn Canadians that aboriginal people 'have a right to be frustrated, concerned, angry – anger that's building and building.'[21] Others encourage unilateral declarations of native sovereignty. Chief Terry Nelson of the Roseau River First Nation in Manitoba and a contender in July 2009 for the office of grand chief of the Assembly of First Nations declared, 'It's time to quit being loyal Canadians ... There are only two ways to deal with the white man. Either you pick up the gun or you stand between him and his money.'[22] When Senator Romeo Dallaire at a meeting of the Senate Committee of Aboriginal People suggested to then retired prime minister Paul Martin that if '[the native people] ever coalesced [as a militant force] ... could they not bring this country to a standstill?' Paul Martin replied, 'My answer and the only one we all have, is we would hope not.'[23]

A quick review of the core facts of aboriginal life in Canada is startling.[24] If the 'root cause theory of insurgency' – a critical social failure in a significant portion of the population of a state will eventually give rise to a serious internal security problem and even to an insurgency – is valid, then Canada has reason to take precautions in matters of internal security.[25] The theory is challenged by examples of major social failures in some states that did not or has not yet spawned an insurgency. New research, particularly the work of the Oxford scholar Paul Collier, refined the general theory, adding to it the notion of 'feasibility.' He explains that where demographic, territorial, and a state's dependence on the export of a prime resource (in Canada, natural gas, petroleum, and hydroelectric energy – about 20 per cent of GDP) is combined with the root cause factors, insurgencies become feasible. Where, he argues, an insurgency is feasible, then it is likely to occur.[26]

Canada's vulnerability to radical, militant aboriginal leaders' threats has been demonstrated in small-scale confrontations at Oka, Burnt Church, Awkwasasne, Caledonia, Desoronto on the main rail lines between Quebec City and Windsor, and more than once in blockades on Highway 401. Native leaders in the West have 'noticed' the link between vast stretches of railway lines and 'the white man's money.'[27] It is alleged that the Conservative government made a hurried land claims deal with the chief of the Roseau First Nations after threats against the transcontinental railway system were allegedly made by native leaders in Manitoba.[28]

Canada's sovereignty is vulnerable and an insurgency is feasible, particularly since the Canadian economy remains dependent on resource-based production (25 per cent of the nation's GDP), and its transportation infrastructure is undefended and probably indefensible. Many reserves in the West and in northwestern Ontario and in northern Quebec sit astride or adjacent to the east-west lines of communications and transportation on which Canada's national economy depends. They sit next door to most of the major sources for Canada's resource industries and on the north-south lines that take them to the industrial bases in Ontario and Quebec and British Columbia. They also sit astride the oil, natural gas, and hydro lines that fuel southern Canada and a good deal of the United States.

Northern Quebec and the James Bay power generation facilities are particularly vulnerable. Insecure hydroelectric transmission lines from the facilities run south for nearly a thousand kilometres. On the prairies, the natural gas and oil pipelines are the great vulnerability. The thousands of kilometres of above-ground lines and compressor/transfer stations that keep things flowing are all unprotected. A few kilos of explosives would put most of these systems out of action. Radical elements and criminal gangs do not have to control the entire territory to cripple Canada. They just have to make raids on the isolated lines from the sanctuary of their reserves.[29]

There are few ways to redress these vulnerabilities or to substitute other things to diminish the harmful consequences of disruptions to critical resource networks. There are today nowhere near the police and military resources that would be needed to protect them continuously throughout the year. For example, the entire prairie region is patrolled by just 4,100 Royal Canadian Mounted Police officers, who are trained to police small towns and the highways outside the major cities, much like the Ontario Provincial Police in Ontario. Their widely scattered, small detachments in an internal security emergency would be more a security liability than a security asset.

In previous internal emergencies involving First Nation people, as at Oka in 1990, for example, local police forces proved unable to maintain or restore order and the CF were deployed into the community 'in aid of the civil powers.'[30] This 'aid' as defined in the National Defence Act is a standing commitment of the CF. If Canada faced an organized uprising like the one suggested by Senator Dallaire, it would present the CF and the government with a problematic situation. Rethinking and rebuilding national police, intelligence, and military capabilities to deter and respond to the threats coming from the aboriginal community is merely a prudent measure in the circumstances.[31]

Gangland Canada

It is estimated by Criminal Intelligence Service Canada that as many as 750 national and transnational criminal organizations were active in Canada in 2009.[32] In every province except Newfoundland, home-grown, aboriginal, and 'ethnic' criminal gangs are expanding into smaller towns and recruiting more aggressively, creating successor generations of members. Expansion, competition for 'trade' and new members, and a general sense that they are untouchable because of 'the sensitive political optics of aboriginal issues'[33] is increasing the number of incidents and the level of violent behaviour across Canada, on reserves and in cities, which is in turn spilling over into peaceful, settled aboriginal and non-aboriginal communities. Police, courts, and jails are struggling to address the problem. In most provinces, but especially in the West, many prisons are dominated by native gangs and cults. They are very dangerous places, which police officers refer to as 'gangland community colleges.'

Intelligence reports indicate that native gangs are composed mostly of young, armed, and ruthless men. These gangs differ in structure from region to region – more like conventional organized crime in the East, especially along the Ontario/Quebec/U.S. borders, where the main business is smuggling.[34] In the East, the gangs (native and non-native) are more entrepreneurial and actually run large supply chains to service their drug, alcohol, tobacco, and firearms smuggling. They also launder money on a significant scale. As with some reserves in the West, some in the East provide safe havens for these and other illegal activities.

Canadian security services may be falling behind the actual development of some of these aboriginal and other 'ethnic-based' gangs, especially in Toronto and Vancouver, where gangs are evolving into political organizations – or 'third-generation criminal gangs.'[35] That is to say, they are beginning to organize and function on political lines to advance their power and interests and to shelter their members and organizations from authorities.

In Canada, police and civilian courts act to counter organized crime and criminal gangs. The police, however, are not adequately structured and trained to deal with increasingly militant gangs. They will inevitably require (as they have in the past) 'assistance' from the CF, if only in equipment such as aerial surveillance resources, armoured vehicles, and explosive-ordinance disposal capabilities. Today, the CF provides continual assistance to the Canadian Coast Guard and Border Services, and the demand for these services will certainly increase in the future.

The open question for Canada is whether the planned improvements in current standards of living for the aboriginal communities on reserves and more aggressive police actions against all types of criminal gangs and their activities can be developed and implemented fast enough and deep enough to avert an 'apprehended insurgency' from becoming a serious challenge to the government of Canada.

What is not at question, however, is the significant security efforts underway in Canada and in the United States – and by extension in Mexico and the Caribbean region – aimed at combating transnational criminal organizations in North America. Furthermore, these efforts increasingly demand the full-time support of national military units in ways and duration never before anticipated. The Canadian Forces are today on duty supporting border security units and the Coast Guard. They continually provide major combatant ships and aircraft 'backup' support to Immigrations Canada and major air and naval operations to interdict illegal drug, weapons, and contraband operations on the Atlantic and Pacific Coasts and in Eastern Canada border areas. While these operations might seem to some to be merely extensions of traditional police matters, they are now considered within the CF as defence of Canada missions and defence of North America missions conducted in cooperation with the United States.[36]

A Canadian Forces Expeditionary Force Model: Building on Experience

The CF national defence mission should encompass specifically or in some combination the defence of Canada, the defence of North America in cooperation with the armed forces of the United States (and possibility in the future, with the armed forces of Mexico), and the conduct of any other undertaking that Canadian governments by their own 'voluntary acts' may assume in cooperation with friendly nations or under any *effective plan* of collective action by international organizations.

While this chapter has emphasized the western hemisphere as the primary focus of attention, a robust expeditionary capability should allow for deployment wherever the Canadian government may determine. The question remains, however, about the extent of the capabilities of such a force – whether it should be a nominal capability that allows Canada to 'show the flag,' or sufficiently robust for significant military action. Obviously the combat force deployed in Afghanistan possessed a 'robust' joint capability, and as such provides an indicator of the level of capability that is appropriate for a responsible middle power such as Canada. However, the Afghanistan example is limited in that it is primarily an air/land force without a significant sea component.

When we turn to the possibilities of a true joint air/land/sea capability expeditionary force for Canada, we can begin by looking at the national models currently in use. These range from, at the upper end, the forces deployed by the United States Navy and Marine Corps, to the middle-power model of the United Kingdom's Royal Navy, Royal Marines, and Parachute structure, to those of a relatively limited nature.

The model provided by the Joint Rapid Reaction Force of the United Kingdom is instructive, in that its successful 2000 military intervention in Sierra Leone (Operation Palliser) provides one of the few cases in which a middle power was able to deploy a robust expeditionary force, involving the deployment of about 4,500 personnel,[37] capable of a self-contained joint force intervention in a 'failing state,' and it did so in such a manner as to restore stability in that state and provide the opportunity for other whole-of-government forces, as well as civilian interventions from the international community for humanitarian and developmental assistance, to prevent the 'failing state' from becoming a 'failed state.'

The Operation Palliser concept of operations included an initial deployment by air of the Spearhead Battalion of the Joint Rapid Reaction Force, which is based on an infantry battalion of approximately

650 personnel, together with supporting units. In this case it was the 1st Battalion of the Parachute Regiment. The initial deployment was followed by that of an Amphibious Ready Group carrying the 600-strong 42 Royal Marine Commando, plus supporting troops including Royal Artillery, Royal Engineers, SAS, and other elements.

The Amphibious Ready Group was built around the two aircraft carriers: HMS *Illustrious*, which provided a command platform and Harrier fighter aircraft for air force protection, and HMS *Ocean*, which provided a platform for both armed and transport helicopters, as well as accommodation for the Royal Marines battle group. The two frigates, HMS *Chatham* and HMS *Argyll*, provided naval force protection and acted as escorts. The three auxiliary oiler replenishers (AORs) – RFA *Fort Austin*, RFA *Fort George*, and RFA *Brambleleaf* – provided tanker refuelling support for the task group. The two Landing Ships Logistics, RFA *Sir Bedivere* and RFA *Sir Geraint*, provided support, fuel, and logistics for the ground forces. The Landing Ships Logistics have since been replaced by Landing Ship Docks (Auxiliary) (LSD[A]); the Largs Bay class is a recent U.K. Royal Fleet Auxiliary design, which displaces about sixteen thousand tons.

The U.K. task force intervention restored stability to Sierra Leone and thus must be viewed as a successful force structure model for such operations. Consequently this chapter develops a hypothetical robust Canada First Expeditionary Force model based on the U.K. precedent.

The centre of the CFEF would be a Landing Platform Helicopter (LPH), which would fill the role exercised by HMS *Ocean* in the Sierra Leone campaign. It was not felt that an air projection aircraft carrier would be needed in the areas in which the CFEF amphibious task force might be called upon to deploy, though this could be modelled if required. An LSD(A) would be required to provide logistics support to the ground component of the CFEF. With the addition of the LPH, there would be no requirement for the joint capabilities of the currently planned Joint Support Ships, so they could be replaced by much more economical AORs. Naval force protection would be provided by existing CF frigates and destroyers – though we should note that four destroyers, instead of the current three, would be required to provide command and control as well as area air defence against air attack to Atlantic and Pacific task forces as well as the CSEF, with one held in reserve for refit/maintenance at all times.

In summation, the navy order of battle would be increased by one destroyer, one LPH, one LSD(A) and four AORs; three Joint Support

Ships would be dropped, since their naval replenishment function would be filled by the four AORs, and their sealift capability by the much larger LPH and the LSD(A). The number of frigates (twelve) and submarines (four) would be unchanged. The army would be increased by one light expeditionary brigade, while the air force would experience no change in its structure. In the context of a reoriented Canadian national defence strategy, as outlined in this chapter, key capabilities for the CFEF in support of an international whole-of government / 3-D (defence, diplomacy, and development) strategy are further detailed in table 12.1.

Costing the CF Expeditionary Force

The Conservative government's *Canada First Defence Strategy* notes that 'the cost of increasing military strength by 1,000 regular personnel is about $150 million annually.'[38] *Making Sense Out of Dollars*, the National Defence publication from May 2008, provides total military ($5.2 billion) and civilian ($1.4 billion) pay figures that, when divided by the total numbers of military (66,737) and civilian (25,000) positions, indicate that a civilian position cost approximately $56,000 in 2007/8, or 72 per cent of a regular position cost of $78,000.[39] It does not provide equivalent data for the calculation of an average Reserve position cost. The annual *Departmental Performance Review* does provide data, but its base is not identical to that of the other document. *Departmental Performance Review 2007–2008* shows planned Reserve strength of 24,750 and a Reserve pay budget of $540,456,000, for an average position cost of $21,800 or 28 per cent of a Regular position.[40]

Accordingly we can estimate the cost of expanding the CF by 1,000 civilian positions should be about $108 million annually, and expanding the CF by 1,000 Reserve positions should cost about $33 million annually.

While we have not attempted to do a detailed establishment study, we feel that something in the order of an increase of fourteen thousand Regular positions, six thousand Reserve positions, and five thousand civilian positions would be necessary to create the additional expeditionary brigade and ships crews for the CFEF, and to bring the existing brigades up to a war establishment so that rotations could be handled by a brigade group without having first to transfer persons in to make up shortfalls before deployment, as is currently the case. A preliminary estimate is that this would result in cost increases of $2.1 billion for the

Table 12.1.   Key capabilities for the CFEF

Operational capabilities
- A Canadian Forces headquarters to provide to the chief of Defence Staff the technical and personnel means to fulfil his or her duties, to provide operational direction to the CF, and to build future military national defence capabilities
- Training, command, control, support, and maintenance units and personnel to sustain CF operations and training missions
- A CF regular/reserve force operational combat-training establishment capable of providing a 'surge–training capacity' to rapidly augment and/or reinforce and build new and additional capabilities to support CF operational missions
- A national joint space-based and unmanned aerial vehicle intelligence collection system
- An intelligence system capable of interpreting in real time surveillance data collected along Canadian borders and in Canadian sea, land, and air territories

Maritime capabilities
- Three frigate-based, maritime helicopter–equipped task forces supported by command and logistical vessels
- A multi-purpose joint amphibious task force capable of carrying and supporting up to an infantry battalion battle group on operational deployments in the western hemisphere
- A four-boat submarine task force
- A maritime special forces unit trained for seaborne interdiction missions
- An Arctic and offshore (coastal and inland waters) armed patrol capability

Land capabilities
- Three deployable, multi-capable, counter-insurgency brigade groups, each of approximately four thousand personnel consisting of three infantry battalions, as well as an armoured regiment, an artillery regiment, a combat engineer regiment, and a service battalion
- A multi-capable, rapidly deployable, light brigade equipped and trained for air- and sea-transported interventions in counter-insurgency, peacekeeping, and disaster relief operations.
- A 'special forces operations' regiment, supported by integral air transport and intelligence subunits

Air capabilities
- An air combat capability, including air refuelling, capable of continuous operations over the sea approaches to Canada and in Canadian coastal regions and in the Arctic
- Strategic and tactical fixed-wing and rotary-wing transport capabilities to support CF operations in Canada and in the western hemisphere
- A maritime and land-based fixed-wing and unmanned aerial vehicle intelligence system
- A fixed-wing and rotary-wing search and rescue capability

---

increase in Regular positions, $0.198 billion for Reserves, and $0.540 billion for civilians, for a total personnel-related increase of $2.838 billion.

As for operations and maintenance, the *Canada First Defence Strategy* projects that – whereas Personnel costs will account for 51 per cent of

Table 12.2.   Instrumental annual cost of CFEF, 2009–10

Category	Cost increase ($B)
Personnel	2.838
Operations & maintenance	2.050
Capital	0.700
Total	5.590

the total defence budget – Infrastructure and Readiness will account for 8 per cent and 29 per cent, respectively. Accordingly, we can estimate that the annual CFEF Infrastructure cost increase would be 8/51 of the annual Personnel cost increase and that the CFEF annual Readiness cost increase would be 29/51 of the annual personnel cost increase. This would result in an increase of $0.444 billion for Infrastructure and $1.609 billion for Readiness for a total of $2.05 billion.

The adoption of accrual accounting makes the calculation of the incremental capital costs of the CFEF somewhat difficult, since the total accrual life of the equipments in some cases goes beyond the CFDS/CFEF period. We see this in the CFDS comment on the $20 billion cost of the 'New Major Fleet Replacements': 'This figure represents the capital costs of the New Major Fleet Replacements during the twenty-year period reflected in the chart. The total capital costs of these platforms amortized over their useful life, which extend beyond this twenty-year period, amount to $45–50 billion.'[41]

Following the accrual budgeting approach would lead us to adopt the budget divisions of the CFDS with capital at 12 per cent of the annual budget, or 12/51 of the personnel cost increase, which would result in a capital cost increment of $700 million.

As table 12.2 illustrates, the incremental annual cost of the CFEF strategy would amount to $5.59 billion in fiscal year 2009/10. This would raise the total CFDS plus CFEF defence budget from $20.993 billion to $26.583 billion – an increase of 26.6 per cent – and would raise defence spending from 1.3 per cent to 1.6 per cent of the economy.

A 'Cash-Based' Capital Budget

An alternative (and traditional) 'cash-based accounting' approach would use the inflation-adjusted total costs of the capital assets modelled to this point. However, this method is complicated by the impact

Table 12.3. Summary of CFEF cost

Category	$B
Capital: naval	3.020
Capital: land	2.064
Capital: air	–
Personnel	2.976
Operations and maintenance	2.159
Total	10.219

of defence inflation, which is considerably greater than civilian inflation. A 2006 RAND study reports that 'in the past 50 years, annual cost escalation rates for amphibious ships, surface combatants, attack submarines, and nuclear aircraft carriers have ranged from 7 to 11 percent.'[42]

This paper has adopted the mean of those figures as the defence inflation figure to be used. The methodology selects the final cost of a representative platform and calculates the total compounded inflation, depending on the number of years from the date the contract was let to the present, and then corrects for the current exchange rate between the Canadian dollar and the currency in which the representative platform was contracted.

The CFEF model does not include incremental increases for the Air element. An initial estimate of the incremental capital equipment increase for the Land element would be about $2.063 billion.[43] The Navy's additional platforms cost estimates are one additional destroyer at $1.733 billion,[44] an LSD(A) at $0.342 billion,[45] an LPH built to commercial standards at $0.993 billion and four AORs for a subtotal total of $1.862 billion.[46]

This would result in summary table 12.3, which does not include smaller capital equipment or infrastructure projects.

Conclusion

Canada is on the cusp of a fundamental reorientation of its domestic internal security and its foreign and defence policies, driven by changing domestic and international circumstances, resource limitations, and the political evolution of Canada and Canadian society. Governments simply do not have the resources (at a mere 2 per cent of GDP) to devote to a national defence strategy that would effectively encompass the future demands of the nation's two defence imperatives – the defence of Canada and the defence of North America in cooperation with the United States – while at the same time helping to guard Europe, responding to worldwide UN military commitments, and guarding the 'near-at-home' Caribbean and Latin America regions.

The government has chosen to concentrate Canada's defence and security resources in the western hemisphere and is changing course, steering out of the now secure North Atlantic and into the increasingly turbulent waters of the Arctic Ocean and the Caribbean Sea. This is a prudent, justifiable, and affordable policy choice. Progressing steadily towards a viable, integrated, and harmonized defence and security strategy and building the capabilities to implement it should be achievable within the budgets forecasted by the present Conservative government for the post-2011 era,[47] assuming these budgets are adjusted continually for national and especially defence inflation over time.

NOTES

1 Prime Minister Harper and President Obama: Joint Press Conference, Ottawa, 19 Feb. 2009.

2 As quoted in Canada, Department of Foreign Affairs and International Trade, *Canada and the Americas: Priorities & Progress* (Ottawa: DFAIT, 2009), 3.

3 Qtd in George Stanley, *Canada's Soldiers: The History of an Unmilitary People* (Toronto: Macmillan, 1960), 294.

4 Jean Chrétien's defence policies reflected the Laurier Doctrine tellingly: 'Every government is under constant pressure to spend more and more on defence. In our case, the pressure came from the American government . . . arms merchants, military lobbyists for whom no amount of money is ever enough. The [CF] always claim it needed more tanks, and guns, more submarines and destroyers, more bombers and helicopters, but I wasn't sure that its self-interest was the same as the national interest.' Jean Chrétien, *Jean Chrétien: My Years as Prime Minister* (Toronto: Alfred A. Knoff, 2007), 303.

5 Defence white papers and ministers' public statements on the need to build strong national defence capabilities abound. Minister of National Defence John McCallum, for instance, declared in October 2002, 'We must be prepared to defend our citizens, our economy, our infrastructure, our economic system, and even our way of life,' even as the Liberal government continued to neglect in every federal budget the need to build military, diplomatic, and security capabilities for these purposes. As quoted in Douglas L. Bland,

ed., *Canada without Armed Forces?* (Montreal and Kingston: McGill-Queen's University Press, 2004), x.

6 See Paul Chapin, *Security in an Uncertain World: A Canadian Perspective on NATO's New Strategic Concept* (Ottawa: Conference of Defence Associations Institute, Canadian Defence and Foreign Affairs Institute, 2010).

7 Myth one, Canada (Lester Pearson) invented peacekeeping, therefore Canada must guard forever the holy chalice and participate in every UN mission. Myth two, peacekeeping is a selfless activity undertaken in the interests of the global community. Myth three, Canada never has advanced and cannot advance its national interests by waging war or by joining alliances outside the dictates of the UN – peacekeeping is not warfare. Myth four, the mandate of the Canadian Forces is 'peacekeeping.'

8 Qtd in Douglas L. Bland, ed., *Canada's National Defence,* vol. 1, *Defence Policy* (Montreal and Kingston: McGill-Queen's University Press, 1997), 20 (emphasis added).

9 Canada, Department of National Defence, *Canada First Defence Strategy* (Ottawa: DND, 2008); and *Canada and the Americas: Priorities & Progress.*

10 See, for example, Canada, Department of Foreign Affairs and International Trade, 'Seizing Global Advantage: Canada's Commercial Engagement in Latin America and the Caribbean,' http://www.international.gc.ca/commerce/strategy-strategie/m2.aspx; and Canada, Canadian International Development Agency, 'The Americas,' http://www.acdi-cida.gc.ca/acdi-cida/ACDI-CIDA.nsf/En/NIC-5510467-KBV.

11 Andrew Rasiulis and Sara Fortin, 'Military Training Assistance Program,' *On Track* 14, no. 2 (Summer 2009): 39–41. And Michelle Collins, ed., 'Americas Strategy Includes Military Drug Ops,' *Embassy,* 25 Mar. 2009; and Patrick Lennox, 'After Afghanistan: Maritime Options for the Future of Canadian Global Engagement,' *Canadian Naval Review* 5, no. 2 (Summer 2009): 4–9.

12 Interview, Ottawa, June 2009.

13 Rasiulis and Frotin, 'Military Training Assistance Program,' 40.

14 Confidential interviews, Ottawa, February 2010.

15 Canada, Department of National Defence, 'Western Hemisphere Policy: The Americas,' http://www.forces.gc.ca/admpol/americas-eng.html.

16 Canada, Department of Foreign Affairs and International Trade, 'Minister of State Kent Visit, Venezuela and Bolivia,' news release, 19 Jan. 2010.

17 Canada, Department of Foreign Affairs and International Trade, 'Minister of State Kent Concludes Successful Visit to Cuba,' news release, 17 Nov. 2009.

18 On the rapidly growing criminal insurgency in Mexico, see, for instance, John Baram, 'An "Iron River of Guns" Flows South,' *Security Management*

(June 2008) http://www.securitymanagement.com/article/iron-river-guns-flows-south; 'State of Siege: Mexico's Criminal Insurgency,' *Small Wars Journal* (Aug. 2008): 1–12; and Colleen Cook, *Mexico's Drug Cartels* (Washington, DC: Congressional Research Services, February 2008). By some reliable reports, the criminal cartels have already moved across the U.S.-Mexican border and conducted armed raids on U.S. police and border guards and rivals in the drug trade. See Hal Brands, *Mexico Narco-Insurgency and US Counterdrug Policy* (Carlisle, PA: Strategic Studies Institute, US Army War College, May 2009), 13; and Max G. Manwaring, *State and Nonstate Associated Gangs: Credible 'Midwives of New Social Orders'* (Carlisle, PA: Strategic Studies Institute, U.S. Army War College, May 2009).

19 Brian Mulroney, 'Canada and the OAS, 20 Years Later,' *National Post*, 9 Mar. 2010.

20 Centre for Hemispheric Defense Studies, '12 Questions for the Deputy Assistant Secretary of Defense for the Western Hemispheric Affairs Frank Mora,' 12 Jan. 2010, http://www.ndu.edu/chds/news.cfm?action=view&id=57&lang=en.

21 Phil Fontaine, grand chief of the Assembly of First Nations, *CTV News*, 15 May 2007.

22 Terrance Nelson, chief, Roseau River First Nation, Manitoba, *CTV News*, 15 May 2007.

23 Senate of Canada, Committee on Aboriginal People, Ottawa, 8 Apr. 2008.

24 Canada, Statistics Canada, 'Aboriginal Peoples in Canada in 2006' (Census Year 2006) (Ottawa: Statistics Canada, 2008). Although the 2006 census is generally accurate, Statistics Canada warns in various sections that the data are cautionary, especially in a census where the target population is allowed without qualification to 'self-identify' at each census and where some Aboriginal groups such as some First Nations refused or discouraged members from joining a Canadian government process.

25 Readers will recall the armed 'apprehended insurgency' launched by the Front de libération du Québec (FLQ) in the early 1970s that required the deployment of the CF to bring it under control.

26 Paul Collier, *The Bottom Billion* (Oxford: Oxford University Press, 2007). See also Paul Collier, 'Ethnic Civil Wars: Questioning the Received Wisdom,' *Harvard International Review* 28, no. 4 (Winter 2007) http://hir.harvard.edu/ethnic-conflict/ethnic-civil-wars.

27 *When Justice Fails, Stop the Rails*, a video that calls for blockades like those staged in Tyendinaga, Ontario. *CTV.ca News Staff*, 16 May 2007.

28 'Prentice Denies Protest Threat Prompted Land Deal, *CTV.ca News Staff*, 24 June 2007.

29 Brian MacDonald, *Canada–US Defence Relations and Critical Infrastructure Protection*, Atlantic Council of Canada, paper 7/10 (2001).

30 For detailed research on the Oka crisis and the CF, see Timothy C. Winegard, *Oka: A Convergence of Cultures and the Canadian Forces* (Kingston: Canadian Defence Academy, 2008).

31 For a current depiction of Senator Dallaire's warning, see Douglas L. Bland, *Uprising* (Toronto: Blue Butterfly Books, 2010).

32 Canada, Criminal Intelligence Service Canada, *09 Report on Organized Crime* (Ottawa: 2009), http://www.cisc.gc.ca/annual_reports/annual_report_2009/document/report_oc_2009_e.pdf.

33 Interviews, Ottawa, 2008–9. See also Michael C. Chettleburgh, *Young Thugs: Inside the Dangerous World of Canadian Street Gangs* (Toronto: HarperCollins Publishers, 2007).

34 Established Aboriginal gangs in Alberta – the Red Alert, the Indian Posse, and the Alberta Warriors – are based mainly in Edmonton and Calgary. In Saskatchewan, the Native Syndicate controls Regina, while the Indian Posse controls Saskatoon. In Manitoba, the main gangs are the Manitoba Warriors, the Indian Posse, and the Native Syndicate.

35 See, for example, Hal Brands, 'Third-Generation Gangs and Criminal Insurgency in Latin America,' *Small Wars Journal* (July 2009): 1–9; Max Manwaring, *Street Gangs: The New Urban Insurgency* (Carlisle, PA: Strategic Studies Institute, US Army War College, March 2005); and John P. Sullivan, 'Transnational Gangs: The Impact of Third-Generation Street Gangs in Central America,' *Air & Space Power Journal* (July 2008), http://www.airpower.au.af.mil/apjinternational/apj-s/2008/2tri08/sullivaneng.htm.

36 Confidential interview, Ottawa, 2009.

37 Andrew Dorman, 'Operational Concepts and Doctrine – Sierra Leone: A Case Study in the Royal Navy's Contribution to Joint Warfare,' *World Defence Systems* 10, no. 1 (2007): 52–4.

38 DND, *Canada First Defence Strategy*, 15.

39 Canada, Department of National Defence, *Making Sense out of Dollars*, 2007–2008 Edition (Ottawa: DND, 2008), 49, 63, http://www.admfincs-smafinsm.forces.gc.ca/fp-pf/msd-add/2007-2008/nde-dmdn-eng.asp. These military and civilian pay figures do not include the cost of pension contributions or of personnel-related O&M costs such as travel, food, clothing, education of dependents, tuition, medical, rental of living quarters, and rental of buildings and facilities for education, training, and recreation.

40 Canada, Department of National Defence, *Departmental Performance Report, 2007–2008* (Ottawa: DND, 2008), 28, 30, http://www.tbs-sct.gc.ca/dpr-rmr/2007-2008/inst/dnd/dnd-eng.pdf.

41 DND, *Canada First Defence Strategy,* 12n2.

42 Mark Arena, Irv Blickstein, Obaid Younossi, and Clifford A. Grammich, *Why Has the Cost of Navy Ships Risen? A Macroscopic Examination of the Trends in U.S. Naval Ship Costs over the Past Several Decades* (Santa Monica, CA: RAND Corporation, 2006).

43 The initial estimate (low) of the capital cost of the Light Brigade can be made by adding one-third of the capital cost of the Medium Support Vehicle System project of $1.089 billion, and one-third of the value of the Family of Land Combat Vehicles (FLCV) projects valued at $5.1 billion. These figures can be found in Canada, Department of National Defence, *2009–2010 Report on Plans and Priorities* (Ottawa: DND, 2009), table 10a; and 'Government of Canada to Renew Fleet of Land Combat Vehicles,' *DND News Release,* 8 July 2009, http://www.forces.gc.ca/site/news-nouvelles/ news-nouvelles-eng.asp?id=3040.

44 The Canadian Association of Defence and Security Industries estimate a budget of $26 billion for fifteen ships of the Canadian Surface Combatant class, or $1.733 billion per ship. See CADSI, *Sovereignty, Security and Prosperity: Government Ships – Designed, Built and Supported by Canadian Industry,* Report of the CADSI Marine Industries Working Group (Ottawa: CADSI, May 2009), 9.

45 The UK National Audit Office reports the total cost for four ships of the LSD(A) class at 2006 was £596 million. Converted to Canadian dollars at an exchange rate of 1.77 per pound and adding an annual three-year defence inflation rate of 9 per cent, produces an estimated 2009 cost of C$342 million per ship. This may be a low figure. See United Kingdom, National Audit Office, *The Landing Ship Dock (Auxiliary) Project HC 98-III,* Report by the Comptroller and Auditor General, Session 2007–2008 (London: National Audit Office, 2007).

46 Jeremy Olver reports a 1993 cost of £154 million for the LPH and a 1998 cost of £100 million for the AOR, converted to Canadian dollars at an exchange rate of 1.77 per pound and adding an annual fifteen-year and ten-year defence inflation rate of 9 per cent, respectively, produces an estimated 2009 cost of C$993 million for the LPH and C$421 million per AOR. See Olver, 'The Royal Navy Postwar,' http://www.btinternet. com/~warship/. With the addition of the AORs, the navy would be able to forgo the Joint Support Ships, which have an estimated cost – based on the *2009–2010 Report on Plans and Priorities* – of $1.728 million.

47 Interestingly, though media attention to Budget 2010–11 focused on the government's declared intention to 'slow the rate of increase' of the defence budget, they paid no attention to the information supplied in the Main Estimates 2010–11 that were quietly tabled in the House the

day before the Budget Speech. Part 1 of the Main Estimates for 2010–11 actually showed a $1.862 billion, or 9.7 per cent, increase year-over-year. While $822 million of that total represented extra funding provided for the Afghanistan mission, which will cease with the 2011–12 fiscal year, the remaining increase of $1.02 billion represented an increase of 5.4 per cent – substantially ahead of the 2.6 per cent annual growth promised in the *Canada First Defence Strategy*. See Canada, Treasury Board, *Main Estimates*, 2010–11 (Ottawa: 2010), 13, table 9: International, Immigration and Defence programs, http://www.tbs-sct.gc.ca/est-pre/20102011/me-bpd/docs/index-eng.pdf.

13 WMD Proliferation, Missile Defence, and Outer Space: A Canadian Perspective

JAMES FERGUSSON AND
DAVID S. MCDONOUGH

Canadian concerns over proliferation of weapons of mass destruction (WMD) are unlikely to subside or fade in the post-9/11 era. The failure to discover a *substantial* WMD program in Iraq,[1] while appearing to vindicate a more sanguine approach to manage and control the WMD threat, should not overshadow the inexorable proliferation of WMD technology to state and non-state actors alike. North Korea and Iran remain serious proliferation challenges, with the former twice demonstrating its nuclear capabilities (2006 and 2009) and the latter quite open in its desire for a nuclear fuel cycle capable of generating weapons-grade fissile material. It would also be imprudent to dismiss the possibility that groups with a clear willingness to undertake mass-casualty terrorist attacks could – by their own devices or in cooperation with hostile regional proliferators – be armed with WMD in the future.

Canada is certainly not immune to a direct attack, sitting as it does within the 'second inner ring' if not exactly at the 'bullseye' of the terrorist target, nor would its national interests be unaffected by the consequences of an attack elsewhere. Canadian policymakers are fortunately familiar with the dangers of WMD, having lived 'along the flight path' between the nuclear arsenals of two superpowers long before it was in the 'inner ring' of the terrorist target,[2] and the country proved quite active in the non-proliferation, arms control, and disarmament (NACD) discussions of the Cold War. Yet Canada would do well to recognize the differing characteristics of the WMD threat in the current strategic environment – in which the 'horizontal proliferation' of WMD to rogue states and international terrorist groups takes precedence over the 'vertical proliferation' of nuclear weapons among the established nuclear powers. This does not mean that one should simply ignore the dangers of the sizable and modernizing arsenals of these major powers. But it does mean that Canada should acknowledge that the threat of a catastrophic nuclear exchange involving thousands of weapons has receded and the possibility of a much smaller use of WMD has arguably increased, and adapt its NACD policies accordingly.

This chapter seeks to re-examine Canada's policies towards WMD proliferation and offer suggestions for this particularly salient component of its overarching national security strategy. It begins with an overview of the current threat, with specific reference to how proliferation may affect Canada's national interests. Any renewed Canadian approach in dealing with WMD should recognize the potential strategic utility of ballistic missile defence (BMD). As such, this analysis will provide further examination of Canada's potential role in BMD and conclude with an analytical excursion on how Canadian participation in some future missile defence project could intersect with strategic developments in outer space.

Proliferation and Canada's National Interests

WMD was initially associated with nuclear weapons, given the genuinely massive destructive effects of its atomic and thermonuclear variants. Yet there was an understanding that technological advancement could make other types of weapons adaptable to mass destruction, notably with the addition of biological (viruses, bacteria, and toxins), chemical (blister, nerve, and other agents) and radiological weapons. Biological weapons are the only non-nuclear type of WMD that approach a strategic nuclear capability. Yet biological agents are also difficult to weaponize and disseminate. They are vulnerable to passive defences and meteorological conditions,[3] and often their prolonged incubation period limits their utility for strategic attacks against civilians, though incapacitating agents and toxins like botulinum can have tactical utility. In contrast, chemical weapons do not approach the lethality of either nuclear or biological weapons, and face comparable dissemination and vulnerability problems as bioweapons; while potentially employable in a tactical battlefield capacity, their effectiveness would be severely degraded against protected troops. Radiological 'dirty bombs' rely on conventional explosions to disperse the radioactive material and are generally envisioned as a potential threat emanating primarily from terrorist groups.

The most devastating, if not necessarily likely, WMD scenario facing Canada remains a nuclear exchange involving the major nuclear powers, which could involve the direct targeting of Canadian centres or, in the case of a more limited strike against the United States, result in radioactive fallout drifting into Canadian territory. The need to manage vertical proliferation – in which quantitative or qualitative changes in the nuclear arsenals of these states could abet strategic instability and increase the probability of nuclear war – formed a pillar within Canada's NACD policies during the Cold War.[4] But Canada needs to recognize that the threat posed by vertical proliferation, especially as it concerns the American, Russian, and Chinese nuclear arsenals, has fundamentally changed. Few envision a severe nuclear crisis taking place in the foreseeable future, with perhaps the sole exception resulting from a China-U.S. military confrontation over Taiwan. Despite all three countries modernizing their strategic forces, it is still far from apparent that there is an incipient arms race – the hostile intentions for any such action-reaction phenomenon is simply not present.[5] Of course, this does not mean that vertical proliferation has become totally benign. The launch-on-warning postures in the United States and Russia, and perhaps someday in China, do increase the possibility of an inadvertent or accidental nuclear war, while unchecked vertical proliferation could eventually encourage the transition to a more virulent sort of geostrategic rivalry. But it does mean that vertical nuclear proliferation, while certainly not risk free, is no longer as salient an issue.

Canada's most pressing security challenge is the proliferation of WMD technology and weapons to states and non-state actors beyond the major nuclear powers. Nuclear arsenals have long since proliferated to Israel, Pakistan, and India. A number of states already have suspected offensive biological and chemical weapon capabilities, and some seem intent in adding nuclear weapons to their WMD arsenal; and perhaps most worrisome, these 'latent proliferators' have seemingly advanced covert nuclear programs under a facade of adherence to the Non-Proliferation Treaty – as North Korea openly accomplished and Iran (and possibly others) are possibly following. The A.Q. Khan network, involved in trading nuclear technology with a number of developing states, has also brought into question the utility of current supply-side measures. These second-tier proliferation networks reflect another worrisome trend – the presence of non-state actors as both suppliers of *and* recipients for WMD technology. Terrorist groups like al Qaeda have shown both a clear interest in WMD and a clear willingness to commit mass-casualty attacks, and it would not be absurd to imagine that a future terrorist group will eventually be able to overcome technological hurdles to develop an effective WMD capability – or to acquire weapons (such as the infamous Russian 'suitcase nuke') from the black market.

Proliferation to these rogue states and non-state actors poses a direct threat to Canadian national security interests. Terrorists could employ WMD against Canadian centres with disastrous results, potentially as a 'proof of possession' attack in order to coerce the United States.[6] The possibility of a rogue state supplying WMD to terrorist proxies, haemorrhaging weapons in the event of a state collapse, or undertaking a 'bolt-from-the-blue' attack, unlikely as these scenarios may be, cannot be discounted. Canada might also find itself in a U.S.-led military conflict with a proliferating state, in which case intra-war deterrence becomes far more uncertain. It would not be difficult to imagine an adversary employing chemical weapons in a tactical capacity on the battlefield or pre-delegating the use of nuclear or biological weapons to strike regional American allies or North America as a last-ditch deterrent – or simply to enact revenge against its enemies and, given the prospect of nuclear retaliation, its own population as well.[7] The strategic implications are undoubtedly significant; proliferators may be seen as unable to be deterred by the threat of nuclear retaliation. And the capacity to threaten the United States directly, in the absence of a viable damage-limitation capability, could undermine the willingness of the United States to intervene in regional conflicts and protect allies from threats of nuclear blackmail.

Canadian security would be most directly endangered by the use of WMD against its industrial centres and population, whether civilians at home or soldiers fighting in a WMD environment. But our national interests could also be adversely affected in more indirect ways. Aside from the possibility of fallout from radioactive contamination or biological contagions, a WMD attack on the United States would likely result in a dramatic tightening of the Canada-U.S. border, with catastrophic consequences for the cross-border traffic underpinning our economy; the collapse of the current international trading system itself might not be unimaginable. Canada would also probably need to adapt to a seismic shift in American grand strategy; and whether the Unites States turns inward towards neo-isolationism or pursues ever more ferocious military policies abroad, the results will likely prove equally consequential for global order. One should also keep in mind that a direct attack on the United States might not even be necessary – a regional conflict involving WMD in South Asia or the Middle East or even an acceleration of horizontal proliferation could itself result in a gradual shift towards such a future.

Canada has traditionally relied on a number of multilateral non-proliferation agreements – the Non-Proliferation Treaty, Chemical Weapons Convention, the Biological and Toxin Weapons Convention, the Missile Technology Control Regime, the Nuclear Suppliers Group, among others – to contain the horizontal spread of WMD. There have also been notable successes in reversing this trend, including the denuclearization of South Africa, Ukraine, Kazakhstan, and Belarus; the Libyan decision to renounce its WMD programs; the curtailment of the nuclear ambitions of Brazil, Argentina, and a number of American allies; and the effective elimination of Iraq's WMD *ambitions* with the 2003 Iraq War. Yet it is also clear that the growing number of multilateral agreements within the non-proliferation regime have not stopped proliferation, and it is even debatable whether it has even slowed this trend – especially given the presence of countries with suspected biological and chemical weapon capabilities that are party to the chemical and biological weapons conventions and the evidence of latent nuclear proliferation abetted by the Non-Proliferation Treaty agreement itself – a dangerous loophole that no Additional Protocol will likely fully close.

Canada should continue its historic tradition of supporting the existing non-proliferation regime.[8] But reliance on these agreements, while likely necessary to prevent the further spread of WMD technology, can no longer contain this threat, and fortunately Canada has begun to recognize this fact. The country committed $1 billion over ten years for the G8 (Group of Eight) Global Partnership against the Spread of Weapons and Materials of Mass Destruction, which expands the U.S. cooperative effort to safeguard and destroy Russia's WMD stockpiles and ensure personnel involved in its massive WMD complex are properly employed. It is also a participant of the Proliferation Security Initiative, a loose 'coalition of the willing' to intercept the transport of WMD and their delivery systems, while following the American lead closer to home by strengthening border security against the WMD terrorist threat. Meanwhile, Canada has shown clear willingness as a Nuclear Supplier Group member to support the Indo-U.S. Nuclear Agreement, which is a tentative step towards accepting the reality that WMD in the hands of some countries (India) are less risky than in the hands of others (North Korea); this is especially significant, given Canada's historic involvement in India's nuclear program and pioneering role in nuclear export controls.

Other initiatives to deal with WMD proliferation will likely prove more controversial. The United States, for instance, has increasingly turned to counter-proliferation as an important supplement to its traditional support for the non-proliferation regime. Counter-proliferation would ensure that the United States has some protection against the WMD threat, most notably with active and passive defences, as well as counterforce capabilities (conventional and nuclear) to deter the use of WMD or pre-emptively destroy them. Canada has found some of these initiatives worthwhile, most notably with the Proliferation Security Initiative and the need for passive defences and consequence management, but it also retains some serious concerns. Active defences like BMD have long been considered anathema to Canada's traditional NACD policies, and the same can be said of recent U.S. nuclear weapon developments, such as the refinement of its hard-target kill capability, the development of prompt 'global strike,' and the now stalled efforts at low-yield bunker-busters. Indeed, these initiatives are seen as synergistic components for a purported U.S. first-strike capability,[9] and, as such, destabilizing to the fragile strategic balance with Russia and China; their deleterious impact on the non-proliferation regime is meanwhile criticized as a key driver for horizontal proliferation.

Yet Canada should keep in mind that it has greater latitude to support initiatives that might have been seen as dangerous in the Cold War. Russia and China may rhetorically object to these initiatives and even adopt modest measures to secure their arsenals' survivability, but this does not entail the beginnings of an arms race, nor does it increase the possibility of a nuclear crisis that could realistically result in a nuclear war. It is also likely that these U.S. strategic initiatives could be formulated to minimize any lingering first-strike anxiety in both Moscow and Beijing and minimize their current reliance on launch-on-warning.[10] And given the overwhelming conventional military disparity between the United States and proliferating states, it is absurd to assume that the sizable nuclear capabilities of established powers is the crux behind a rogue state's WMD ambitions. Simply put, the retention of nuclear weapons and the nuclear targeting of non-nuclear states, while contrary to the precepts of the Non-Proliferation Treaty itself, are unlikely to significantly increase the value of WMD for these proliferators. Even that small risk should, however, be weighed against the value that counter-proliferation could have in buttressing deterrence, ensuring a proportional pre-emptive or retaliatory strike if required, and providing a modicum of protection in the event of deterrence failure – not to mention reassuring U.S. allies on the credibility of its extended deterrence guarantees and thereby dampening their own potential nuclear ambitions.[11]

BMD, Outer Space, and Canada's Options

As a function of the relationship between geography and technology, the primary (if not only) direct military threat to Canada, its population, and its industrial centres is found in aerospace.[12] In recognizing this primacy during the Cold War, Canada, in conjunction with the United States, invested significant resources and established the bi-national North American Aerospace Defence Command (NORAD) to meet the initial threat posed by long-range Soviet bombers. With the onset of the ballistic missile age, the relevance of the air-breathing threat to Canada and North America declined, notwithstanding its partial rejuvenation with the advent of air-launched cruise missiles in the 1980s. Nonetheless, ballistic missiles armed with nuclear warheads emerged as the direct military threat by the 1960s, and in the absence of the capacity to intercept incoming ballistic missile warheads, Canada relied upon the U.S. strategic retaliatory deterrent to ensure its security.[13] In so doing, successive Canadian governments accepted the fundamental premises of nuclear deterrence and mutual assured destruction as the only means to prevent a devastating nuclear strike against Canadian targets. Moreover, they also uncritically accepted the idea that any attempt to defend against a ballistic missile attack would exacerbate vertical proliferation and undermine the stability of the mutual deterrence relationship between the United States and the Soviet Union.

Yet the political-strategic conditions that informed assumptions about mutual deterrence requirements during the Cold War have disappeared. WMD proliferation has emerged as a major security concern, with fears that proliferating states, specifically North Korea and Iran today, will acquire the capability to target North America with – in the worst case scenario – nuclear-tipped intercontinental ballistic missiles. Finally, the United States has developed and deployed a range of BMD systems in direct response to the strategic implications of proliferation. In the post–Cold War strategic world, marked by both WMD proliferation and rapidly maturing BMD technologies, Canadian thinking and policy has remained fully entrenched in the past. Defence options, either to deter or manage deterrence failure, are implicitly left to Canada's allies, and the defence of Canadian cities and industrial centres from a potential attack by a new nuclear state is effectively left in the hands of the United States. During the Cold War, North America was part of an integrated Soviet target set, such that any attack on Canada would likely have coincided with an attack on the United States. Canada could therefore credibly rely upon U.S. strategic retaliatory forces to deter any such attack. This was in contrast to concerns about the credibility of the U.S. extended strategic nuclear deterrent to North Atlantic Treaty Organization (NATO) – Europe, which informed continuous debates about NATO nuclear strategy and provided a rationale for independent French and British nuclear forces to ensure the coupling of U.S. strategic nuclear forces to the defence of Europe.[14]

Today, Canadian policymakers have implicitly assumed that the credibility of the extended U.S. nuclear umbrella remains in place and has been further supplemented by U.S. missile defences. Canada can rely on both to protect its cities and industrial centres, even though it has no input into U.S. strategic decision-making, defence priorities, or missile defence strategy. It is simply assumed that these new nuclear states will either view North America as a single integrated target set or target only the United States, given the limited size of their future strategic arsenals. Moreover, it is assumed as a function of current technology and the polar trajectories of incoming warheads from East Asia (North Korea) or the Middle East (Iran), that the United States will have no choice but to defend Canadian centres from an attack, which could be intentional or simply the result of poor guidance systems. Given the location of the current (and perhaps final) land-based missile defence layers – Fort Greely in Alaska, Vandenberg Air Force Base in California, and in the future possibly in Europe – unless U.S. early warning and warhead-tracking capabilities are able to identify the specific target of an incoming warhead prior to the point at which an interceptor can be launched, the United States will have no choice but to intercept every warhead in succession in order to ensure that U.S. centres are defended. If, however, Canada is conceived and specified as a separate independent target by such states, and/or U.S. capabilities are able to identify the actual target prior to the initial or subsequent interceptor attempts, then Canadian vulnerability to strategic threats and attack will be high, and its ability to rely on the United States questionable.

The United States, as the global superpower and leading Western nation, is likely to be the primary target for these new nuclear states as a means to deter American intervention. There would be little value in directly threatening Canada, as it would not intervene without its

American ally. Nonetheless, these states might perceive some utility in a direct, separate, independent threat to Canada, and indeed attack a Canadian target as a warning to the United States, thereby enhancing the credibility of its deterrent threat and potentially affecting the U.S. strategic calculus. Whether the United States in such a circumstance would explicitly threaten nuclear retaliation and indeed carry out the threat if a Canadian centre was destroyed with no direct physical damage to the United States would be an open question in the minds of all parties concerned, especially if the attacking nuclear state had sufficient capabilities to retaliate itself. Similarly, depending upon the size of their nuclear arsenals, relative to American BMD capabilities, one must wonder if the United States would expend one or more interceptors to defend a Canadian target if that meant the loss of a significant capability to defend the United States against a subsequent attack.[15] This assumes, of course, a U.S. capacity to identify the specific target of the initial attack.

In effect, Canada faces an extended deterrence dilemma potentially similar to that of the Europeans. U.S. President Franklin Roosevelt may have included Canada within the ambit of the American defence umbrella in 1938, but the exact meaning and nature of the umbrella today and in the future is an open question. As such, Canada faces two options to ensure its security and defence. It can choose to develop its own small, independent nuclear deterrent, although the probability that any government would even contemplate such an option is as close to zero as one can imagine. Alternatively, it can acquire its own limited BMD capabilities as a hedge against strategic uncertainty.

In addition to providing for its own defence, a Canadian missile defence capability would also provide a significant contribution to the defence of the United States. Envisioning one or two Canadian interceptor sites (in the East and West respectively) to defend Canadian centres, these sites would in effect provide an additional layer of defence for the continental United States against 'leakers' – those ballistic missiles that have flown through the current U.S. BMD layers. For this reason alone, the United States would be willing to transfer the technology to Canada and potentially share in the costs of the sites, as it has long done in NORAD. This contribution to the defence of North America would also likely lead the United States to add missile defence into the bi-national mission of NORAD, thereby facilitating Canadian input into the operational missile defence strategy and provide an avenue for substantive Canadian participation in any potential future NATO missile defence arrangement.

A limited Canadian BMD capability thus serves two major security interests. It provides a hedge against strategic uncertainty produced by proliferation, and it makes a significant contribution – psychologically and functionally – to the integrated defence of North America. Such a defence also provides a damage-limitation capability in worst-case scenarios of a strategic adversarial relationship between the United States and the major nuclear powers. As a limited capability, it would also not contribute to fears that BMD would destabilize these strategic relationships, even though such fears are often greatly exaggerated, and completely theoretical in being divorced from any significant political considerations governing the use of force.[16] Finally, such a capability has significant value relative to another area of growing strategic significance for Canada – outer space.

Today, no nation possesses the capability to threaten or attack Canada from dedicated strike platforms on orbit in outer space. Ballistic missiles would transit through outer space on their way to North American targets, but these missiles have never been conceptualized as a space strike weapon. However, intercontinental ballistic missiles do represent a capability to strike at targets located on orbit in outer space, as most recently demonstrated by the Chinese anti-satellite test in 2007.[17] Nuclear proliferators developing ballistic missile capabilities to threaten North America are simultaneously developing the means to destroy vital military and commercial satellites on orbit. Both North Korea and Iran have already demonstrated a fledgling capability to launch objects into space.[18] Nuclear weapons provide a crude, indiscriminate means to destroy satellites within their blast radius or render them inoperable through radiation and electromagnetic effects over a wide swath of orbital space. Satellites are also very vulnerable because of their predicable orbital paths, and they generally lack sufficient hardening against such effects.[19]

These states also have major incentives to develop the capability to threaten satellites on orbit. American and increasingly other Western military forces, including Canada's, have become increasingly dependent on space-based communication, earth observation, and navigation (the Global Positioning System) satellite systems, military and commercial, as vital force multipliers. Western economies have also become dependent on space, such that any loss of services would have a significant economic effect. In contrast, neither the North Korean, nor Iranian, nor other future proliferators' militaries or economies are dependent upon space, so the costs of such an attack would be marginal to their own interests. Threatening to attack these services in space thus may have deterrent value during a political crisis, and attacking them in the case of war may significantly degrade Western military capabilities and provide a means for them to strike at the Western economies, without fear of nuclear retaliation if nuclear weapons are employed.

While satellite vulnerability is clearly recognized in the United States, and likely to be identified in the Canada's forthcoming updated National Defence Space Policy and Strategy, neither the United States nor Canada has significant means to respond. Active defence measures raise the spectre of the weaponization of outer space, which directly conflicts with Canadian policy. Passive defensive measures, such as hardening, on-orbit manoeuvring, stealth, and a rapid reconstitution capability are very costly with current technology, especially for commercial operators, whose profit margins are small. For Canada in particular, the costs of space, especially in relation to other defence investment demands on a historically constrained budget, have significantly restricted Canada's role in outer space to the margins.[20]

Beyond its reliance upon commercial systems, Canada has depended largely upon access to U.S. military space to meet its security needs. The NORAD relationship with U.S. Space Command served as the primary conduit for Canadian access, the most recent example being Canadian involvement in the U.S. space-based infrared sensor program under the planned U.S. Space Tracking and Surveillance System. The Canadian strategy was to make limited niche investments, including personnel, to exploit the U.S. Space Command–NORAD relationship to obtain Canadian access to U.S. strategic thinking and planning regarding military space. However, this conduit ended with the U.S. decision to merge U.S. Space Command with U.S. Strategic Command in 2002, with the commander of NORAD thereafter dual-hatted as commander of U.S. Northern Command rather than Space Command.

This strategy is also at issue as a function of the missile defence question. Like missiles, BMD is generally conceptualized outside the military space file. Yet missile defence relies significantly on space assets. The U.S. Defence Support Program of infrared sensors in geosynchronous orbit plays a vital role in identifying ballistic missile launches and cueing the ground-based ballistic missile warning radars for target tracking. In the future, the Space Tracking and Surveillance System will provide in-flight warhead tracking, radar cueing, and target discrimination for missile defence batteries. The U.S. Space Surveillance Network, currently consisting of ground-based sensors, and in the future space-based sensors, ensures the ability to discriminate between existing satellites and space debris from hostile warheads, and will also support the Space Tracking and Surveillance System. Finally, it has long been recognized that the most effective means to intercept missiles is during their launch or boost phase, and an ideal location for boost-phase intercept is from space-based platforms (although there are no current U.S. development programs for space-based interceptors – kinetic or exotic – underway).

This is the third benefit of Canadian active engagement in missile defence. Besides providing defence for Canadian centres against emerging proliferation threats and making a significant contribution to the defence of North America, it promotes Canadian access to U.S. military space, and with it, a direct relationship with U.S. Strategic Command. This is not to suggest, however, that Canada should not invest in outer space capabilities and depend solely upon U.S. military space, as in the past. Investment in significant national capabilities, such as the future Radarsat Constellation, will provide significant value for Canadian national interests, especially in monitoring its national territory, and make a significant contribution to North American defence and overseas military operations. When combined with significant niche contributions to larger U.S. systems, such as Project Sapphire, Canada will acquire a significant role in the future issues concerning the military use of outer space, especially with regard to proliferation implications and responses, which in turn, will positively affect its relationship with the dominant strategic and space power – the United States.

Conclusion

For too long, Canadian national security strategy regarding NACD has been dominated by diplomatic efforts within multilateral agreements that make up the overarching non-proliferation regime. Successive Canadian governments have largely eschewed direct engagement on the defence side of the equation. To the question of what to do if non-proliferation efforts fail, the Canadian answer has been to delegate responsibility to its allies in general, and the United States in particular. Simply put, Canada has rejected counter-proliferation as a national interest. Horizontal proliferation may be a security priority in keeping with its importance among allies and the international community, but beyond domestic anti-terrorism and border security initiatives, defensive and counter-offensive military options have been largely rejected, or ignored.

Canada's largely one-dimensional NACD policy is at odds with its primary national security interest to defend and protect its territory, citizens, and economic well-being. In this regard, it is a conceptual hangover from the Cold War in which Canada had little choice but to rely upon the U.S. strategic deterrent in response to vertical proliferation, and play on the diplomatic margins. As new threats emerge from proliferating states and the possible acquisition of WMD by non-state actors, new Canadian responses are required and viable, given technological developments, to meet the nation's fundamental national security interests. In effect, the conceptual categories that determined Canada's NACD policies of the past have collapsed, and Canadian policies need to be developed on an integrated multi-dimensional basis, which includes military options.

While there are a range of defence and military choices to be entertained across the spectrum, including effective cruise missile defences, direct engagement in North American BMD ensures the defence of Canada against the emerging threat posed by current and future WMD proliferators in the fluid strategic environment. It also signals a firm Canadian commitment to the bi-national defence of the continent – a long-standing vital national security interest – and in combination with limited investments into defence space assets promotes a major role for Canada in the militarily and economically vital realm of outer space. Investments in BMD and outer space are also affordable, especially given the significant benefits they provide to Canada's national security and the likelihood of cost-sharing arrangements with the United States.

Naturally, ballistic missile defence in particular, to a lesser degree outer space defence investments, and the entire notion of counter-proliferation will meet with domestic opposition employing old Cold War rhetoric of contributing to arms races and subservience to the United States. Nonetheless, the strategic world has changed. Canadian decision-makers need to be sensitive to the potential impact of BMD and outer space on the established nuclear powers and the future relationship among them. But this sensitivity should not be an excuse to cede the defence of Canada to its superpower neighbour and relegate Canada to the margins in confronting the strategic threats of today and tomorrow.

NOTES

1 The Iraq Survey Group did not find substantial WMD programs or the large quantities of weapons and stockpiles that many scholars and intelligence analysts suspected. But it did find evidence that Iraq continued

WMD-related research and retained an ability to quickly reconstitute its chemical and biological weapon programs once the sanctions regime was lifted.

2 The terms *second inner ring* and *bullseye* have been frequently used by Canadian Senator Colin Kenny, and have appeared in prominent reports in his Standing Senate Committee on National Security and Defence. The phrase 'along the flight path' was coined by the late David Cox in reference to the fact that, in the event of a nuclear exchange between the United States and the Soviet Union, intercontinental bombers on either side would traverse Canadian airspace.

3 Yet these vulnerabilities can be mitigated. The United States successfully performed a number of biological weapon field tests in the 1950s and 1960s, while the Soviet Union had genetically engineered immune/UV-resistant biological agents and developed refrigerated warheads and specialized dispersal systems for their ballistic missiles to maximize delivery effectiveness.

4 Canada supported U.S. nuclear policies to buttress Allied deterrence against the Soviets, but also supported arms control measures meant to mitigate the dangers of their nuclear arsenals. For a good account, see Douglas Ross, 'Arms Control and Disarmament and the Canadian Approach to Global Order,' in *Canada's International Security Policy*, ed. David Dewitt and David Leyton-Brown, 251–90 (Toronto: Prentice Hall Canada, 1995).

5 China is increasingly modernizing its arsenal of ballistic missiles, while Russia has begun deployment of its next-generation intercontinental ballistic missiles that will have multiple independently targetable re-entry vehicle warheads and potentially new manoeuvring re-entry vehicle warheads designed to penetrate missile defences. Yet these should be seen as measures to only recalibrate the strategic balance – though there are certainly other political, bureaucratic, and technological reasons for their development.

6 As noted in Douglas Ross, 'Foreign Policy Challenges for Paul Martin: Canada's International Security Policy in an Era of American Hyperpower and Continental Vulnerability,' *International Journal* 58, no. 4 (Autumn 2003): 554.

7 This 'Hitler in the bunker' scenario could have arisen during the 1990–1 Gulf War. Iraq had deployed aerial bombs and SCUD missiles armed with biological and chemical weapons, and pre-delegated control of these weapons in the event of a cut in command and control links – as would have happened with a U.S. military drive to Baghdad. Chemical weapons could have been used against coalition troops, but a more worrisome possibility was a bio-weapon attack against Israel and consequent Israeli nuclear retaliation. See

Amatzia Baram, 'An Analysis of Iraqi WMD Strategy,' *Nonproliferation Review* 8, no. 2 (Summer 2001): 25–39.

8 Canada had historically developed significant technical expertise on WMD verification. This expertise was facilitated by creation of the Verification Research Unit in the Department of Foreign Affairs and International Trade, though this unit was discontinued in 1996.

9 See Keir Lieber and Daryl Press, 'The End of MAD? The Nuclear Dimension of US Primacy,' *International Security* 30, no. 4 (Spring 2006): 7–44. For an excellent critique, see Bruce Blair and Chen Yali, 'The Fallacy of Nuclear Primacy,' *China Security* (Autumn 2006): 51–77.

10 The United States could reduce its hard-target kill capability and reliance on launch-on-warning for a significant portion of its strategic nuclear arsenal, especially its sea-based force, while retaining both BMD and a number of highly accurate, low-yield and earth-penetrating bunker-busters. This 'limited counterforce capability' could be used for prompt 'global strikes,' but would not pose a significant 'decapitation' or silo-busting threat to Russia or China. A responsive nuclear infrastructure would be critical, as it would ensure that the United States has the capability to make rapid changes to its nuclear force posture if required and even more sizable reductions in its nuclear weapons stockpile.

11 The issue of comparative risk is forcefully made in Frank Harvey, *Smoke and Mirrors: Global Terrorism and the Illusion of Multilateral Security* (Toronto: University of Toronto Press, 2004).

12 The prospects of a land invasion of Canadian territory by a hostile nation are near zero, as few, if any, nations have the capacity to project and sustain land forces on the continent of North America. Notwithstanding the security importance of the sea lines of communication to Canada's economy and its ability to support forces deployed overseas and allies, maritime military threats to Canada also take on an aerospace form, whether these are long-range carrier-based strike aircraft or naval platforms capable of launching ballistic or cruise missiles.

13 The United States did develop a modest damage-limitation capability during the brief operation life of the Safeguard Anti-Ballistic Missile system. The single Safeguard site deployed near Cavalier, North Dakota, consisting of thirty long-range Spartan, and seventy short-range Sprint nuclear-tipped interceptors as allowed under the 1974 Protocol to the ABM Treaty, was declared operational in the spring of 1975, and subsequently cancelled in the fall of 1975.

14 Once the Soviet Union acquired the ballistic missile capability to target the United States, the credibility of the U.S. threat to commit suicide to defend its European allies was at issue. While neither NATO, nor the French,

nor the British possessed an 'assured destruction' capability, each could
threaten to inflict significant damage on the Soviet Union by destroying
its major cities. In so doing, the Soviet Union would be crippled, with the
United States undamaged and strategically dominant. In such a scenario,
the Soviet Union would likely face little choice but to strike at the United
States, thereby directly engaging U.S. strategic retaliatory forces. In effect,
NATO, France, and the United Kingdom each ensured the credible coupling of U.S. strategic nuclear forces to deter war in Europe. For an overview, see Lawrence Freedman, *The Evolution of Nuclear Strategy*, 2nd ed.
(London: Macmillan, 1989).

15 One cannot imagine an American president attempting to explain to the
U.S. public why a Canadian city was saved at the loss of a U.S. city. Indeed,
this was arguably implicit in the negotiations between Canada and the
United States on Canadian BMD participation in 2003–4, when the United
States refused to give any specific commitment to the missile defence
of Canada. James Fergusson, *Déjà vu All over Again: Canada and Ballistic
Missile Defence 1954–2009* (Vancouver: University of British Columbia
Press, Studies in Canadian Military History, 2010).

16 The basic argument was that missile defences generated fears of surprise
attack, thereby creating incentives for the parties to adopt a first-strike posture in the case of a crisis. Strategically, it assumed that the first act of war
would be a nearly simultaneous massive nuclear attack by both parties,
thereby destroying each other. Political considerations determining military actions were simply rejected in favour of technological determinism.

17 The United States deployed a kinetic-kill weapon launched by an F-15, and
the Soviet Union a co-orbital hunter-killer satellite as their respective anti-
satellite weapons during the Cold War.

18 All of North Korea's three-stage long-range ballistic missile tests, beginning
in 1998, have been justified by the regime as peaceful satellite launches. Iran
launched its first satellite into low earth orbit in February 2009.

19 All satellites are hardened or shielded to some degree to deal with natural radiation effects in outer space. But this is insufficient to deal with the
effects of a nuclear attack, except for dedicated military satellites, which
are likely to be sufficiently hardened or shielded.

20 Reflecting this, the first dedicated Canadian military satellite is expected
to be launched into space in 2012. Project Sapphire consists of a single
space-based optical sensor for the surveillance of space. For an overview of
Canada and national security space, see James Fergusson and Steve James,
Canada, National Security and Outer Space (Calgary: Canadian Defence and
Foreign Affairs Institute, 2007).

14 Counter-Capability and Counter-Motivation: A Counterterrorism Strategy for Canada

ALEX S. WILNER

Saad Khalid garnered the nickname 'Abu Canada' (Father of Canada) while participating at a makeshift terrorist training camp in Ontario in December 2005. The nom de guerre originated from the red toque emblazoned with the word *Canada* Khalid wore as he took part in obstacle courses, paintball games, shooting practice, and other outdoor exercises.[1] Three-and-a-half years later, Khalid would appear before a Brampton, Ontario, courtroom and enter a guilty plea to aiding a Canadian terrorist cell preparing bombs for attacks in Toronto. He was eventually handed a twenty-year prison sentence, becoming the second individual convicted on terrorism charges in connection to the 2006 arrest of the 'Toronto 18.' Court documents reveal an intricate plot that was to culminate in the detonation of explosive-laden vans against the Toronto Stocks Exchange, the Canadian Security Intelligence Service's (CSIS) headquarters, and other targets. The group's strategic rationale, discussed at a 2006 meeting, was to 'screw [Prime Minister Stephen] Harper, the government and the military' and force Canada to 'withdraw its troops from Afghanistan.' Canada would capitulate, a member explained, 'because it [was] not tough like Britain or the United States.'[2]

The Toronto case is a stark reminder of the evolving nature of contemporary Islamist terrorism. Paralleling trends in other Western countries, the 2006 plot is marked by the involvement of citizens born, raised, and/or educated within the country they plan to attack. Self-radicalized, these individuals independently finance and plan acts of terrorism with little support from international groups. Most frightening, home-grown terrorists are nearly indistinguishable from other citizens: they share their society's language, cultural characteristics, and national and social mores. And yet the Toronto suspects vehemently rejected Canada's national values and, in trading ballots for bullets, threatened its liberal-democratic political system and challenged its open and inclusive society. In targeting other Canadian citizens, they came to see their compatriots as legitimate targets. And in tying their own local struggle to al Qaeda's global war with the West, the Toronto 18 sided with a consortium of international actors that have placed Canada, the United States, and their friends and allies on one side of an enduring and near-cosmic socio-political struggle.

This last development is the most troubling. In the decade since al Qaeda's attack on New York City and Washington, DC, terrorism has emerged as a pre-eminent global security concern, and counterterrorism has acquired unprecedented importance in the making of policy. Despite tactical successes against al Qaeda at the international level – perhaps best epitomized by the daring U.S. Special Operations raid that killed Osama bin Laden in May 2011 in Abbottabad, Pakistan – al Qaeda–inspired Islamist terrorism is on the rise globally. This suggests that the conflict with al Qaeda has entered a second, ideological front for the very hearts and minds of Westerners and implies further that the organization remains a potent, resilient, and driven adversary.

This chapter investigates how terrorism threatens Canadian national interests and suggests ways in which counterterrorism policy might be effectively tailored to contend with this security challenge. Focused primarily on al Qaeda and Islamist terrorism, the chapter begins by unpacking contemporary threats into international, regional, and home-grown dimensions. Doing so identifies precisely where and how Canadian interests are threatened. In section two, counterterrorism is broken down into its two primary processes – counter-capability and counter-motivation – helping to illustrate the range of strategies and policies that will be needed to effectively confront al Qaeda. In the final section, these two counterterrorism processes are applied to each of the three dimensions of Islamist terrorism, illustrating the many (and diverse) approaches Canadian counterterrorism must adopt if it is to properly contend with emerging threats.

Al Qaeda: International, Regional, and Home-grown Dimensions

For the purpose of this chapter, terrorism is defined as the use of indiscriminate violence against non-combatants by non-state actors with the purpose of generating fear in order to signal, communicate, and/or achieve particular socio-political objectives. The Canadian Forces, in its 2008 field manual *Counter-Insurgency Operations,* posits that terrorism is utilized 'to intimidate and coerce governments [and] societies.' The importance of terrorism, the manual explains, 'is not in the act itself, but in the message that it sends to various audiences.'[3] These definitions imply that terrorism creates 'psychological repercussions' beyond the immediate victims and that death and destruction may be a secondary objective, a means to other ends.[4] Terrorism is usually employed to address real or perceive socio-political and/or ideological grievances and to promote and achieve local, regional, and international agendas by compelling a stronger adversary to accept demands by threatening further violence. It is also used to communicate strength, capabilities, and resolve, and/or to undermine the legitimacy of a government by laying bear its inability to properly contend with and prevent attacks.

Though 9/11 brought global terrorism to the forefront of international relations, terrorism is not a new development. Nationalist and irredentist organizations have used terrorism for decades in hopes of securing independence, while Marxist extremists, right-wing fundamentalists, and radical environmentalists have relied on terrorism to force socio-political change. Canadians themselves have been victims of terrorism long before 2001. In the 1960s, the Front de libération du Québec (FLQ) used terrorism to wrest a sovereign Quebec from Canada. It bombed the Montreal Stock Exchange, conducted a mail-bombing campaign, and abducted and murdered individual policymakers. In 1985, extremist Canadian Sikhs aligned with Babbar Khalsa were responsible for the deadliest terrorist attack prior to 9/11 when they placed explosives on two aircraft departing Vancouver International Airport; one bomb detonated mid-flight on Air India Flight 182 and killed 280 Canadians. Direct Action (aka the Squamish Five) conducted small attacks across Canada in the 1980s as part of its anti-capitalist campaign, while eco-terrorists associated with Earth First! and the Earth Liberation Army used sabotage, tree spiking, and arson to destroy resource extraction infrastructure and intimidate individuals. The recent bombings of EnCana pipelines in British Columbia are a case in point.

Yet it was the severity and gravity of 9/11 that caught the world's, and Canada's, attention. While it is false to suggest that terrorism began with al Qaeda, its 2001 attack signified a shift in terror's momentum. With 9/11, al Qaeda demonstrated that a relatively small, ill-equipped, non-state organization could carry out an attack that retained the destructive potential once reserved to states alone. Its sheer contempt for human life and ability to identify, penetrate, and attack so-called soft spots in the single most powerful state in the world – to say nothing of the fanatical devotion of its suicide operatives – suggested that mass-casualty terrorism on the scale of 9/11 could and would be repeated. The idea that al Qaeda might develop chemical, biological, radiological, and nuclear weapons – as other groups, namely Japan's Aum Shinrikyo, had already done – suggested further that the traditional conceptions of state power and security had evolved.

Al Qaeda and its Islamist allies represent a multifaceted security challenge. Islamist terrorism connotes both religious and political characteristics. While its adherents rely on religious principles to guide their actions, Islamist terrorism is nonetheless rooted in socio-political aspirations, with its primary objective the establishment of Islamic governance over particular territories and the propagation of strict interpretations of sharia law. Importantly, political power rather than religion is the genesis of the violence. As Fawaz Gerges explains, 'Religion became [the jihadist] tool for political mobilization.' While regional Islamist political systems, like Taliban Afghanistan, present day Sudan and Gaza, and parts of Somalia and Pakistan are 'clothed in Islamic dress,' they are nonetheless fashioned along the constructs of power and territorial and socio-political control. 'There is nothing uniquely "Islamic,"' Gerges concludes, about these cases, 'except the rhetoric and the symbolism.'[5] Al Qaeda's foremost goal is the consolidation of the global Islamist movement, which it pursues by supporting like-minded groups, attacking Western interests, and facilitating the establishment of Islamist regimes.

Of all contemporary terrorist threats, al Qaeda is Canada's primary security concern. On 9/11, it was directly responsible for the death of twenty-four Canadians. The organization has threatened Canada directly on five occasions, including a 2006 communiqué promising an 'operation similar to New York, Madrid, London and their sisters.'[6] Its regional franchises have also killed and injured Canadians. Al Qaeda in Iraq, for instance, killed two Canadians in its 2003 bombing of the UN headquarters in Baghdad and abducted another two in 2005. An April 2011 bombing of a popular tourist cafe in Marrakesh, Morocco, likely carried out by associates of al Qaeda in the Islamic Maghreb, killed Montrealer Michal Zekry (pregnant at the time of her death) and her husband, Messod Wizman. Its Indonesian ally, Jemaah Islamiyah, killed two Canadians in its 2002 Bali attack, injured three more in 2005, and another two in 2009. In Niger, two Canadian diplomats were captured and delivered to al Qaeda in the Islamic Maghreb in 2009.[7] In Afghanistan, Canada's military and diplomatic corps face a number of groups like the Taliban, the Islamic Movement of Uzbekistan, the Tora Bora Military Front, Hezb-i-Islami Gulbuddin, and Tehrik-i-Taliban that are ideologically and tactically allied with al Qaeda. And, as recent events in Ontario suggest, al Qaeda inspires Canadian citizens to carry out attacks within the country. These examples highlight the diffuse nature of the threat. Internationally, the organization attacks Western interests at home and abroad. Regionally, it supports violent sub-state Islamist groups in Africa, Asia, and the Middle East by offering structural, financial, tactical, and ideological assistance. And within Western states, al Qaeda motivates and assists radicalized citizens to attack their compatriots.

At each level of abstraction, al Qaeda threatens Canadian national interests.[8] Internationally, it directly threatens the welfare and well-being of Canadians and our friends and allies by organizing attacks against Western assets. Al Qaeda's 2006 liquid bomb plot, for instance, was an attempt to destroy transatlantic aircraft, including two Air Canada flights with service from London to Montreal and Toronto, which would have killed hundreds of Canadians and thousands of others. Regionally, it supports local insurgent efforts that destabilize states. It does so in Saudi Arabia, Iraq, Algeria, Afghanistan, Pakistan, Indonesia, Yemen, Somalia, and elsewhere, with the hope of helping like-minded groups wrest control from governments. In exchange for its assistance, al Qaeda is allowed to establish safe havens from which it can train operatives and organize international attacks. Al Qaeda's regional struggle is also an ideological one: in destabilizing governments, it hopes to consolidate a transnational Islamist political system that is in many respects an affront to democracy and liberal ideals like the rule of law and individual rights. Al Qaeda–sponsored totalitarian regimes, like the Taliban of Afghanistan, are the antithesis of Canadian values and represent a threat to Canada's humanitarian interests. Finally, at home, al Qaeda's virulent ideology indoctrinates Canadians and compels them to attack other citizens to promote the organization's broader socio-political goals. Canadians who internalize this ideology also espouse anti-democratic ideals that undermine Canada's political ideology, historical narrative, and related value systems. As a report by the Dutch General Intelligence and Security Service posits, the process of societal rejection and 'extreme isolationism' threatens democratic political systems because it 'gradually harm[s] social cohesion and solidarity' while undermining fundamental human rights.[9]

Unpacking the manner in which al Qaeda physically and ideologically threatens Canadians adds nuance to the contours of the security challenge and helps identify the responses that are required to defend Canadian interests. It also allows Canada to focus its strategic priorities. While Canadians are right to condemn terrorism always and everywhere as an affront to our fundamental values, and while the government should do its utmost to reiterate openly that terrorism is never justified under any circumstance, it is a strategic reality that some terrorist threats, like al Qaeda, are more pressing than others. The point is that Canadian counterterrorism prioritizes international, regional, and home-grown challenges and ensures decision-makers have a range of responses that address the whole spectrum of potential threat scenarios.

A Two-Pronged Defence: Counter-Capability and Counter-Motivation

The 9/11 attacks prompted the immediate establishment of a comprehensive and international counterterrorism coalition. Canada was an early part of that effort. On 12 September 2001, alongside its eighteen North Atlantic Treaty Organization allies, Canada invoked Article V of the North Atlantic Treaty, pronouncing al Qaeda's attack on the United States as an attack against it. The coalition's primary objective was to degrade al Qaeda's military capability. With UN approval, the Taliban regime that provided shelter was removed by force, al Qaeda bases of operation were eliminated, and its leaders and fighters were killed and captured. Despite these losses, al Qaeda survived and eventually regrouped. It did so by partially evolving from a centrally organized and territorially rooted terrorist group into a diffuse ideological movement able to collude with and motivate others to plan acts of terrorism. Al Qaeda's successful transformation was based, in part, on its organizational resilience and a misguided shift in global counterterrorism efforts. That a subset of the U.S.-led counterterrorism coalition turned its attention towards invading Iraq in 2003 added credence to Osama bin Laden's conspiratorial claims that his organization embodied a legitimate and necessary Islamic vanguard against an encroaching Western adversary. The invasion compelled disparate groups and individuals angered by Western intervention to unite and hoist the group's banner.[10] As a result, by 2006, al Qaeda's challenge to Canada and the West had diversified: it threatened physical violence, death, and destruction in the West; galvanized an ideology that was anathema to democratic and humanitarian norms; and assisted insurgencies that destabilized entire regions.

Properly combating al Qaeda requires two distinct though related strategies. First, Canada, in concert with others, must diminish al Qaeda's capability to organize and facilitate terrorism. Second, Canada should undermine the group's ability to motivate would-be supporters at the regional and home-grown level. These approaches – counter-capability and counter-motivation, respectively – represent the twin pillars of a broader counterterrorism strategy and are the basis for a multitude of tactics. For instance, counter-capability approaches are tactical and coercive, the idea being to eliminate the source of power that allows al Qaeda to organize acts of terrorism. Destroying training facilities, targeting terrorist leaders, restricting safe havens, deterring state sponsorship, strengthening state institutions, constricting terrorist financing, and disrupting plots diminish the group's ability to commit acts of terrorism and limit its capacity to assist regional groups. Counter-motivation approaches, on the other hand, challenge the logic and legitimacy of al Qaeda's ideology. They do so by addressing the socio-political and economic factors that help foster support for terrorism, impeding the achievement of al Qaeda's socio-political objectives, fostering and diffusing anti-terrorism norms, and championing and rewarding non-violent behavioural alternatives. These tactics focus on degrading the ideological and practical rationales for terrorism and on denying its efficacy in addressing socio-political grievances.

To tackle this terrorist threat on all fronts, Canadian security policy must integrate both elements of counterterrorism into its strategy. By unpacking al Qaeda into a global, regional, and home-grown phenomenon and presenting counterterrorism as two processes, decision-makers have the ability to decide which element of the broader strategy and in what combination should be given priority and under what circumstance. Combating al Qaeda's role in fostering home-grown terrorism, for instance, will require a set of policies and counter-strategies that are different from combating its alliance with Taliban factions fighting in Kandahar. While military force will at times be required, so too will diplomatic, defensive, and developmental endeavours. The challenge for Canada is to appreciate how best to prioritize and tailor its counterterrorism efforts and find the appropriate strategic balance to respond to al Qaeda's international, regional, and home-grown threat.

Combating al Qaeda's International Dimension

Combating al Qaeda internationally begins by continually diminishing its coercive abilities by militarily engaging the organization and forcing it to take defensive positions. Targeting, killing, and, when possible, capturing al Qaeda leaders will keep the organization disoriented.[11] In discussing the efficacy of precision attacks, Central Intelligence Agency Director Leon Panetta has argued that, 'very frankly, it's the only game in town in terms of confronting or trying to disrupt the al Qaeda leadership.'[12] Though normatively, politically, and legally contentious, targeted killings force al Qaeda facilitators underground, disrupt its command and control mechanisms, and diminish its capabilities.[13] Though it may be too early to accurately assess the exact consequences bin Laden's death will have on the global jihadi movement, the removal of al Qaeda's chief operator, recruiter, and ideologue will almost certainly have a lasting effect. Renewed emphasis should go towards eliminating and/or capturing Ayman al-Zawahiri – bin Laden's replacement – and other top al Qaeda facilitators. Though some of these figures control little of al Qaeda's regional operational planning, their continued freedom embarrasses international efforts and galvanizes its supporters.

Military force alone, however, will not defeat al Qaeda; countermotivational efforts must accompany coercive measures. To this end, an important international element is the continued denunciation of terrorism. Vilifying terrorist violence, in all cases regardless of geography and circumstance, delegitimizes its use. Steven Simon and Jeff Martini suggest that denying terrorist groups the constituent support they need to survive requires a 'marshalling [of] international norms to stigmatize terrorism,' which push the tactic 'farther towards the margins' of acceptable behaviour. The process requires both top-down stimulus (defining what actions are justified at the international level and shaming non-compliance) and bottom-up action (where local community leaders enforce 'habitual compliance' with counterterrorism norms).[14]

On both counts, Canada can play a role. Firstly, Canada collects vital intelligence on Afghanistan that can be utilized by our forces and those of our traditional allies to track, capture, and if necessary, eliminate terrorist leaders. CSIS, the Communications Security Establishment, and the Intelligence Branch of the Canadian Forces are all active in Afghanistan.[15] While the exact nature of this work is not publicly known, there is little doubt that Canadian intelligence officers have an intimate knowledge of the conflict environment and are an asset to counter-capability operations like precision attacks. On the second matter, Canada can help construct, strengthen, and disseminate international counterterrorism norms and regimes. It can use its status with international institutions, like the UN, the Group of Eight (G8), and La Francophonie to reiterate its staunch disapproval of terrorism. Canada can do so by going beyond denouncing al Qaeda to vehemently rejecting all terrorism, always and everywhere. The current government has done so repeatedly.[16] Condemnations against terrorism carry weight domestically and internationally. They illustrate Canada's commitment to fight terrorism wherever it occurs and strengthen counterterrorism norms by affirming Canada's commitment to work with like-minded states in the protection of democracy and the rule of law.

Countering al Qaeda's Regional Resurgence

Countering al Qaeda's resurgence regionally will require a multifaceted strategy. Al Qaeda's popularity with local communities, its ties with regional terrorist groups, and expanding franchises are a serious security concern. Regional diffusion is al Qaeda's best chance to regain territorial control and rebuild its military capabilities. Reversing the group's regional resurgence is therefore a strategic priority for Canada.

First, al Qaeda safe havens and training facilities must be dismantled. At times, this will require Western military force, as is occurring today in Afghanistan, Iraq, Pakistan, and Somalia. Other times, indigenous militaries can be prompted to do so themselves, as is taking place in Algeria, Saudi Arabia, Indonesia, Yemen, and Egypt. Harassing al Qaeda weakens its territorial consolidation. The case of al Qaeda in Iraq is informative. A 2007 American troop surge of over thirty thousand soldiers is credited – alongside the establishment of anti–al Qaeda Awakening Councils – with having diminished its base of operations. According to U.S. Ambassador Ryan Crocker, the troop surge helped defeat al Qaeda's Iraq franchise by assisting Iraqis themselves 'to forcibly resist' al-Qaeda and by assuring them that 'the coalition was there in support of their efforts.'[17] By 2008, al Qaeda lost its foothold, and violence dropped to below 2004 levels.

Second, al Qaeda's growing popularity with local communities must be addressed. The strategic goal should be to persuade local Islamists to sever their ties with al Qaeda. Doing so diminishes the threat of terrorism, constricts terrorist ranks, and reduces its reach. Events in Libya illustrate how disassociation might work. Local Islamists associated with the Libyan Islamic Fighting Group (LIFG) renounced a 2007 merger with al Qaeda and were, until political instability rocked North Africa, politically addressing their grievances with the Libyan government. The LIFG's strategic reversal stemmed from a desire to re-emphasize local efforts, like the establishment of an Islamic state, rather than international ones, like waging global jihad at al Qaeda's behest. Importantly, in September 2009, the imprisoned leaders of the LIFG prepared a religious refutation, *Corrective Studies in Understanding Jihad, Accountability, and the Judgment of People*, that contradicted al Qaeda's rationales for terrorism.[18] In exchange, the Libyan government released LIFG prisoners, began dismantling Abu Salim prison (where, reportedly, over a thousand militants were killed in the 1990s), and established 'compensation tribunals' to address historical wrongdoings.[19]

While LIFG's decoupling from al Qaeda likely stanched the organization's regional diffusion, the Libyan civil war that began in February 2011 (ongoing as of this writing) greatly complicates long-term assessments. For starters, it is difficult to gauge how many members of the LIFG credibly and sincerely broke ranks with al Qaeda. In fact, around the time of the 2007 merger, a 'surge' of Libyan foreign fighters travelled to Iraq to join the group. According to the Combating Terrorism Center, Libya ranked second (behind only Saudi Arabia) as the country of origin of al Qaeda in Iraq's foreign fighters between 2006 and 2007. But as a per capita measurement, Libya contributed far more fighters than any other country.[20] Some of these militants are likely to have returned home to Libya following the demise of al Qaeda in Iraq. Second, it has become increasingly apparent that former members of the LIFG (including those who had allied themselves with al Qaeda) have joined the Libyan 'rebels' fighting Colonel Muammar Gaddafi. Importantly, according to the Combating Terrorism Centre report, nearly 90 per cent of Iraq's Libyan fighters were recruited from the cities of Darnah and Benghazi, currently the stronghold of the anti-Gaddafi rebel force. While developments are ongoing and the leadership and exact make-up of the rebel force remain unclear, there is mounting suspicion that LIFG and al Qaeda members are actively present.[21] What this means for al Qaeda's future in North Africa is uncertain.

Third, the group's ideology must be delegitimized and its regional supporters de-radicalized. This can be done by encouraging theologians and former al Qaeda allies, like members of the LIFG, to challenge al Qaeda on religious and ideological grounds. A number of prominent jihadi scholars have retracted their support for terrorism in recent years. For instance, in 2007, Sayyid Imam Sharif (aka Dr Fadl), a one-time leader of Egypt's Islamic Jihad and an early al Qaeda ideologue, retracted his commitment to bin Laden. In articles published in Egypt, Dr Fadl argued, 'We are prohibited from committing aggression, even if the enemies of Islam do that' and explicitly forbade the practice of *takfir* (in which apostate Muslims are identified and targeted) along with the killing of non-Muslims in Muslim countries and members of non-Sunni Muslim sects.[22] Saudi scholars Sheikh Su'ud al-Rushud and Sheikh al-Askar followed, condemning al Qaeda's use of religious edicts that permitted suicide attacks. 'The act of "killing the soul" sanctified by Allah,' they argued, brings upon the 'individual committing suicide suffering from Allah.'[23] Another Saudi Sheikh, Salman al-Awdah (al-Ouda), attacked bin Laden on television for killing hundreds of thousands of civilians.

By 2008, al Qaeda was forced to expend half its airtime defending its legitimacy. Bin Laden himself reiterated that 'the Muslim victims who fall during the operations against the infidel Crusaders ... are not the intended targets,' and Zarwahiri countered Dr Fadl in a lengthy treatise.[24] Alongside these criticisms, a number of de-radicalization programs have sprung up over the past two years. In Saudi Arabia, Egypt, and Indonesia, for instance, captured militants are placed into education programs in which they are given lectures by prominent scholars and participate in courses that contradict and ridicule al Qaeda on religious and political precepts.[25] The combined effect of delegitimization and de-radicalization is the turning of militants away from terrorism and a restriction of its recruitment base.

Fourth and finally, Western policies that galvanize communities susceptible to al Qaeda's ideology should be addressed. To this end, rebuilding Iraq and Afghanistan, stabilizing Somalia, Sudan, and Lebanon, and promoting a cessation of conflict between Palestinians and Israelis should be rigorously sought. The democracy movements that sprang up in Tunisia, Egypt, Libya, and elsewhere in the Middle East in early 2011 should also be bolstered. To be sure, these are lofty and complicated goals, yet inaction on the factors that propagate terrorism only strengthens al Qaeda.

Canada can rebuff al Qaeda's growing regional presence in a number of ways. First, Canada's military, diplomatic, and developmental efforts in Afghanistan impede its local resurgence. While critics of the Afghan mission posit that fighting the Taliban and countering al Qaeda are two separate endeavours, these groups think otherwise.[26] Other groups fighting in Canada's field of operations – like the Islamic Movement of Uzbekistan, the Tora Bora Military Front, and Hezb-i-Islami Gulbuddin – are all al Qaeda allies. As a result, Canada's Afghan mission might be properly understood as one part of the global effort to counter al Qaeda's regional presence. By bolstering Kabul's fledgling democratic government, training the Afghan National Police and Afghan National Army, and assisting international and indigenous counterinsurgency efforts, Canada eliminates a potential al Qaeda sanctuary. At the very least, it ensures that the Taliban and others cannot effectively operate in the country and forces al Qaeda to expend time, energy, and personnel reinforcing its allies rather than planning acts of international terrorism.

Similarly, Canada can assist other governments to assert sovereign control over their borders by helping them construct viable governing, policing, and judicial institutions. Canada has already done so in Iraq, by rebuilding and training police forces and assisting in the construction of a constitution, and could add its diplomatic weight behind similar efforts in Somalia, Pakistan, Egypt, Tunisia, and Lebanon. Canada's military involvement in Libya, as a result of UN Security Council Resolution 1973 and the establishment of a NATO-enforced 'no-fly' zone, deserves mention as well. While the military mission is ongoing and its achievement, as of April 2011, remains uncertain, the danger for Canada and its allies is clear. Failure to stabilize a post-Gaddafi Libya risks giving al Qaeda and other militant Islamists room to consolidate local support. Already there is concern that Libyan arms – pilfered from their caches by the rebel movement – might fall into terrorist hands.[27] The greatest fear is that terrorists will acquire sophisticated shoulder-fired anti-aircraft missiles, like those launched in 2002 against an Israeli passenger aircraft departing Mombasa, Kenya. Shoring up and assisting a post-conflict regime in Libya will be critical. None of these ventures alone will eradicate al Qaeda, but piecemeal successes are an important step in reducing the threat of global terrorism.

Second, Canadian diplomatic efforts can help facilitate the sort of rapprochement that took place in Libya between the LIFG and the government. In Afghanistan, for instance, Canada is involved in 'flipping' elements of the Taliban, compelling groups and individuals to cease their support for terrorism and al Qaeda in exchange for economic opportunities and access to the political system. By sponsoring national reconciliation programs, like Afghanistan's Allegiance Program and Program Takhim e-Solh, Canada can help in conflict resolution.[28] Canada can also financially support individual de-radicalization programs. These programs, while based and organized overseas, serve Canada's national interests because the international delegitimization of al Qaeda and the de-radicalization of its foot soldiers diminish its global standing and thin its ranks.

Third, Canada can help ensure Canadians themselves do not inadvertently or purposefully support and assist foreign terrorist organizations. While it occurs rarely, an increasing number of Canadian citizens have turned up fighting in regional conflicts. In May 2007, a Canadian purportedly intent on undertaking jihad in Afghanistan was arrested in Kabul. In January 2008, Canadian Mohammed Jabarah was sentenced to life in prison in the United States for a 2001 embassy plot, while his brother Abdel died in a 2003 firefight in Saudi Arabia.[29] Canadians have also been reportedly killed in both Pakistan and Somalia.[30] And other Canadians are suspected of having trained with and/or joined other groups fighting in Algeria, Lebanon, Chechnya, and Iraq.[31] Canada's domestic security apparatus should do its utmost to impede Canadians from joining foreign terrorist groups and should locate, monitor, and obstruct recruiters active in the country. When Canadians do show up on foreign battlefields, the government should rigorously investigate the process that got them there.

Finally, Canada should ensure that its official list of terrorist entities reflects global trends. According to Public Safety Canada, the listing of an entity is 'a very public means' of identifying a group associated with terrorism. When listed, an entity's property and finances are subject to seizure, and it becomes a criminal offence to 'knowingly participate in or contribute to ... any activity' that enhances the ability of the group in question. Canada's current list includes forty-two organizations. While al Qaeda has long been listed, its franchise in Iraq is not, and its affiliates in Yemen were added only in late 2010. The Taliban is also missing, though it is identified as an ally of other listed entities, including Gulbuddin Hekmatyar and Hezb-i-Islami Gulbuddin. Canada should take steps to update its list of foreign terrorist organizations more regularly. Al Qaeda's rapid evolution and growing association with regional groups deserves Canada's full attention.

Combating Al Qaeda's Home-grown Appeal

Home-grown Islamist terrorism is a worldwide phenomenon. It is marked, first and foremost, by the participation of radicalized citizens and long-term residents born, raised, and/or educated in the country targeted with violence. An expansive study of several hundred European Islamist terrorists found that over 90 per cent were residents of a European country and almost 60 per cent held European citizenship.[32] A defining characteristic is the manner in which al Qaeda 'inspires' Westerners to target their compatriots. With a little encouragement, individuals predisposed to accept al Qaeda's ideology radicalize and independently prepare acts of violence.[33] Since the 2004 Madrid bombings, in which seven of the twenty-one individuals convicted were Spaniards, several dozen home-grown attacks have been carried out and/or foiled in North America, Europe, and Australia. Recent trends suggest al Qaeda has taken notice and has shifted its resources towards directly facilitating home-grown attacks. Its goal is to go beyond inspiring radicalized Western Islamists to assisting them. A growing portion of al Qaeda's Internet propaganda, for instance, is now produced in English, tailored specifically to resonate with Anglo-Saxon audiences. In July 2010, al Qaeda in the Arabian Peninsula began publishing a sophisticated, English-language propaganda magazine online.

Furthermore, Western citizens who participated in regional conflicts are now returning home. Some individuals are likely to have been purposefully dispatched by al Qaeda and others to help organize attacks in their countries of origin. This appears to have been the case with Najibullah Zazi's 2009 plot to attack New York City's subway, Faisal Shahzad's 2010 car bombing at Times Square, New York, and Taimour Abdulwahab al-Abdaly's 2010 suicide attack in Stockholm, Sweden. Western foreign fighters are al Qaeda's prize possession – they have 'clean passports' that allow them to more easily slip into Western countries and have cultural and linguistic backgrounds that help them infiltrate unnoticed. Developments like these represent an emerging crossroad at which al Qaeda's international role facilitates home-grown terrorism.

Canada, too, is threatened by home-grown terrorism and has citizens fighting overseas. As of April 2010, fourteen Canadians have been found guilty under Canada's Anti-Terrorism Act, thirteen of whom were inspired by al Qaeda. The list of perpetrators includes Ottawa-native Mohammad Khawaja, guilty of building detonators for attacks in the United Kingdom; Quebecer Said Namouh, an al Qaeda sympathizer; and eleven members of the Toronto 18, a home-grown cell planning bombing atrocities in and around Toronto. Of these convicts, four are serving life sentences and four are serving ten years or more. Another five Canadians are awaiting terrorism trials stemming from arrests conducted in 2010 and 2011 in Alberta and Ontario.

Countering home-grown terrorism in Canada will require managing threats. First, home-grown organizations must be tracked and dismantled, suspected terrorists identified, arrested, and tried. Canada's police force is an essential component of this process. Canadian communities are protected by nearly ninety thousand police and Royal Canadian Mounted Police (RCMP) officers, who have a keen sense of the socio-political intricacies that mark their environments and are well positioned to assist CSIS in domestic counterterrorism. Training even a fraction of Canada's police force in counterterrorism will provide a network of active intelligence gatherers in all of Canada's major cities. Second, because home-grown cells often have contacts, affiliates, and members living in other Western countries, honing international counterterrorism, intelligence-sharing, and policing partnerships is critical. The 2006 arrests in Ontario, for instance, were supported by cooperation among enforcement agencies in Canada, the United States, Denmark, Britain, Bosnia, and Bangladesh.[34] Not all of these partners are traditional Canadian allies. To ensure that critical intelligence is shared in a timely fashion, Canada must effectively manage its bilateral and multilateral security relations.

Third, foiling plots and imprisoning would-be Canadian terrorists requires robust human intelligence, which is obtained from personal interaction with individual cell members. Mubin Shaikh and Shaher Elsohemy, for instance, were two police informants who helped thwart the Toronto 18 plot. Compelling individuals like Shaikh and Elsohemy to participate in investigations requires building ties between Canadian security services and the broader Canadian Muslim community. Ottawa should work with community leaders to build a consensus on security, welfare, and individual well-being that would help establish a common security agenda and assist in information sharing.[35] CSIS's regional director for Toronto, Andy Ellis, did so in August 2008 when he invited Muslims for a public meeting at the Meadowvale Community Centre in Mississauga, Ontario, and asked his audience to help 'de-demonize' Canada's security agencies. In December 2008, a team of RCMP officers battled a group of young Muslims on a Toronto soccer pitch. The friendly match was followed with a discussion on national security issues.[36] Alongside outreach, Ottawa should also develop strategies to inform Canadian communities about the realities of Canada's security environment. The RCMP's National Security Youth Outreach Program, for instance, engages youths about national security issues. As part of the program, the RCMP offers presentations and workshops for university and high school students and contributes speakers to conferences. Other government agencies, like the Department of National Defence through its Security and Defence Forum, engage the Canadian public with conference organizations, panel discussions, seminars, lectures, and keynote addresses. These endeavours give Canadians a frank assessment of the evolving security environment and introduce the strategies devised to protect Canadian national interests.

Finally, Canada needs to develop a national de-radicalization strategy. The first step is to gain a better appreciation for how and why Islamist radicalization occurs in the West and trace its development in Canada more specifically. By appreciating how the processes of radicalization work, intervention, de-radicalization, and socio-political reintegration can take place.[37] De-radicalization programs, like those developed overseas, should be constructed in Canada and tailored to address radicalization in this country. The first such program, the Specialized De-Radicalization Intervention program at the Masjid el Noor mosque in Toronto offers 'treatment and counselling' to young Muslims attracted to al Qaeda's ideology, and through education, dialogue, and debate attempts to disseminate 'anti-terror values' within Canada's Muslim community.[38] Ottawa should support and broaden these efforts. Likewise, the recent imprisonment of a number of Canadian Islamists suggests research into prison radicalization might also be needed to gauge whether or not Canada's general prison population is at risk of radicalization. A number of cases from the United States and Europe suggest that jailed Islamists can radicalize other prisoners and plan acts of violence from behind bars.[39] Ensuring similar developments do not take place in Canada is a priority.

Conclusion

An effective Canadian counterterrorism strategy must take into account the evolving nature of terrorist threats. While weakened, al Qaeda is Canada's primary concern. The organization continues to plan acts of violence against Western interests, colludes with regional groups to destabilize governments, and inspires and facilitates Western radicalization and home-grown terrorism. It is the essential protean enemy. Combating it will require the development and application of a multitude of military, diplomatic, developmental, and ideological approaches that not only target its coercive capabilities but undermine its ability to motivate others to participate in terrorism.

NOTES

1 'Statement of Uncontested Facts – R. v. Saad Khalid,' *Globe and Mail*, 3 Sept. 2009.
2 Ibid.
3 Canada, Department of National Defence, *Counter-Insurgency Operations* (Kingston: Army Publishing, 2008), 2-16–17.
4 Frank Douglas, 'Waging the Inchoate War: Defining, Fighting, and Second-Guessing the "Long War,"' *Journal of Strategic Studies* 30, no. 3 (2007): 391–420; Bruce Hoffman, *Inside Terrorism* (New York: Columbia, 2006), 40; Bruce Hoffman and Gordon McCormick, 'Terrorism, Signaling, and Suicide Attack,' *Studies in Conflict & Terrorism* 27 (2004): 248–51.
5 Fawaz Gerges, *Journey of the Jihadist: Inside Muslim Militancy* (Toronto: Harcourt, 2007), 11–14, 39–45.
6 Stewart Bell, 'Al-Qaeda Warns Canada,' *National Post*, 28 Oct. 2006.
7 Olivia Ward, 'Tribesmen, Angry over Uranium Resources, Nabbed Diplomats, Then Passed Them to Al Qaeda,' *Toronto Star*, 23 Apr. 2009.
8 The author first explored this typology in 'Canada's Role in Combating al Qaeda: International, Regional and Homegrown Dimensions,' *Strategic Datalink* no. 11 (July 2009): 1–6.
9 Netherlands, General Intelligence and Security Services, *The Radical Dawa in Transition: The Rise of Islamic Neoradicalism in the Netherlands* (Zoetermeer, Netherlands: GISS, 2007), 9–12.
10 United States, Director of National Intelligence, *National Intelligence Estimate – Trends in Global Terrorism: Implications for the United States* (Washington, DC: DNI, Apr. 2006). For example, Algeria's Salafist Group for Preaching and Combat became al Qaeda of the Islamic Maghreb. Al Qaeda in Iraq followed suit, and franchises were established in Pakistan, Lebanon, Yemen, Libya, the Sinai Peninsula, West Africa (Mauritania, Chad, and Niger), Saudi Arabia, Gaza, and elsewhere.
11 Over the past few years, there has been heavy attrition in al Qaeda's international leadership: al Qaeda's Abu Laith al-Libi, Abu Sulaiman al-Jasiri, Abu Jihad al-Masri, Midhat Mursi al-Sayid, Abu Wafa al-Saudi, British-born Rashid Rauf, along with the Taliban's Baitullah Mehsud, were

targeted in Pakistan and Afghanistan, and Saleh Ali Saleh Nabhan and Abu Ghadiya were killed in Somalia and Syria, respectively.

12 Leon Panetta, speech to the Pacific Council on International Policy, Los Angeles, 18 May 2009.

13 Alex Wilner, 'Targeted Killings in Afghanistan: Measuring Coercion and Deterrence in Counterterrorism and Counterinsurgency,' *Studies in Conflict & Terrorism* 33, no. 4 (Apr. 2010): 307–29.

14 Steve Simon and Jeff Martini, 'Terrorism: Denying Al Qaeda Its Popular Support,' *Washington Quarterly* 28, no. 1 (2004): 132, 135.

15 Senate of Canada, *Proceedings of the Standing Senate Committee on National Security and Defence,* issue 2, 29 May 2006.

16 During the 2006 Israel-Hezbollah conflict, Canada was instrumental in crafting the G8's statement that blamed Hezbollah for the violence. At the *La Francophonie* summit, Canada singularly vetoed the organization's statement because it acknowledged Lebanon's suffering while ignoring Israel's. The Canadian rejection stood, gained support from France and Switzerland, and a balanced resolution was issued by summit's end.

17 'Assessing the Surge: A RUSI Interview with Ambassador Ryan Crocker,' *RUSI Journal* 152, no. 2 (2007): 36.

18 Mohammed Ali Musawi, *A Selected Translation of the LIFG Recantation Document* (London: Quilliam, 2009).

19 Camille Tawil, 'Libyan Islamists Back Away from al-Qaeda Merger,' *Terrorism Monitor* 7, no. 17 (June 2009): 5–6; Evan Kohlmann and Josh Lefkowitz, 'Dossier: Libyan Islamic Fighting Group,' *NEFA Foundation* (Oct. 2007): 1–22; and 'Briefs,' *Terrorism Monitor* 7, no. 29 (Sept. 2009): 1–3.

20 Joseph Felter and Brian Fishman, *Al-Qa'ida's Foreign Fighters in Iraq: A First Look at the Sinjar Records* (West Point, NY: Combating Terrorism Center, 2007), 7–10.

21 See Stewart Bell, 'Libyan Rebels' Islamist Ties Cause Concern: Report,' *National Post,* 29 Mar. 2011; Mark Landler, Elisabeth Bumiller, and Steven Lee Myers, 'Washington in Fierce Debate on Arming Libyan Rebels,' *New York Times,* 29 Mar. 2011; Praveen Swami, Nick Squires, and Duncan Gardham, 'Libyan Rebel Commander Admits His Fighters Have al-Qaeda Links,' *Daily Telegraph,* 25 Mar. 2011.

22 Ronald Sandee, 'Core Al-Qaida in 2008: A Review,' *NEFA Foundation* (Apr. 2009): 1–16; Lawrence Wright, 'The Rebellion Within: An al Qaeda Mastermind Questions Terrorism,' *New Yorker,* 2 June 2008.

23 Asaf Maliach, 'Saudi Religious Scholars Come Out against Al-Qaeda's Use of Religious Edicts Permitting Suicide Attacks against Muslims,'

International Institute for Counter-Terrorism, 2007, http://www.ict.org.il/ NewsCommentaries/Commentaries/tabid/69/Articlsid/154/currentpage/13/ Default.aspx.

24 Peter Bergen and Paul Cruickshank, 'The Unraveling: The Jihadist Revolt against bin Laden,' *New Republic,* 11 June 2008; Sandee, 'Core Al-Qaida in 2008,' 11–12.

25 Omar Ashour, 'De-Radicalization of Jihad? The Impact of Egyptian Islamist Revisionists on Al-Qaeda,' *Perspectives on Terrorism* 2, no. 5 (Mar. 2008): 11–14; and Stewart Bell, 'Toronto Mosque Offers "Detox" for Extremists,' *National Post,* 11 Feb. 2009.

26 Before his 2007 elimination, Mullah Dadullah, the Taliban's most senior Afghan leader, stated bluntly, 'We and Al-Qaida are as one. If we are pre-paring attacks, then it is likewise the work of Al-Qaida, and if Al-Qaida is doing so, then this is also our project.' Interview with Mullah Dadullah, *NEFA Foundation* (10 May 2007). Maulvi Omar, a Tehrik-i-Taliban Pakistan leader, suggested that 'the Taliban and Al-Qaida have become an ideol-ogy ... those fighting in foreign countries are called Al-Qaida, while those fighting in Afghanistan and Pakistan are called Taliban. The aim and objectives of both ... are the same.' Interview with Maulvi Omar, *NEFA Foundation* (29 Aug. 2008). These video interviews are available at http:// www.nefafoundation.org/index.cfm?pageID=33.

27 C.J. Chivers, 'Experts Fear Looted Libyan Arms May Find Way to Terrorists,' *New York Times,* 3 Mar. 2011.

28 See Fotini Christia and Michael Semple, 'Flipping the Taliban: How to Win in Afghanistan,' *Foreign Affairs* 88, no. 4 (July–Aug. 2009): 34–45; Brian Fishman, *Dysfunction and Decline: Lessons Learned from Inside Al-Qa'ida in Iraq* (West Point, NY: Combating Terrorism Center, US Military Academy, 2009); Joanna Nathan, 'A Review of Reconciliation Efforts in Afghanistan,' *CTC Sentinel* 2, no. 8 (Aug. 2009): 11–14.

29 See *CBC,* 'Calgary Man Arrested in Kabul,' 11 May 2007; Alan Feuer, 'Canadian Gets Life in Qaeda Bomb Plot,' *New York Times,* 19 Jan. 2008; and Bruce Riedel and Bilal Saab, 'Al Qaeda's Third Front: Saudi Arabia,' *Washington Quarterly* 31, no. 2 (2008): 33–46.

30 Stewart Bell, 'Somali-Canadians Joined Fight in Horn of Africa: Report,' *National Post,* 25 July 2007; and Colin Freeze, 'Pakistan Probes Deaths of Alleged Canadian Militants,' *Globe and Mail,* 3 Sept. 2008.

31 Ian MacLeod, 'The Warning Lights Are All Blinking Red,' *Ottawa Citizen,* 23 Feb. 2008; Integrated Threat Assessment Centre, 'Is Canada Next?' Intelligence Assessment 06/23, 13 Apr. 2006 (Unclassified – For official use only).

32 Edwin Bakker, *Jihadi Terrorists in Europe: Their Characteristics and the Circumstances in Which They Joined the Jihad* (The Hague: Netherlands Institute of International Relations, 2006), 36–7.

33 Frazer Egerton and Alex Wilner, 'Militant Jihadism in Canada: Prosecuting the War of Ideas,' Metropolis Project, Justice, Policing, & Security, Feb. 2009) 7–12, http://canada.metropolis.net/pdfs/militant_jihadism_in_canada_e.pdf; Alex Wilner and Claire-Jehanne Dubouloz, 'Homegrown Terrorism and Transformative Learning: An Interdisciplinary Approach to Understanding Radicalization,' *Global Change, Peace & Security* 22, no. 1 (Feb. 2010): 33–51; and Alex Wilner, 'Enemies Within: Combating Homegrown Terrorism in Canada,' Atlantic Institute for Market Studies (Sept. 2008), 1–32.

34 Robert Mueller, remarks to the City Club of Cleveland, Ohio, 23 June 2006.

35 Christen Eddy and Eric Rojas, 'Analysis: Home-grown Canadian Terrorism,' The Center for Policing Terrorism, Manhattan Institute for Policy Research (Jan. 2007).

36 Stewart Bell, 'Ottawa Using Intervention to Extinguish Extremism,' *National Post*, 31 Jan. 2009; Colin Freeze, 'CSIS Wants Help from Ordinary Muslims,' *Globe and Mail*, 25 Aug. 2008; Colin Freeze, 'Mounties 4, Muslims 4,' *Globe and Mail*, 3 Dec. 2008.

37 Alex Wilner and Claire-Jehanne Dubouloz, 'Transformative Radicalization: Applying Learning Theory to Islamist Radicalization' *Studies in Conflict and Terrorism* 34, no. 5 (2011): 418–38.

38 Bell, 'Toronto Mosque Offers "Detox"'; 'Radical Detox Program in Canada Draws Reactions,' *Al Arabiya News*, 11 Mar. 2009. See also Sayyid Ahmed Amiruddin, testimony, Special Senate Committee on Anti-Terrorism, Ottawa, Canada, 4 Oct. 2010.

39 Alex Wilner, 'From Rehabilitation to Recruitment: Islamist Prison Radicalization in Canada,' *True North* 3 (Oct. 2010): 1–38.

Conclusion

DAVID S. MCDONOUGH

There is an unfortunate tendency for strategy – and strategic studies more broadly – to be an under-appreciated field of inquiry among policymakers and scholars, and not only in middling powers like Canada. Even the United States would often mistakenly conflate strategy with the characteristics of certain weapons in its decades-long struggle against the Soviet Union, as can be seen by its frequently arcane discussions surrounding the 'strategic capability' inherent in the latest weapon system, from 'silo-busters' like the MX Peacekeeper to strategic defences against air-breathing or atmospheric threats. Technological solutions to the Soviet challenge, as astute commentators would frequently remind the U.S. defence community, were not a panacea or substitute for old-fashioned strategic thinking.[1]

Canada fortunately avoids much of the technological determinism that often fixates policymakers south of the border. Strategic thinking in this country, while not necessarily a tradition built upon the deepest of foundations, is a considerable factor in Canada's policymaking process and in the content of many of its more substantive foreign, defence, and security policies. It is my firm belief, however, that Canada – which continues to grapple with an array of important issues at a time when its own relative position as a *middle* power is under increasing strain – would benefit from a framework capable of identifying and balancing a country's means (national instruments) and ends (political goals) in pursuit of a national security strategy or grand strategy. As David Haglund argues, grand strategy appears to be 'a more urgent imperative for those states that are not bounteously endowed with the material attributes of power.'[2]

Our goal for this volume has been to bring together diverse perspectives on how Canada has historically safeguarded its security and might better advance its national interests by adopting a more strategic approach to its foreign and defence policies, and in so doing, provide the beginnings of a grand strategy or national security strategy that would allow this increasingly 'middle-aged power,' to borrow John Holmes's words, to steer with some sense of direction in the uncertain currents of the post-9/11 world.[3]

Charles Doran and David Pratt set the stage for this volume by providing guidelines to formulate an effective and successful Canadian grand strategy. As they note, a grand strategy needs to be flexible and cognizant of changing circumstances and structural shifts, and lest national unity crises take place, also obtain the broad acceptance of its citizens. It should provide sufficient unity and predictability to transcend changes in governing parties, as well as be informed by a clear conception of the country's national interests, threats, and underlying values. Lastly, policymakers are obligated to provide capabilities to meet its strategic objectives, thereby avoiding the 'capability-commitment gap' that has so long plagued Canada's national defence strategy.[4]

The importance of identifying a country's interests and values is picked up in the chapter by Don Macnamara, who argues that policymakers should seek to advance Canada's core national interests in national security, economic prosperity, a stable international order, and the projection of the country's values, the last of which refers to such fundamental values as democracy, rule of law, individual freedom, and human rights. As he concludes, Canada would benefit from a national security strategy or grand strategy that is informed by core national interests and Canadian values, cognizant of American national security interests and strategic policies, and aware that Canada's security capabilities have been underfunded in recent years.

This theme is also expanded upon in Hugh Segal's chapter. As he concludes, there is an urgent need to develop an expeditionary capacity and development assistance to combat global violence and poverty, and thereby secure the 'balance of freedoms.' Such a foreign policy goal nicely combines Canada's interest in international order and the projection of its values concerning freedom (from both 'want' and 'fear') and human rights. And as Segal makes clear, this will also require allocating significant resources to the defence, diplomacy, and development (3-D) portfolios, all the while uniting and synergizing these diverse elements of national power with an integrated strategic planning structure.

There is little doubt that Canadian grand strategy and its national interests begin on the 'home front.' As described in Craig Stone's chapter on Canadian defence procurement, the Canadian Forces has an indirect, overlooked, and important role in advancing the goal of economic prosperity. Given the aging character of many of its major platforms, such as fighter aircraft and naval vessels, and its clear need for equipment acquisitions as the Afghan campaign finally comes to an end, it seems to be a prudent time to situate this long-term procurement process within a larger strategic framework that is concerned not only with the military capabilities themselves, but also with domestic industrial benefits that can be accrued from their acquisition. The military procurement process should help ensure the continued competitiveness and viability of Canadian industry and economy, and especially those key defence industrial sectors that are crucial for procurements in the future.

A core mission for Canada's grand strategy in general and the military in particular, which should be reflected as its recapitalization proceeds apace, is to safeguard Canadian territory and populace. This point is taken up in Elinor Sloan's detailed overview of Canada's homeland security and defence policies. Successive Canadian governments have re-emphasized the role of the Canadian military in the defence of Canada, especially as it pertains to the maritime approaches and the Arctic. But, as she goes on to explain, post-9/11 institutional changes and policy initiatives have gone beyond the military to include other departments and agencies operating in close coordination with the Canadian military in buttressing homeland security. Canada may be inclined by its own strategic culture to focus on the 'forward defence' of its international commitments, as Macnamara argues, but its grand strategy should be equally concerned with the defence and security of its homeland, not least of which as a means for 'defence against help'[5] – to mitigate the possibility of unilateral U.S. actions to safeguard its own security, which could in turn endanger Canada's sovereignty and economic prosperity.

Similarly, it is important to recognize that the security on the home front can be achieved truly only in close cooperation with Canada's superpower neighbour to the south. Beginning with the 1940 Ogdensburg Declaration, which resulted in the Permanent Joint Board of Defence, successive Canadian governments have concluded a series of important agreements with the United States on continental defence, though these arrangements have generally been informal and loosely institutionalized.

Joseph Jockel and Joel Sokolsky make clear that even the North American Aerospace Defence Command, perhaps the most integrated of Canada-U.S. defence arrangement, is largely concerned with a narrow set of activities and will likely continue to be less than comprehensive – at least, if the modest inclusion of maritime warning in the 2006 renewal is any indication. Instead, looser bilateral Canada-U.S. defence arrangements will be the norm in the post-9/11 period.

As Jockel and Sokolsky go on to argue, a return to such a historical trend provides the United States with greater flexibility and freedom in its policies, while offering Canada – always sensitive to encroachments on its sovereignty – a sense of distance from its sometimes overwhelming ally. A Canadian grand strategy should therefore recognize that a loose working relationship with the United States may actually be in Canada's national interest. This does not mean that greater integration on some key areas of the relationship should not be attempted; as shown in the chapter by Fergusson and McDonough, cooperation on ballistic missile defence represents one potentially useful avenue of cooperation. But it does mean that policymakers should be wary of the proposition that anything less that tight integration could result only in significant harm to the relationship.

Canada's grand strategy needs to adapt not only to the vagaries of U.S. policies through a return to looser bilateral arrangements, but also to important developments of its traditional Euro-Atlantic region of interest. Canada does have an interest in pursuing a partnership on economic and non-military matters with the European Union. As argued by Alexander Moens, however, it would be amiss to do so at the expense of Canada's vital interest in the North Atlantic Treaty Organization (NATO). Canadian policymakers, while grappling with the country's grand strategy, should be aware of NATO's important role in maintaining European stability, especially in light of recent Russian intransigence, and in projecting military force in expeditionary, 'out-of-area' operations beyond the strict confines of Europe itself. But as he concludes, in a theme that is taken up in subsequent chapters, Canada needs to ensure that future NATO military missions remain limited in scope and purpose.

Canada should be well aware that, even as it maintains its trans-atlantic connections with NATO and a new partnership with a more self-confident European Union, this should not come at the expense of its relationship with other key regions. As Thomas Adams ably documents, there has been a notable shift – in global economic power and international security issues – towards the Asia-Pacific, in particular Northeast Asia. Canada's core national interests may be threatened by developments in that region; international trading routes may be disrupted, thereby threatening its prosperity, while even more serious challenges are posed by a rising China and the proliferation of weapons of mass destruction (WMD). As Adams makes clear, a Canadian grand strategy should include a closer cooperation with the United States in both engaging and strategically hedging against China; this initiative would certainly benefit from a shift in Canada's naval assets and posture towards the Pacific theatre.[6]

Policymakers, even as their attention is increasingly divided between the Atlantic and Pacific regions, should ensure that Canada's grand strategy does not overlook regions further afield. Douglas Goold, for instance, ably documents the growing importance of South Asia. While often overshadowed by developments in East Asia, it would be prudent to recall that South Asia is strategically relevant for many of the same reasons (a rising power, WMD proliferation, economic markets and trading routes, and significant diasporas living in Canada), in addition to its propensity for both terrorism and failed states, and contiguity with Central Asia and the Persian Gulf. Canada's nearly decade-long commitment to Afghanistan, a country closely entwined with South Asia's security dynamic, is an important testament to the region's likely growing importance as the twenty-first century unfolds. As he concludes, Canada would benefit from closer defence cooperation with the major regional states – especially Pakistan and India – and should situate these linkages in a larger multilateral context in order to maximize its influence.

Both Adams and Goold point to the benefits of naval and expeditionary power projection capabilities in the Pacific and South Asian regions, respectively. This point was also clearly reflected in Macnamara's proposition of a Canadian strategic cultural inclination towards forward defence operations, as well as in Segal's and Adams's recognition that Canada should have an important role in the development of a global expeditionary capacity. As policymakers formulate an overarching grand strategy for Canada, they should recognize that Canadian national interests may require the deployment of military force – in addition to diplomatic, development, and other instruments of statecraft, and likely in conjunction with key allies – for expeditionary operations abroad. This can entail the deployment of 'boots on the ground,' as has been clearly on display in Afghanistan for the last decade, or it can result in the sort of air and maritime deployments that currently take part in the NATO-led military enforcement of the no-fly zone over Libyan airspace.

With a keen eye to post-Afghan deployments, David Bercuson and J.L. Granatstein delineate principles to guide Canadian military expeditions into the future. Prior to any deployment, the mission should have a clearly defined political objective, involve a debate in Parliament, and be authorized through a vote in the House of Commons. Once the military is deployed, parameters need to be negotiated with its allies and must include local Canadian command and a 'political-administrative' chain of command all the way to the prime minister. Lastly, any Canadian military expeditions should have at the very least the support of the United States and be made to follow – as much as it is feasible – the principle of Canadianization, whereby the military is equipped and transported by Canada and supported in the field by Canadian arms.

Canada's expeditionary commitment to stabilization operations is unambiguously on display in its front-line combat role as part of the UN-mandated and NATO-led International Security Assistance Force for Afghanistan. And despite the end of a combat role in this commitment, with Canadian troops now in a less onerous training mission, it would be prudent for Canadian officials to recognize that any future expeditionary missions will likely have many of the same issues concerning the requirements for and efficacy of stabilization. In that regard, as Ann Fitz-Gerald makes clear, Canada needs to further expand the strategic capacity of the departments and agencies involved in the 3-D approach to stabilization, and ensure greater harmonization of their respective strategic plans. As she goes on to note, while Canada has shown itself strategically astute in linking the stabilization mission with its national interests and values, executive- and Cabinet-level agreement on Canada's approach to stabilization would provide a greater foundation for any future missions.

Previous chapters have noted the importance for Canadian grand strategy to place increasing and simultaneous attention to a diverse number of regions, from Europe to South Asia. Douglas Bland and Brian MacDonald, expanding on a point raised by Moens and others, argue for greater selectivity and prudence in Canada's international commitments and military deployments. In what they have termed the 'Claxton Doctrine,' named in honour of Minister of National Defence Brooke Claxton (1946–54), the authors go on to prescribe a greater strategic attention on Canada's immediate vicinity – North America and increasingly the western hemisphere – and a more flexible, 'voluntarist' approach to expeditionary operations elsewhere. Canada may still have interests in other regions and may need to deploy expeditionary forces beyond the strict confines of the western hemisphere, perhaps as part of a NATO or UN operation. But the decision to do so would be voluntary and decided upon on a case-by-case basis.

Given Canada's demonstrated propensity for expeditionary operations and forward security, policymakers should begin thinking more seriously on the possible consequences of such overseas adventurism, not least of which is the danger of asymmetrical attacks involving WMD or anti-satellite weapons. Canada has already begun preparing for such an eventuality, primarily by investing in passive defences, consequence management, and diplomatic efforts to prevent the weaponization of space. But as James Fergusson and David McDonough argue, it may be time to think about participating in more controversial endeavours. Missile defences, for instance, would be a useful means to deter WMD coercion and blunt a WMD missile attack, and Canadian participation in a continent-wide missile defence system – perhaps with its own interceptor site – might be a prudent course of action. And as anti-satellite weapons proliferate, it may be equally wise for Canada to work with the United States in proactively confronting such a challenge.

Lastly, Canada needs to continue working with its allies in responding to the global terrorist threat that bedevils policymakers in Ottawa and elsewhere. Alex Wilner, for instance, outlines a Canadian counterterrorism strategy for Canada involving a multidimensional effort – in close cooperation and coordination with key allies – that targets different levels of the al Qaeda threat (international, regional, and homegrown) and includes an equal emphasis on counter-capability and counter-motivation targeting – the elimination of non-state groups' capability to pursue terrorist attacks and the mitigation of the motivational urge driving actual and potential terrorists. This may require the deployment of an expeditionary military force abroad, but it will also require Canada to bring to bear ideological, economic, and indeed all instruments of national power, in concert with her allies, for the successful conclusion of the 'war on terror.'

Admittedly, the formulation of a single, coherent, and synergistic grand or national security strategy for Canada remains a difficult if important task. But the basic elements for such a strategy have certainly been brought together in this collection, whether in the guidelines and heuristic framing devices offered in the first section; the domestic and continental policies offered in the second section; the reminder on how Canada should approach diverse regions in the third section; guidelines for expeditionary missions and Canadian military force structures offered in the fourth section; or the different ways that Canada should approach diverse security issues, risks, and threats in the fifth section.

Some of the prescribed strategies and policy recommendations offered in this book may be complementary, while others may prove contradictory or at least be more difficult to integrate. Indeed, it is doubtful whether the authors themselves would necessarily agree with the diverse perspectives and prescriptions offered here. Nevertheless, this volume certainly fulfils its goal of providing the foundations for a Canadian strategic approach to national and international security. The difficult job of actually crafting and formulating a grand or national security strategy for Canada remains with the country's talented officials, diplomats, and defence planners, and it is our hope that the collected insight and strategic wisdom gathered in this volume serves as a useful guide in their important task.

NOTES

1 Perhaps the most notable critic of U.S. technological determinism as a substitute for – rather than complement to – strategic thinking is Colin Gray. For an overview, see his *Modern Strategy* (Oxford: Oxford University Press, 1999).

2 David Haglund, *The North Atlantic Triangle Revisited: Canadian Grand Strategy at Century's End,* Contemporary Affairs no. 4 (Toronto: Irwin Publishing / Canadian Institute of International Affairs, 2000), 7.

3 John Holmes, *Canada: A Middle-Aged Power* (Toronto: McClelland and Stewart, 1976).

4 See R.B. Byers, *Canadian Security and Defence: The Legacy and the Challenges,* Adelphi Paper 214 (London: International Institute for Strategic Studies, 1986).

5 Nils Ørvik, 'The Basic Issue in Canadian National Security: Defence against Help, Defence to Help Others,' *Canadian Defence Quarterly* 11, no. 1 (Summer 1981): 8–15.

6 This would reflect a similar American re-orientation of its military and nuclear forces towards the Pacific. See David S. McDonough, 'The US Nuclear Shift to the Pacific: Implications for "Strategic Stability,"' *RUSI Journal* 151, no. 2 (Apr. 2006): 64–8.

Contributors

Thomas Adams is an executive associate at Kreab Gavin Anderson in Beijing, China, a global public relations and communications partnership, advising corporations and other organizations on issues of strategic importance in business, finance, and politics. Previously, he was research officer at the Canadian Institute of Strategic Studies and then research program officer at the Canadian International Council (CIC) in Toronto and a member of the CIC Strategic Studies Working Group. He holds an MA in political science from the University of Alberta in Edmonton. He specializes in Sino–Canadian relations and has edited numerous publications and authored articles for *Strategic Datalink, On Track, International Journal, SITREP,* as well as numerous op-eds and letters in the Canadian print media.

David J. Bercuson has been the director of the Centre for Military and Strategic Studies at the University of Calgary since January 1997 and is also the director of Programs of the Canadian Defence and Foreign Affairs Institute. In 1988, Bercuson was elected to the Royal Society of Canada, and in May 1989 he was appointed dean of the Faculty of Graduate Studies at the University of Calgary. In 1997 he was appointed special advisor to the minister of national defence on the future of the Canadian Forces. He was a member of the minister of national defence's Monitoring Committee from 1997 to 2003. In 2004 he was appointed to the Order of Canada. He has published on a wide range of topics specializing in modern Canadian politics, Canadian defence and foreign policy, and Canadian military history. His most recent book is *The Fighting Canadians: Our Regimental History from New France to Afghanistan* (2009).

Douglas L. Bland (lieutenant colonel, retired) is professor and chair of the Defence Management Studies Program in the School of Policy Studies, Queen's University. His research is concentrated in defence policymaking and management at national and international levels, the organization and functioning of defence ministries, and civil–military relations. Bland is a graduate of the Canadian Army Staff College, the NATO Defence College at Rome, and holds a doctorate from Queen's University. Among other works, he wrote *The Administration of Defence Policy in Canada 1947–84* (1987), *Chiefs of Defence: Government and the Unified Command of the Canadian Armed Forces* (1995), and (with Sean Maloney) *Campaigns for International Security: Canada's Defence Policy at the Turn of the Century* (2004). In January 2010, he published his first book of fiction, *Uprising*, which presents an apocalyptic vision of frustrated, disfranchised, and well-armed aboriginals who take on Canada by striking at the country's underbelly – its vulnerable energy resources.

Charles F. Doran is the Andrew W. Mellon Professor of International Relations and director of the Center of Canadian Studies at the Johns Hopkins School of Advanced International Studies, Washington, DC, and a senior associate at the Center for Strategic and International Studies. His first book (1971) established the power cycle theory of state rise and decline in relative power, and foreign policy role (changing structure of the system) as the foundation for grand strategy. Doran has also conducted major studies on oil politics and regional instability since 1970, directing the McArthur Foundation project on Persian Gulf energy security at the Middle East Institute (1988–91). He has given the Alistair Buchan Club Lecture (Oxford), the Claude T. Bissell lectures (University of Toronto), and a series of invited lectures at the Sorbonne (Paris I). He received the Governor General's International Award for Canadian Studies (1999) and the Distinguished Scholar Award (Foreign Policy) from the International Studies Association (2006).

James Fergusson is the director of the Centre for Defence and Security Studies, a professor in the Department of Political Studies at the University of Manitoba, and a senior research fellow with the Canadian Defence and Foreign Affairs Institute. He teaches courses in international relations, strategic studies, and foreign and defence policy, with an emphasis on Canada. His recent publications include *Canada and Ballistic Missile Defence 1954–2009: Déjà vu All Over Again* (2010), and (with Wilson Wong) *Military Space: Current Issues* (2010), and *Beneath the Radar: Change* *and Transformation in the Canada–US North American Defence Relationship* (2009). He has testified on several occasions to the Standing Committee on Foreign Affairs and International Trade and the Standing Committee on National Defence and Veteran's Affairs. He was also a member of the Defence Science Advisory Board, and the honorary colonel of the Canadian Forces School of Aerospace Studies.

Ann M. Fitz-Gerald is an associate professor in Cranfield University's Department of Engineering Systems and Management and the associate dean (Research). She holds degrees in commerce, international relations, war studies, and security and defence management. She serves on the boards of the Institute for Research on Public Policy, Saferworld, the CIC's Strategic Studies Working Group, and the Security Sector Advisory Group for U.K. Trade and Investment. She is also the chair for the International Working Group on National Security. Ann has worked on national security, security sector reform/management, and joined-up government issues for seventeen years and is widely published in this field. Her work has included the facilitation of national security strategy processes in post-conflict, developing, and developed states. Her most recent book is an edited volume, *From Conflict to Community: A Combatant's Return to Citizenship* (2005). She is academic leader of the MSc Security Sector Management and leads Cranfield University's research programs in security sector management, stabilization, and national security.

Douglas Goold is senior editor at the Asia Pacific Foundation of Canada. Previously, he was a senior fellow with the Canadian International Council and the president of the CIC and its predecessor, the Canadian Institute of International Affairs. He is the former editor of the *Globe and Mail's Report on Business* and *Report on Business Magazine*, as well as a long-time national columnist. Goold is the co-author of *Peace without Promise: Britain and the Peace Conferences, 1919–1923* (1981) and *The Bre-X Fraud* (1997), and has written a book on the Canadian banks. He recently completed a study for the CIC entitled, 'Doing Business in India: Success, Failure and the Prospects for Canada.' In 2011, he appeared before the Standing Senate Committee on Foreign Affairs on the rise of Russia, India, and China. Goold has a PhD in modern history from St John's College, Cambridge. He completed two Killam Postdoctoral Fellowships at the University of British Columbia and taught at the Universities of Alberta and Victoria. He is on the Advisory

Board of Glendon College, York University, and on the India Committee of the Ontario Chamber of Commerce.

J.L. Granatstein taught Canadian history for thirty years, is a senior research fellow of the Canadian Defence and Foreign Affairs Institute, was director and CEO of the Canadian War Museum, and writes on Canadian military history, foreign and defence policy, and politics. Among his publications are *Canada's War: The Politics of the Mackenzie King Government, 1939–45* (1975, 1990); *The Generals: The Canadian Army's Senior Commanders in the Second World War* (1993, 1995; new edition, 2005); *Canada's Army: Waging War and Keeping the Peace* (2002, 2004); *Who Killed the Canadian Military?* (2004); *Whose War Is It? How Canada Can Survive in the Post-9/11 World* (2007); and *Who Killed Canadian History?* (1998, 1999; new edition, 2007).

Joseph T. Jockel is a professor and head of Canadian Studies at St Lawrence University, Canton, New York. He is also co-editor of the *International Journal*, the scholarly quarterly of the Canadian International Council in Toronto. Jockel is the author or co-author of several books and many articles on Canadian defence policy and Canada–U.S. relations. Among other works he is the author of *No Boundaries Upstairs: Canada, the United States and the Origins of North American Air Defence* (1987) and *Canada in NORAD, 1957–2007: A History* (2007).

Brian MacDonald (colonel, retired) is a graduate of the Royal Military College of Canada and York University. He is a prominent media commentator on security and defence, counting hundreds of television, radio, and speaking appearances. His international conference papers have included Kings and Emmanuel Colleges of Cambridge University; the German Armed Forces University, Munich; the Beijing Institute for International Strategic Studies; the Shanghai Institute for International Studies; and the Atlantic Treaty Association in Budapest, Copenhagen, Edinburgh, Paris, Slovenia, Washington, and Ottawa. He has edited nineteen books and authored one, *Military Spending in Developing Countries: How Much Is Too Much?* (1997). He is the senior defence analyst at the Conference of Defence Associations and a member of the Board of Directors of the CDA Institute.

Don Macnamara, OMM, CD, DScMil, a specialist in national and international security affairs and strategic intelligence analysis, retired as a brigadier-general after thirty-seven years in the RCAF and Canadian Forces. For the last half of his military career he was doing and teaching strategy, strategic analysis, and planning in National Defence Headquarters, the Canadian Forces College, and the National Defence College. On retirement, he joined the faculty of the Queen's University School of Business and for over twenty years taught international business in the Commerce and MBA programs, and in Queen's Executive Development Centre, directing the Public Executive Program for ten years. Now living in Sidney-by-the-Sea, BC, he is chair of the Board of Governors of the Royal Military College and honorary colonel of the Canadian Forces College in Toronto. He also is a member of the Air Command Advisory Council, the Board of the Canadian International Council, and chair of the CIC Strategic Studies Working Group.

David S. McDonough is a SSHRC post-doctoral fellow in the Department of Political Science (Balsillie School of International Affairs) at the University of Waterloo. He completed a PhD in political science at Dalhousie University in 2011 and is a research fellow at Dalhousie's Centre for Foreign Policy Studies. He is a recipient of the SSHRC Canadian Graduate Scholarship (2006–9), the SDF Dr Ronald Baker Doctoral Scholarship (2009–10), and Killam Doctoral Scholarships (2008–11). He held positions at the Canadian Institute of Strategic Studies, the Royal Canadian Military Institute, and the International Institute for Strategic Studies. He has published widely on international security in *International Journal, RUSI Journal, Strategic Survey, Orbis, Journal of Military and Strategic Studies, Canadian Naval Review, SITREP, Strategic Datalink,* and *Third World Quarterly,* and a monograph in the IISS Adelphi Paper series titled *Nuclear Superiority: The New Triad and the Evolution of Nuclear Strategy* (2006).

Alexander Moens is a professor of political science at Simon Fraser University, a senior fellow at the Fraser Institute in the Centre for Canadian–American Relations, and a fellow in the Canadian Defence and Foreign Affairs Institute. He is the author of *The Foreign Policy of George W. Bush: Values, Strategy, Loyalty* (2004) and *Foreign Policy under Carter* (1990), as well as several edited books on NATO and European security, and Canadian–American relations. He co-edited *Immigration Policy and the Terrorist Threat in Canada and the United States* (2008). Moens has published in Canadian, American, and European journals and newspapers. Recently published papers on Canada–U.S. relations include *Canada and Obama: Canada's Stake in the 2008 U.S. Election* (2008) and *Measuring Parliament's Attitude towards Canada-U.S. Cooperation* (2009). Recently published articles on NATO include 'Afghanistan and the Revolution in Canadian Foreign Policy,' *International Journal* 63, no. 3 (Summer 2008).

David Pratt is an independent consultant. Most recently, he spent five months in Baghdad as a senior parliamentary expert with the USAID-sponsored Iraq Legislative Strengthening Program – the largest legislative capacity-building project in the world. From 2004 to 2008, he served as special advisor to the secretary general of the Canadian Red Cross (CRC), where his focus was on humanitarian issues. He also led the CRC's Auxiliary to Government project, which promoted a new relationship between the CRC and governments at all levels. In 2007, Pratt delivered the three-part Ross Ellis Memorial Lectures on the question 'Is There a Grand Strategy in Canadian Foreign Policy?' Pratt served as an elected representative at the municipal, regional, and federal levels for sixteen years. He was first elected to the House of Commons in 1997 and was chair of the Standing Committee on National Defence and Veterans Affairs from 2001 to 2003. He served as Canada's thirty-sixth minister of national defence in 2003–4.

Hugh D. Segal spent several decades in the private and public sectors before being appointed to the Canadian Senate in 2005. He is a former president of the Institute for Research on Public Policy, and he remains a senior fellow and lecturer at Queen's University. He also sits on corporate and public boards, as well as serving on not-for-profit and charitable organizations. Since being appointed to the Senate, he has served on Senate committees for Foreign Affairs and International Trade, Agriculture and Forestry, and Aboriginal Affairs, and on the Special Committee on Anti-Terrorism. In 2003, he was named to the Order of Canada; in 2004, he received an honorary doctorate from the Royal Military College; and in 2005, he was appointed an honorary captain of the Canadian Navy. He has authored numerous books and articles on public policy and on the Conservative party, and prior to his Senate appointment, he was a regular commentator on the CTV, PBS, and CBC television networks.

Elinor Sloan is associate professor of international relations in the Department of Political Science at Carleton University, and is a former defence analyst with Canada's Department of National Defence.

She received her MA (international affairs) from the Norman Paterson School of International Affairs at Carleton University, Ottawa, in 1989, and her PhD (international relations) from the Fletcher School of Law and Diplomacy at Tufts University, Boston, in 1997. Sloan's research interests include U.S. and Canadian defence policy and military capabilities, ballistic missile defence, NORAD, the Arctic, NATO, and peacekeeping. She is the author of five books, including *Security and Defence in the Terrorist Era*, 2nd ed. (2010) and *Military Transformation and Modern Warfare* (2008).

Joel J. Sokolsky is principal and professor of political science at the Royal Military College of Canada. He received his PhD in political science from Harvard University. He has been the author, co-author, and co-editor of a number of books, monographs, and articles. His most recent works include 'Canada and NATO: Keeping Ottawa In, Expenses Down, Criticism Out ... and the Country Secure' (with J. Jockel), and 'A Larger "Footprint" in Ottawa: General Hillier and Canada's Shifting Civil–Military Relationship, 2005–2008' (with P. Lagassé). Sokolsky is a senior fellow at the Queen's University Centre for International Relations and holds an appointment with the Queen's Department of Political Studies. He is a member of the Canadian navy's Strategic Advisory Group and a research affiliate at the Strategic Studies Program of the Massachusetts Institute of Technology. He has served as a consultant to several government offices and represented Canada on the Secretariat Working Group of the NATO / Partnership for Peace Consortium of Defence Academies and Security Studies Institutes.

Craig Stone is the director of Academics at the Canadian Forces College, Toronto, and an associate professor and head of the Department of Defence Studies at the Royal Military College of Canada. He holds an MA and PhD in war studies from the Royal Military College of Canada. He has published on Australian and Canadian defence industrial base issues, Canadian defence policy, and Canadian defence procurement, and he recently completed an edited collection on the public management of defence in Canada. He retired from the Canadian Forces in 2005 after serving over twenty-nine years as an artillery officer.

Alex S. Wilner is a senior research fellow at the Center for Security Studies at the ETH Zurich (Swiss Federal Institute of Technology). Born in Montreal, he completed his PhD in 2008 at Dalhousie University and holds an MA, also from Dalhousie. He was a recipient of SSHRC and DND/SDF Dr Ronald Baker Doctoral Scholarships and received the 2008 Transatlantic Post-Doc Fellowship for International Relations and Security. He is a research fellow with the Centre for Foreign Policy Studies, the Atlantic Institute for Market Studies, and the Macdonald-Laurier Institute. Wilner has published on a variety of subjects, including failed and fragile states, Israeli–Iranian relations, deterrence theory, counterterrorism and counterinsurgency, targeted killings, political radicalization, and home-grown and international terrorism. His work has appeared in the *Journal of Strategic Studies, Studies in Conflict and Terrorism, Global Change, Peace & Security, Canadian Naval Review, Journal of Military and Strategic Studies, Israel Journal of Foreign Affairs, International Journal, CIC Strategic Datalink, National Post,* and the *Globe and Mail.*

Index

123 agreement. *See* Canada-India Nuclear Cooperation Agreement
2004 *National Security Policy*, 46, 51, 73, 102, 131, 215–16, 218, 220–2
2005 *International Policy Statement*, 103, 175, 195, 200, 204
3-D (defence, diplomacy, and development), 51, 179, 184, 210, 218–19, 222, 243, 290, 294
9/11, ix, 3–5, 16–17, 33, 57, 100, 102, 122, 124, 127, 132, 170, 194, 271–2, 274; post-9/11, 58, 96, 99, 103, 111, 128, 143, 253, 290–2, 300

aboriginals, 73, 237–40, 298, 302
Abyssinia, 60
Aerospace Industries Association of Canada, 85
Afghan National Army, 151, 186, 216, 280
Afghanistan, ix, 3, 14–15, 33–4, 38, 50–3, 61–3, 67, 98, 145–7, 150–2, 155, 171, 175, 177–9, 182–3, 185–6, 193–4, 200–2, 204, 206, 209, 211, 213–17, 220–2, 229–32, 241, 269, 272, 279, 280–1, 293–4, 297, 302; Allegiance Program, 281;
Canadian aid to, 147, 177–9, 213, 220; Canadian fatalities, 147, 178; Independent Panel on Canada's Future Role in Afghanistan, 147, 214; public support, 179, 194, 216; terrorists, 122, 142, 146, 153, 182, 273, 276–7, 280–1; training mission, ix, 16, 63, 151, 178–9, 186, 280, 294. *See also* International Security Assistance Force (ISAF); Taliban
Africa, 53, 57, 162, 170–1, 179, 273; African Union, 210; North Africa, 17, 278. *See also* South Africa
aid of the civil powers, 12, 104, 239
Air Canada, 273
air surveillance, 67, 122, 205
airplane hijackings, 99, 121–2, 124
airport security, 101, 112
al-Awdah, Salman, 279
al-Qaeda, 153, 178, 201, 255, 270–85, 295
al-Rushud, Su'ud, 279
al-Zawahiri, Ayman, 276, 279
Alaska Boundary Dispute, 27
Alberta, 32, 121, 283, 297, 299
Alexander, Christopher, 178